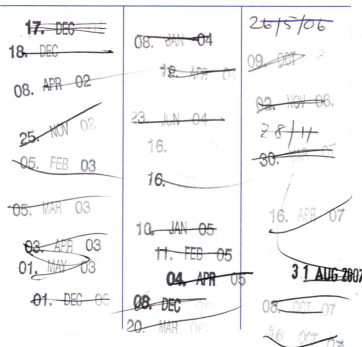

PITTI
IMMAGINE

UNIFO

ORDER AND D

)RM

$ORDER

edited by Francesco Bonami, Maria Luisa Frisa, Stefano Tonchi

CHARTA

Graphical Project
Giorgio Camuffo

Graphical Coordination
Gabriele Nason
Daniela Meda

Senior Editing
Emanuela De Cecco

Editorial Coordination
Elena Carotti

Editing
Sara Tedesco
Harlow Tighe

Translations
Steve Piccolo

Press Office
Silvia Palombi Arte & Mostre

Cover
Wolfgang Tillmans, *Lutz, Alex,
Suzanne & Christoph on Beach*,
1993.
Courtesy Galerie Daniel Buchholz,
Cologne

391.04 BON

Edizioni Charta
via della Moscova, 27
20121 Milano
Tel. +39-026598098/026598200
Fax +39-026598577
e-mail: edcharta@tin.it
www.chartaartbooks.it
www.artecontemporanea.com/charta

Printed in Italy

UNIFORM
ORDER AND DISORDER

Stazione Leopolda, Florence
January 11 – February 18, 2001

P.S.1 Contemporary Art Center,
Long Island City, New York
May 20 – September 23, 2001

Project produced and promoted by
Pitti Immagine

*Pitti Immagine is committed to
implementing projects that
promote the growth and diffusion
of modern artistic and aesthetic
culture related to fashion. Its
research activities address themes
that take fashion into broader
cultural and social environments.
Uniform. Order and disorder
conducts its investigation within
the anthropology of fashion,
analyzing one of its constituent
elements.*

Project Manager
Lapo Cianchi

Public Relations
Sibilla della Gherardesca

Press Office Coordination
Cristina Brigidini

Press Office
Francesca Tacconi with Elisabetta
Paroli and Francesco Toscano
(Florence)
Alessandra Buompadre (Milan)

Production Secretary
Valeria Santoni (Florence)
Sylvia Chivaratanond (Chicago)

Concept
Maria Luisa Frisa
Stefano Tonchi
with Francesco Bonami

Edited by
Francesco Bonami (exhibition
curator)
Maria Luisa Frisa (editor)
Stefano Tonchi (fashion curator)

Coordination
Emanuela De Cecco
Massimiliano Gioni

Installation Design
Gruppo A12

Art direction
Studio Camuffo

Research
Brunella Caccaviello, Livia Corbò,
Emanuela De Cecco, Massimiliano
Gioni and Sabino Pantone (Milan),
James Sherwood (London),
Matthew Lyons (New York),
Rebecca Voight (Paris)

Special Contributions
Cristina Lucchini (textile/fashion)
Kyle Bradfield (fashion installation)

Coordination Design
Anna Pazzagli

General Organization
Antonella Arena
Elisabetta Basilici
Cristiana Busi

Pitti Immagine would like to thank

303 Gallery, New York
Accademia della Guardia di
Finanza, Bergamo
Accademia Navale, Livorno
Agenzia Contrasto, Milan/Rome
Agenzia Grazia Neri, Milan
Andy Warhol Foundation, New York
Archivio Boetti, Rome
Area 51
Arena
Giorgio Armani
Art & Commerce
Avirex
Barbara Gladstone, New York
John Bartlett
Stephen Beale
Benetton
Lina Bertucci
Kurt Brondo
Burberry
Walter Cassidy
Caterina Chiarelli
Chronicle Books, San Francisco
Chrysalys Books
Comando Regione Carabinieri,
Tuscany
Comando Regione Militare Centro
di Firenze
Comme des Garçons
Edizioni Condé Nast
John Connelly
Contemporary Fine Arts, Berlin
Paula Cooper, New York
Corpo Nove
Creative Exchange
Antonio Cristaudo
Grazia D'Annunzio
Massimo De Carlo, Milan
Jeffrey Deitch, New York
Details
Rineke Dijkstra
Dyke Action Machine
EMI Records
Esquire
Cesare Fabbri
The Face
Carlo Fei
Paula Feldman
Gianfranco Ferré
Giusi Ferré
Flash Art
Douglas Fogle
Fondazione Sandretto Re
Rebaudengo
Foster
Gianni Franceschi
Jean Paul Gaultier

Gavin Brown Enterprise, New York
George
Marian Goodman, New York
GQ
David Granger
Lorenzo Greco
Jeff Griffin
Ulrike Groos
Gucci
Guerrilla Girls, New York
Haight Street
Hamid Dabashi
Katherine Hamnett
Hauser & Wirth, Zürich
ID
Ideale Audience International, Paris
Donna Karan
Mike Kelley
Dorling Kindersley
Calvin Klein
Steven Klein
Walter König, Cologne
Michael Kucmeroski
Helmut Lang
Lehmann-Maupin Gallery, New York
Longanesi, Milan
Roxanne Lowitt
Martin Luciano
Augustine Luhring, New York
Mario Lupano
Maharishi
Terry Manduca
Mapplethorpe Estate, New York
Matthew Marks, New York
Paul McCarthy
Liz McQuiston
The Metropolitan Museum of Art,
New York
Migros Museum, Zürich
Moravska Galerie
Museum of Contemporary Art,
Chicago
Museum of Contemporary Art,
San Diego
Naviglio Più, Milan
Wayne Northcross
Nova
Lucy Orta
Out
Maria Pia Paliotto
Salvatore Paliotto
Fabio Paracchini
Maureen Pauley, London
Phaidon Press, London
The Photographers Gallery, London
Cristina Piacenti
Alberto Piaggi

Anna Piaggi
John Paul Pietrus
Pincus Collection, Philadelphia
Plexus Publishing
Prada
Steven Pranica
Publifoto
Emilio Pucci
Ralph Lauren
Ray Ban
Regen Projects, Los Angeles
Andrea Rosen, New York
Italo Rota
Lia Rumma, Naples
Ives Saint Laurent
Fabio Sargentini, Rome
Scuola di Guerra Aerea, Florence
Michele Sernini
Raf Simons
Carlo Sisi
Sonnabend, New York
Franca Sozzani
Mary Spirito
Sportswear Company
Steven Sprouse
Monika Sprüth, Cologne
Stephen Friedman Gallery, London
Stone Island
Studio Guenzani, Milan
Wolfgang Tillmans
Isabella Tonchi
Oliviero Toscani
Vanity Fair
Paola Vannucchi
Gianni Versace
Matthias Vriens
Vivienne Westwood
W
Charlotte Wheeler
Yohji Yamamoto
Zero Production, Berlin

*and also everyone who made this
catalogue and exhibition possible.
It was a complex project that
required the collaboration of
designers, artists, military
insitutions, archives, museums,
corporations, publishers, galleries,
collectors, press offices,
newspapers and individual
enthusiasts. The names are many,
and in order not to cite them all it
was decided to let the book and
exhibition speak for themselves.*

Contemporary fashion always and constantly expresses the world in which it operates in new ways. This occurs through the creative work of designers and the ongoing commercial and organizational experimentation of the industry, but also through the personal interpretations of the individuals who buy fashion and wear it. This complexity of references and subjects makes the study of fashion an open process, requiring curiosity, refinement and different forms of disciplinary expertise. The triptych of exhibitions and books created over the last few years have examined the concrete functioning of the cultural, design and production model of the fashion system, and focused on its capacity to construct a prototype for other sectors and interpret current images and symbols (*Il Motore della moda*, 1998; *Volare. L'icona italiana nella cultura globale*, 1999; *Uomo oggetto. Mitologie, spettacolo e mode della maschilità*, 2000). The research conducted by Pitti Immagine now turns to a specific fashion theme – the uniform – and uses it to analyze a segment of our recent history and an important aspect of our social life.

This investigation has reinforced the authoritative international image of Pitti Immagine, and at the same time Italian fashion as a whole. In addition to its complete working cycle from the production point of view – practically unique on a global level – Italian fashion now demonstrates its capacity to reflect on itself as one of the many creative languages of the contemporary scene. This capacity is the result of the widespread cultural eclecticism and aesthetic sensibilities infused by fashion into an industry that is finely tuned to a world in rapid transformation, and intensely permeated by information flows and global communications. An industry geared towards an increasingly sophisticated, individualistic and despotic consumer.

Mario Boselli
President, Pitti Immagine

Today it is no longer possible to organize fashion fairs by offering sector and media professionals only products and services, without also providing them with contexts in which to communicate their message – something that has become an essential part of a focus on quality. This is why Pitti Immagine has been studying fashion for years, conducting research on themes that associate fashion with the cultural and anthropological spheres. The company's communications program aims at creating events that reflect wider-ranging issues, in which fashion plays a central role not only in terms of aesthetics, but also in terms of cultural content. The exhibition "Uniform. Order and Disorder" represents the latest chapter in our research on the anthropology of fashion, with an analysis of one of its constituent elements. The uniform, its functional nature, its formal qualities, and the ideological values with which it is commonly associated represent a sort of place of origin and controversy for menswear, and a subterranean constant throughout fashion. The love/hate relationship fashion has always experienced regarding the military style is, in a certain sense, analogous to the order/disorder implied in the style itself. This can tell us a lot about what fashion is, and what fashion thinks about itself and its role for the society and individuals that absorb its output. As always, the approach to the theme must be one of many levels. In this case, a special space has been set aside for artists, whose expressive capacities represent a sensitive, profound seismographic reading of contemporary order/disorder – just like fashion, though in a more widespread, intersubjective way. This experimentation with the connections between fashion and other creative languages, and its capacity to add something new to our comprehension of the world in which we live, form the basis for the reasoning behind all the research initiatives carried out by Pitti Immagine.

Raffaello Napoleone
Managing Director, Pitti Immagine

CONTENTS

UNIFORM

Francesco Bonami, Maria Luisa Frisa, Stefano Tonchi

> *A photograph is not only an image (as a painting is an image), an interpretation of the real; it is also a trace, something directly stenciled off the real, like a footprint or a death mask.*
>
> Susan Sontag, "New York Review of Books," 23 June 1977

Images of war. Soldiers advance, inches at a time. Faces, personalities and stories stolen from the void. Faces grimace tensely, masks of the fear that clenches at even the bravest of the brave. They are struggling to get out of the water. Some are already wounded and screaming, crying, protesting against death. Others grip their rifles and aim at the enemy over here, where we are. Where we are watching. Watching an operation of war, subjected to it, and suffering helplessly while gazing at the blind, inexorable event. But this is just the front page of a fashion feature, published last summer in the English monthly *Arena*, under the title "Fashion Is Hell, This Season Khaki Is the Colour to Die For." In a series of shots quoted from *Saving Private Ryan*, fashion photographer Carter Smith reenacts war in all its violence. Smith isolates a small group of soldiers and follows them through ten two-page spreads on their way through a war without a happy ending. The bodies of the youthful heroes lie bleeding on the ground, while the dazed survivors hesitate between losing themselves in total despair or attempting to organize a final, probably hopeless last stand.

Uniform. Order and Disorder begins with the simple realization that menswear is derived from uniforms, along with a large portion of modern dress: industrially-produced garments with standard sizes, designed to be practical, wearable and durable. The various versions of sport/survival fashion over the last few years, for example, have all made military technological research their main point of reference.

Uniform is a modern concept. To make things uniform means to make them equal. Making individuals equal means abolishing distinctions of class and demographics. All the scenarios of the contemporary world are pervaded by a tensing towards globalization, which implies a need for standardization. Mass-produced: the utopia of a better future, a sign of civilization and well-being. The science fiction of the Sixties with men and women in tights and jumpsuits, all in the same garish colors against the backdrop of comfortable, standard-issue robotized housing.

Our idea was to extract from the flow of images produced over the last half century those that made a real mark on our collective "media" mindset. To reinterpret the uniform today as a prototype of male dress, retracing the salient phases of the formation of the fashion system through its protagonists and its forceful utilization of communications media. To analyze the message of the uniform removed from the military context and devoured not only by the creative processes of fashion, but also by the violence of all the "counter-utopias" from the postwar era to the present, absorbed by pop culture and utilized by art as a way of challenging the hegemony of a language of social and aesthetic signs.

This meant that we had to come to grips with the opposite poles of the mythology of the uniform, revealing its impact on the universal icons and global patterns of dress of the last fifty years. Through a mere piece of clothing fashion, art, cinema, music and photography, but also history, politics and many other things coexist in the flow of images that paper the unstable spaces of our already-future present. In a fast-paced, overwhelming system that manages to mix good and evil, utopia and realism, justice and injustice without making any distinctions between the true, the plausible and the false, while producing images that are nevertheless continuously captivating. Until it reaches the formal perfection of the fashion feature published by *Arena*, which in order to display military-style clothing actually reconstructs a terrifying scenario of war.

We decided to let all these figures coexist without hierarchies, from the true images of photo reporting to the artificial, emotional images of cinema, from the pensive formulations of art to the aesthetically pervasive images of fashion. The result is a complex, stratified panorama in which the various planes intercommunicate and intertwine. The path emerged from the free comparison of visual texts, triggering a striking vision of some of today's most powerful myths. We decided not to interrupt this continuous, almost autonomously urgent flow of imagery constructed by association and contrast. Further analysis is left up to the reader, with the aid of essays by scholars, writers and journalists grouped at the center of the volume, providing pertinent suggestions for orientation.

Comentary for the images provided by
Emanuela De Cecco (edc) and Massimiliano Gioni (mg).

Collier Schorr, *Shaving*, 1998.
C-Print, 35 x 28 cm.
Courtesy 303 Gallery, New York.

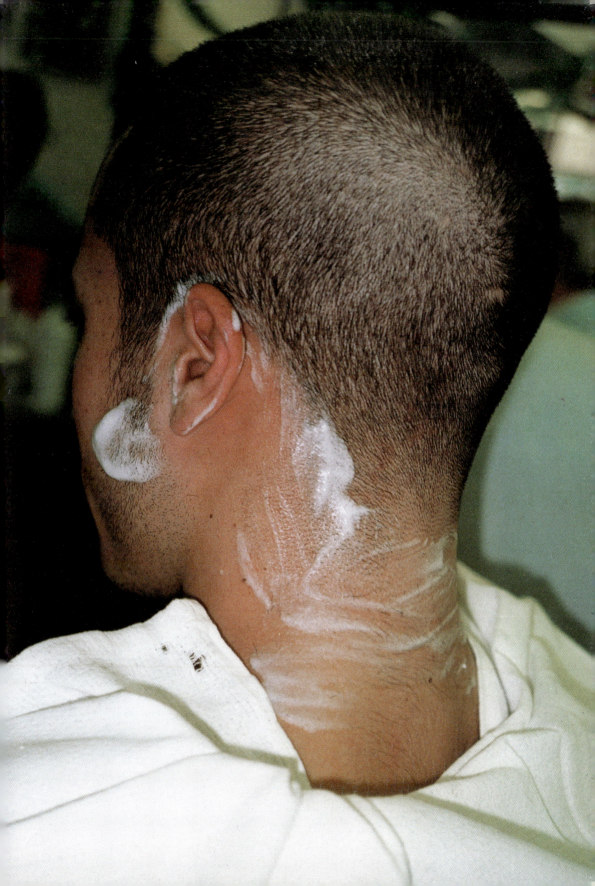

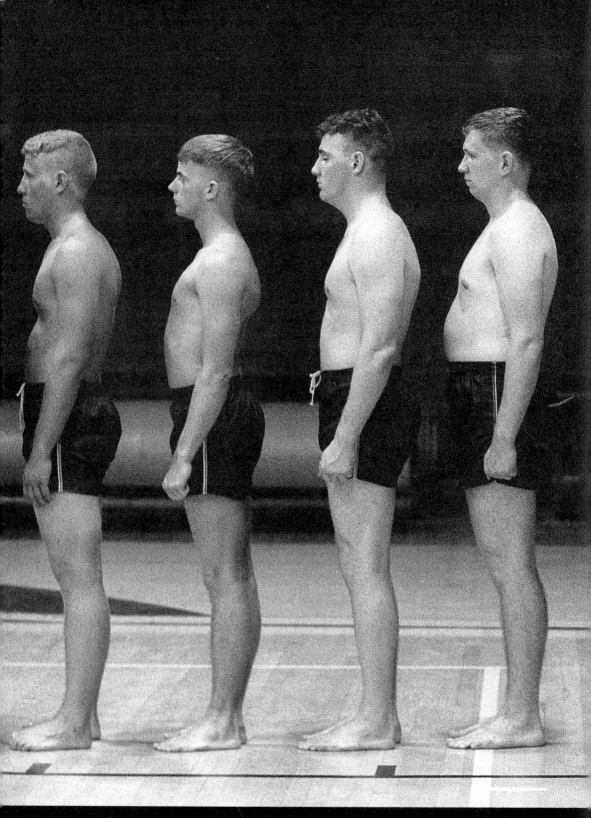

West Point.
© Malloch-Magnum.
Agenzia Contrasto.

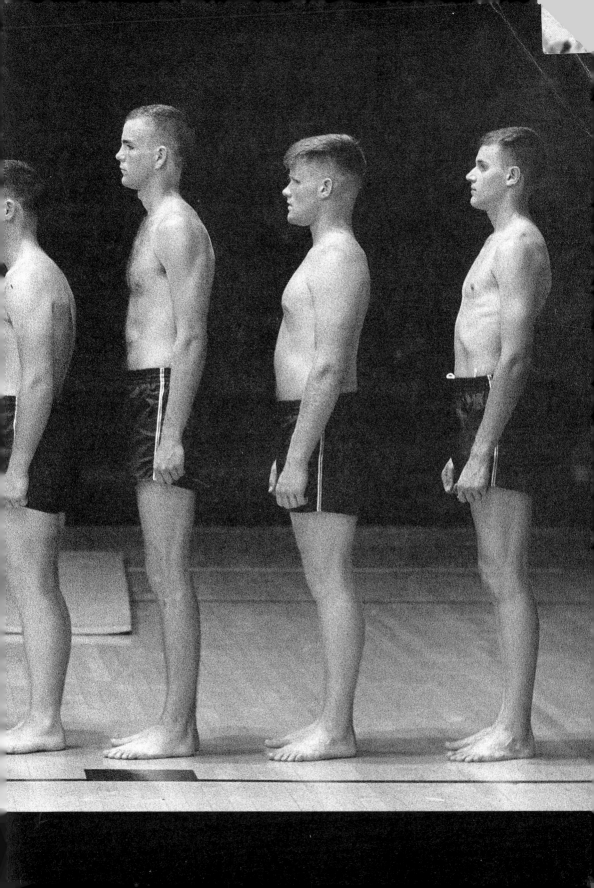

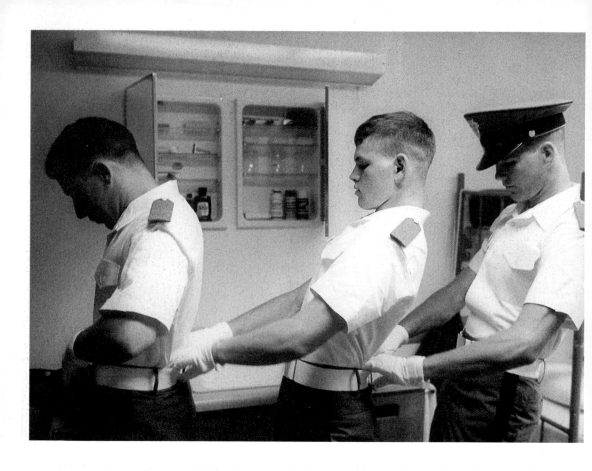

Preceding pages
Foreign Legion.
© John Robert Young Rapho.
Agenzia Grazia Neri.

West Point.
© Malloch-Magnum. Agenzia Contrasto.

New male recruits get clothing issue, 1992.
Eli Red, Magnum. Agenzia Contrasto.

Suddenly the rolling gate rises with a graveyard groan, a rotary screech, I shiver, about thirty young men run out with drooping trousers, untucked shirts, dragging rucksacks full of garments, dropping shoes and slickers. They keep on coming, in twos and threes, in bunches with wasted eyes, slack mouths, the throng never stops emerging in the light of the parade ground, some of them are struggling with their shirts, running, then nothing, just silence, the darkness of the magazine starts to fade, they push us inside...

Endlessly tall shelving reaching up to the invisible ceiling, the pungent smell of mothballs and humidity, an infinite, very narrow corridor between these walls of hanging garments, in the back some soldiers behind a counter, unshaven beards, shouts, over here, move it you bums, let's go, move your ass. You have to shout out your size, get measured, try on the shoes, all-weather boots, shoes for leave, track shoes, service boots. Then into the camouflage suit, out of a shirt, they give me stuff that's too tight, I always ask for the next size, green t-shirts in which I can't even manage to squeeze my arms, it's cold, half naked I put it on, then a pair of very scratchy wool underdrawers, the socks will be children's size, dammit.

Pier Vittorio Tondelli, *PAO PAO*, 1982

Discipline begins, first of all, with the distribution of individuals in space.

Michel Foucault,
***Discipline and Punish*, 1975**

Vanessa Beecroft,
VB 39 US Navy, 1999.
Museum of Contemporary Art, San Diego.
Photo Todd Eberle.

Vanessa Beecroft,
VB 42. Intrepid, The Silent Service, 2000.
Photo Armin Linke.
Courtesy Jeffrey Deitch, New York.

As in any society or tribe, entry in the army is marked by an initiation rite, a fracture that marks the passage from one cultural system to another, underlining, with gestures and symbols, the tacit signing of a contract that involves precise duties, privileges and responsibilities. The haircut is perhaps the most evident sign, imposed by the rules of hygiene but also by causes that are clearly based on ritual, reminders of religious and monastic traditions. Next come the exercises, workouts, training, groupings. As explained in an American basic training manual: "When they are inducted soldiers may be fat, overweight or undernourished. To rebuild the bodies of some, and to help others to adapt to the rigors of military life, an intense program of physical training is required." In keeping with a view that was already widespread in the 1700s, the body of the soldier is a device to be fabricated, clay to be modeled, straightened and stretched, with very precise calculations. The objective, as already expressed in a French ordinance back in 1764, is to erase the body of the peasant, to give him "the air of a soldier." *mg*

naval training base, US west coast

This is a document of what will very soon be history. Next year, the US government is to close this massive naval training base in America's Southwest. It has been the home to new navy recruits since 1914, the local area now completely defined by the grand base that dominates the surrounding landscape.

Granted rare access to a US-forces site in order to document the last days of a naval institution, photographer *Melodie McDaniel* sought to capture the distinctive American tradition of this sort of training facility. Arena Homme Plus has been instructed by the US naval authority not to identify the base – the cold war is long over, although its strictures live on. But for how long? As the parade-ground here falls silent in 1997, does the starched heritage of *An Officer And A Gentleman* fall even further into a sepia-tinted past?

A + 97

"When they report for duty, some recruits are soft, some are overweight and some are underweight. To build some up and trim others down, and to condition all for the rigors of military life, a well planned physical-training program is integrated with other phases of training: military drill, an active outdoor life, good food, good living habits."
Naval training manual

A + 100

A + 101

"Naval Training Base, US West Coast,"
in *Arena Hommes Plus*,
n. 6, autumn/winter 1996/97, pp. 97/104.
Photo Melodie McDaniel.

A + 98

ommander Pitts

Lance Radielli
Ocean Port, NJ

Ernest Gunn
Tacoma, Wash

Kenneth L Gillespie
Omaha, Neb

ick Johnson
hreveport, La

Dick Dale
Little Rock, Ark

James Stubek
Reliance, Wy

Steve Smith
Dallas, Tex

ffrey Beauchamp
tockton, Cal

Laymon Weeks Jr
Odessa, Tex

John R Shortt
San Jose, Cal

Jerry McElroy
Rock Springs, Col

A + 102

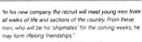

"In his new company the recruit will meet young men from all walks of life and sections of the country. From these men, who will be his 'shipmates' for the coming weeks, he may form lifelong friendships."

Naval training manual

A + 103

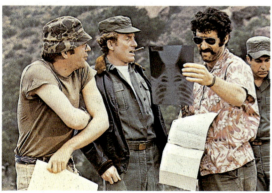

This page, on the left, from top to bottom
Full Metal Jacket, 1987.
Directed by S. Kubrick.
SYGMA/Agenzia Grazia Neri.

Donald Sutherland, Elliot Gould,
in *M.A.S.H.*, 1970.
Directed by Robert Altman.
Shooting Star. Agenzia Grazia Neri.

Streamers, 1983.
Directed by Robert Altman.
Agenzia Grazia Neri.

This page, on the right, from top to bottom
Marine Corps - Parris Island, S.C., 1983.
Agenzia Contrasto.

Marines in training.
Photo James Nachtwey/Magnum.
Agenzia Contrasto.

From top to bottom
"Hard Corps," in *Line*,
spring 2000, pp. 132/141.
Photo Kai Wiechmann.

"The Winds of War," in *Esquire*,
n. 4, April 1999, pp. 106/115.
Photo Noe De Witt.

"Navy Look," in *L'Uomo Vogue*,
n. 171, February 1987.
Photo Klaus Wickrat.

Everything we are called upon to do in the Army requires teamwork, and teamwork is built on a foundation of trust and confidence within units – between soldier and soldier, between leader and led, and between units who see themselves serving side-by-side. That trust and confidence emerges from our daily commitment to our Army values: loyalty, duty, respect, selfless service, honor, integrity, and personal courage. Without trust, there can be no dignity and respect for the individual soldier, and cohesion and morale in our units would suffer.

In the Army, we know that, on our most difficult days, our lives may depend upon the ability and the willingness of the person next to us to perform his or her duty. In combat, soldiers fight for each other. They die for each other. And they carry their fallen comrades out on their backs. The essential questions that are asked in evaluating our peers, our subordinates, and our superiors are simple and fundamental: would I be willing to go to war with you? Would I be willing to put my life on the line for you? Would I be willing to die for you? And when the answers are yes, that is a powerful statement of commitment. There is no higher compliment that one soldier can pay to another.

Eric K. Shinseki
General, United States Army, Chief of Staff, July 2000

Stretch-cotton shirt and
stretch-gabardine tie by Prada.
Opposite: Cotton polo shirt by
Istante; flat-front cotton trousers
by Patrick Cox Wannabe; leather
loafers by Dolce & Gabbana.

KHAKI COUTURE

The stuff of uniforms and work clothes, khaki this season gets
all spiffed up. Actor Matt Damon thrills to the twill.
Photographs by Troy Word. Produced by Guillermo Zalamea.

The weave of khaki contains the inscribed names of soldiers and generals, but also of stylists and fashion victims. In 1848 Sir Harry Burnett Lumsden and William Stephen Raikes Hodson selected it as the fabric for the uniforms of the soldiers stationed in India: with its traditional beige color and cotton and wool fibers, khaki proved to be the ideal fabric for the monsoon climate of the colonies. So much so that the name itself comes from a Hindi word, whose original meaning alludes to the color of dust. An irony of history, an Indian word becomes the emblem of colonial repression: from the first clashes between English and Indians in 1857 to the days of Gandhi, with the South African war in between, the khaki uniform wound up representing conflict and violence between two cultures, a chromatic metaphor for the rise and fall of the British Empire. Not to mention the desert foxes and German soldiers in the African campaign, who for the occasion abandoned the traditional black uniform and donned beige shorts and shirts. In films war is often depicted in khaki tones, from

the *Bridge on the River Kwai* to *Catch 22* and *Mister Roberts*. But this is certainly not the image-bank frequented by fashion designers. In fact, never before as in recent years has fashion flirted so assiduously with khaki, even managing to erase that sensation of boredom and predictability so long associated with the color beige. In the Nineties, in the hands of Chanel, Gucci, Prada and John Barlett, khaki becomes a fabric immediately associated with an idea of a rather demodé luxury, as in those little mohair sweaters that prompt dreams of vaguely Seventies-ish cocktail party atmosphere, martini glasses, brown Op-Art curtains and cool jazz. On the front of functional garments and streetwear we find Calvin Klein, with his 100% khaki line for androgynous models in shirtsleeves like soldiers on leave. Not to mention the explosion of chinos and "dockers" and "avirex" and dress-down Fridays: a new way of living leisure time, with sturdy, slightly wrinkled cotton trousers, aping the soldiers of the Second World War. *mg*

Henry Fonda, James Cagney,
William Powell, Jack Lemmon,
in *Mister Roberts*, 1955.
Snap Photo/JR.
Agenzia Grazia Neri.

John-Paul Pietrus,
Boudicca's Military, 2000.
C-Print, variable dimensions.
Courtesy of the artist.

Preceding pages
"Khaki Couture,"
in *Esquire*,
March 1997, pp. 132/135.
Photo Troy Word.

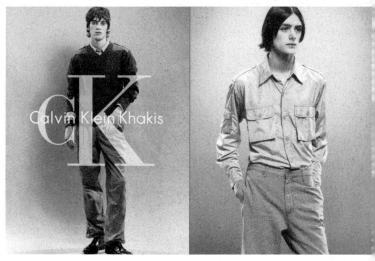

Orson Welles, in *Catch 22*, 1970.
Directed by Mike Nichols.
Snap Photo. Agenzia Grazia Neri.

Calvin Klein advertising, 1996.

"John Bartlett, An American Hero,"
in *Out*, July 1998 (cover).
Photo François Dischinger.

OUT

JOHN BARTLETT
AN AMERICAN HERO

GAYS VOTE REPUBLICAN
UNDRESS FOR BED
CALCULUS OF COCAINE
MINNIE DRIVER FLIES
HIV DRUG SIDE EFFECTS
THE GAY GAMES '98
ARE YOU REALLY FIT?

Adi Nes, *Untitled*, 1999.
C-Print, 90 x 135 cm.

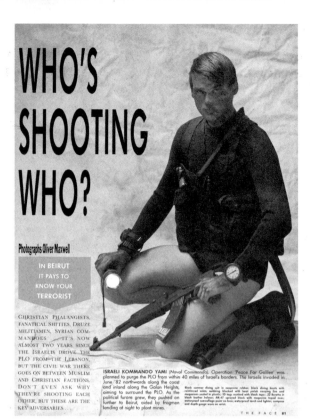

WHO'S SHOOTING WHO?

Photographs Oliver Maxwell

IN BEIRUT
IT PAYS TO
KNOW YOUR
TERRORIST

CHRISTIAN PHALANGISTS, FANATICAL SHIITES, DRUZE MILITIAMEN, SYRIAN COMMANDOES — IT'S NOW ALMOST TWO YEARS SINCE THE ISRAELIS DROVE THE PLO FROM THE LEBANON, BUT THE CIVIL WAR THERE GOES ON BETWEEN MUSLIM AND CHRISTIAN FACTIONS. DON'T EVEN ASK WHY THEY'RE SHOOTING EACH OTHER, BUT THESE ARE THE KEY ADVERSARIES.

ISRAELI KOMMANDO YAMI (Naval Commando). Operation 'Peace For Galilee' was planned to purge the PLO from within 40 miles of Israel's borders. The Israelis invaded in June '82 northwards along the coast and inland along the Golan Heights, aiming to surround the PLO. As the political furore grew, they pushed on further to Beirut, aided by frogmen landing at night to plant mines.

"Who's Shooting Who?"
in *The Face*, n. 75, July 1986.
Photo Oliver Maxwell, styling Elaine Jones.

"Military Gent's,"
in *L'Uomo Vogue*, n. 249, March 1994, p. 120.

Following pages
Rosemarie Trockel, *Balaklava*, 1986.
Wool beret, variable dimensions.
Photo Bernhard Schaub.
Courtesy Monika Sprüth Gallery, Köln.

Matthias Vriens, *Protest/Celebration*, 2000.

military   gent's

Uomo - condot   tiero o uomo-mi-
nistro? Arafat e   Rabin: il fascino
di uno stile perso   nale. Da imitare.

Adi Nes's *Last Supper,* the pages of "Who's Shooting Who?" from *The Face*, and the more recent article "Military Gents," trigger a meaningful interplay among reality, history and art history. While the work of the Israeli artist comes to grips with the traditional iconography of the Last Supper, offering a version in which the sacred side is definitively replaced by the chronicle, in which the conflict between Arabs and Israelis is transfigured and appears on an increasingly flimsy scenario, the pages from *The Face* and *Uomo Vogue* provide an opportunity to extend the discussion to one of the most common communications strategies of fashion and other fields. In the first case we see the uniforms of the factions involved in the civil war between Christians and Muslims in Lebanon. The captions explain the role of each faction, with notes on the details of the clothing, as if they were true fashion accessories. In *Uomo Vogue* the opening with the portraits of Arafat and Rabin is followed by a true fashion presentation and a text describing the styles of the two leaders, with a genealogical analysis: Rabin descends from Roosevelt, Bismark, Cavour, Cicero, Arafat from Che Guevara, Garibaldi, Vercingetorix. In both features, the short-circuit between reality and fiction is determined by the text strategy: the elimination of the differences of sphere is caused by the rhetorical expedients, where the situationist matrix interweaves with the pursuit of glamour at all costs. It is no coincidence that the publication of "Who's Shooting Who?" caused a flood of protest mail from readers, to which the editorial staff of *The Face* replied by blaming the choices on the news staff of the magazine, and by defending the right to invent new modes of information. *edc*

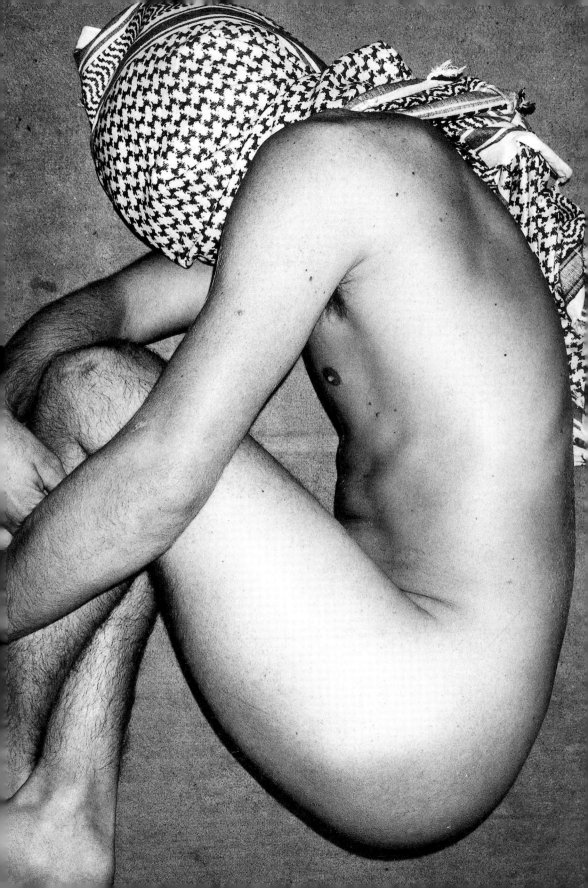

CAMPUS SWEETHEART '68

Margaret Leahy, twenty-three, of San Francisco State College, will be wearing her up-against-the-wall uniform this fall: army surplus helmet; thigh boots for protection when being dragged limp across the campus; culottes, for the same reason; goggles as protection against Mace; Vaseline to seal goggles to face and keep out tear gas; handkerchief dipped in baking soda and water as an antidote against Mace.

by Dan Wynn

Preceding pages
Belfast (Ulster), 9 April 1981.
Photo Michel Philippot/SYGMA.
Agenzia Grazia Neri.

"Campus Sweetheart '68," in
Esquire, September 1968, p. 81.
Photo Dann Wynn.

Identikit Unabomber.

Andres Serrano, Klansman (Great Titan of the
Invisible Empire III), 1990.
Cibachrome, silicone, plexiglas, 152.4 x 125.7 cm.
Courtesy Paula Cooper Gallery, New York.

If you want to know what's behind the balaclava, it's very simple: look at yourself in the mirror.

Subcomandante Marcos
Yo, Marcos, 1994

Milan, 1976. Prison revolt at the San Vittore jail.
Photo Dino Fracchia. Agenzia Grazia Neri.

Belfast, North Ireland, 1981.
Catholics battle British Troops with fire bombs.

THE FACE

DESTROY!

FUCK OFF!

GUCCI

This is the city of the dead
As we lie side by side in bed
I'd do something else instead
But it is the city of the dead.

We went out kickin' around
But you got drunk an' fallen down
An' I wished I could be like you
With the Soho river drinking me down.

In the city of the dead
Fall in love and fall in bed
It wasn't anything you said
Except I know we both lie dead.

What we wear is dangerous gear
It'll get you picked on anywhere
Though we beat up, we don't care
At least it livens up the air.

It is the city of the dead.

The Clash
City of the Dead

The Clash, 1978.
Photo Michael Putland.
Retna/Agenzia Grazia Neri.

The Clash Tribute - Burning London,
Sony, 1999.

The Clash, 1978.
Photo Adrian Boot.
London Features International.
Agenzia Grazia Neri.

Beats and Mods, beaten and beatific. The period is about the same, the clothing and posturing differ. Skinny jackets and sailor-boy looks spread like wildfire among the Beats, with that courteous honor student smile, perhaps to conceal light or heavy drug abuse. Not just the Beatles, but a veritable host of groups and grouplets scattered all over the world, above all in the United States, where music was mixing surf and beat, blues and lysergic guitars. Back in London, the Mods were more or less contemporaries. Born in almost the same year, but fans of the Rolling Stones and the Who, all dressed alike, always in groups: their uniforms were elegant tapered suits, with an army parka. The *Modernists of London* thus took possession of the symbols of British elegance and the aerodynamic icons of the modern era, along with their streamlined Lambretta scooters covered with glittering mirrors. Offspring of the English lower middle class, unprepared for the explosion of consumption, the Mods unleashed their frustrations and dreams of social betterment in urban violence, street fighting, and gang battles against the greasers, rockers and teddy boys. Thirty years later, 1994: Oasis. Same haircut, same parka, naturally in a high-tech voguish update, pre-millenium bug. And the same violence, this time with a nihilistic bent, as imposed by the Nineties label Generation X, apathetic, depressed, demotivated. Without even the excitement of a good rumble over questions of appearance. So there we have it, *Dazed and Confused*, the house organ of a confused, wasted generation: "We're not crazy, we're just bored. If there was something new, new music, a new fashion, at least some new bands, well, sure, I'd go for it right away. But there isn't anything new, we're just bored and we'll end up fighting amongst ourselves". *mg*

Oasis, Sheffield, 22/9/1997.
© Steven Parker Retna.
Agenzia Grazia Neri.

New Colony Six, *Colonization*,
Sundazed, 1994.

September 1965.
© Syndication International,
in Richard Barnes, *Mods!*,
London: Eel Pie Publishing, 1979, p. 83.

From top to bottom, left to right
M. Pesaresi, *Berlino Underground*,
Agenzia Contrasto.

Jack Barron, "Psychedelic Skins,"
in *ID,* n. 97, October 1991, pp. 56/57.

Moscow: skinhead members of the National Party,
founded by Ivanov Kouznitch, 1988.
© Lisa Sarfati. Magnum/Agenzia Contrasto.

Edward Norton and Edward Furlong,
in *American History X*, 1999.
Colorific! Film. Agenzia Grazia Neri.

Following pages
Sarah Lucas, *Concrete Boots*, 1993.
20.3 x 11.4 x 27.9 cm.
Courtesy Barbara Gladstone Gallery, New York.

"West One Searchers,"
in *ID,* n. 37, 1989.
Photo Nick Knight, styling Simon Foxton.

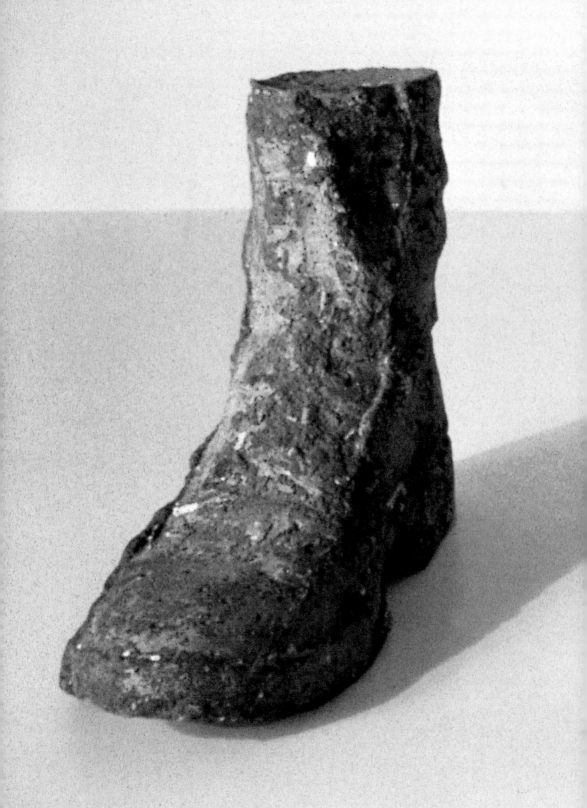

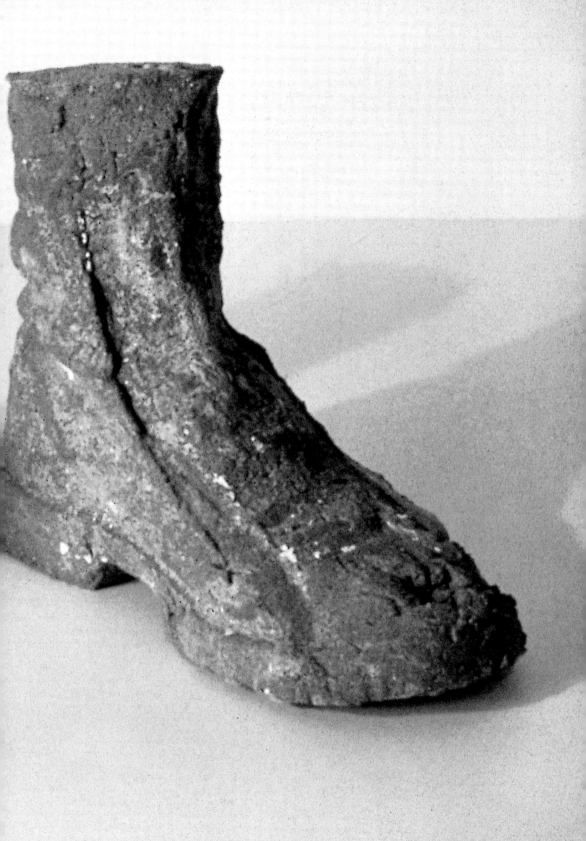

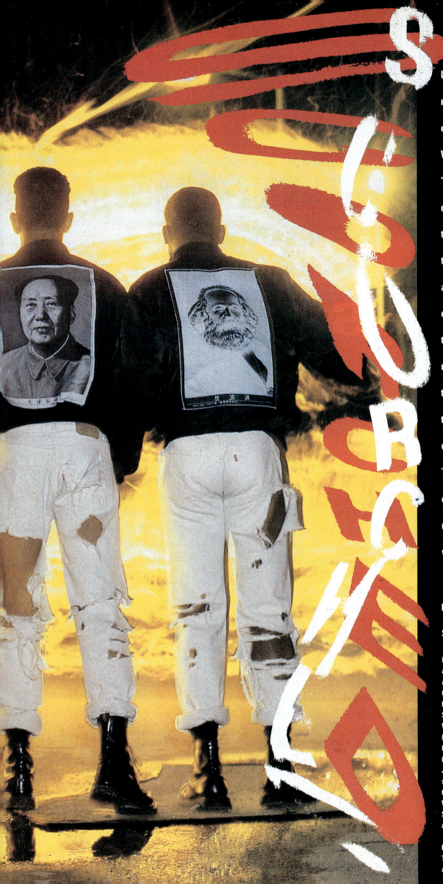

SCORCHED

Urban paranoia surrounds the rumour that London club-runners are re-introducing William The Conqueror's 'Scorch Policy' of burning down hostels of rebellion, or in this case, *competition*. Wearing their hearts on their sleeves and their heroes on the backs of their MA1 Army jackets these nightclub entrepreneurs roam the streets appalled at this wanton disco arson. Will they be next to suffer the wrath of the West One Scorchers? The Soviet butterflies cast their competitors' flyers into the remnants of yet another venue. . . and wonder.

Photograph Nick Knight

Styling Simon Foxton

Black jackets £20 approx, from all Camping and Army shops. Woven Chinese patches £3 each from Gung Ho Book Shop, Gerrard St, London W1. 501's Levis natural (kindly donated by Levis for the ripping of) approx £30, available from Jean Jeanie Oxford St and selected branches through the country, Western Frontier in Selfridges London W1 and Way In at Harrods.

From left to right – EDDIE, TONY, LISTON, VERNON and JAMES.

Preceding pages
Antoine, in Jean-Marie Périer,
Mes Années 60,
Paris: Filipacchi, 1998, p. 94.

Students mourn Jeffrey Glenn Miller,
New York, 1965.
Agenzia Grazia Neri.

Johnny et Sylvie,
in Jean-Marie Périer, *Mes Années 60,*
Paris: Filipacchi, 1998, p. 314.

From top to bottom, left to right
"Private Labels,"
in *Details*, May 1993, pp. 112/119.
Photo Paul Jasmin.

"Fall Guys,"
in *Esquire*, July 1976, p. 107.
Photo Saul Leiter.

Following pages
Prada advertising,
in *L'Uomo Vogue,*
n. 272, July/August 1996, p. 32.

Joseph Beuys, *Filzanzug*, 1970.
Felt, 117.5 x 76.8 x 21.6 cm.
Museum of Contemporary Art, Chicago.
Photo © Museum of Contemporary Art, Chicago.

FALL GUYS

...ase into autumn with
...e fresh, appealing
...othes favored by the
...oung, interesting men
...n these pages. All the
...ings they're wearing
...e loose, easy, and
...onderfully brash.

...spired by a 1942
...nglish aircraft-carrier
...uit, the cotton
...rawstring top and
...nts worn by writer
...Woody Hochswender
...pitomize the fuller,
...portier look for fall. By
...festyle, $50. They're
...ired with rugged
...ction boots by
...aufman, $40. Wear
...is for fun.

...otographed by Saul Leiter

PRADA

Maurizio Cattelan,
La rivoluzione siamo noi, 2000.
Installation.
Migros Museum, Zürich.
Photo Attilio Maranzano.

Joseph Beuys, *We Are the Revolution* 1972.
Silkscreen on polyester, 191 x 100 cm.
Courtesy Studio Guenzani, Milano.

Sarah Lucas, *Self-Portrait*, 1993.
Color photocopy on wrapping paper, 260 x 144.8 cm.
Courtesy Barbara Gladstone Gallery, New York.

L'ESTATE IN DIVISA

A Saint Tropez e a Juan Les Pins abbiamo fotografato il nuovo esercito delle vacanze. La divisa si smitizza ed è un simbolo di libertà, per ironia; è l'antidivisa individuale.

È morta la divisa, W la divisa. Questi anni che hanno decretato l'odio verso gli inquadramenti, l'odio verso le guerre, l'odio verso le gerarchie, proprio questi anni hanno partorito migliaia e migliaia di giovani che prendono a loro simbolo gradi, berretti, camicie, giubbotti di tutti gli eserciti del mondo. L'ironia e la svalutazione si scatenano e tutti questi ragazzi che sono gli amici da molte generazioni a non avere mai vissuto di persona una guerra, tendono a questa privazione di cui non sentono certo la mancanza. Non a caso poi i simboli sono quasi tutti dell'esercito di nazioni in guerra, e l'indefinita ironia diventa preciso e patologico sarcasmo. Amia di libertà è anche osare a tutte queste lotte e scritte e bottoni a pressione anche le magliette pop che inevitabilmente vivono in un'assordante e fraternamente esplosione di colori. Così si completa la vera divisa per le vacanze, reale e autentica anti-divisa; ognuna è un pezzo unico individuale, personalizzato, è un quadro d'autore dove vince la fantasia e la libertà. Tutto questo si tocca con le mani e gli occhi, specialmente appunto a Saint Tropez e a Juan Les Pins dove siamo andati per trovare conferma alle nostre previsioni e proposte, perché sono ancora adesso due posti validi come ottimo punto di riferimento per il « giusto » genere di giovani. In queste due pagine le camicie jeans sono a fianco dei nuovi gradi attaccati alle magliette; il gusto militare è un'idea di tutte le età; le camicie e i blouson arrivano definitivamente dal Vietnam per andarsi al Sennequier con un Pernod tra le mani, ben freddo.

In the protest years the challenge to the reference points of bourgeois society seen as bulwarks of shared values – state, family, religion – obviously also included the institution of the military and, by extension, the uniform. Shirts with tabs and insignia, infantry boots, tundra jackets were stripped of their traditional authority image and worn by young people all over the world, both in political demonstrations and everyday life, becoming a different kind of uniform, of people claiming greater freedom and an end to all wars. This new army, which due to its age bracket had the good fortune not to have experienced war firsthand, had no intention of fighting for territorial borders. Instead, aside from its political demands, the main thrust was

centered on a desire for the essential on a stylistic plane. The possibility of personal interpretation of dress, starting with a common ground: no other garment could respond to this desire as well as a uniform.

With surprising speed the world of fashion and communications caught onto the message, and after having indicated the presence of the phenomenon – see the article in 1971 in *Uomo Vogue* as an example – began to reinterpret it with a procedure that would surely have been appreciated by Roland Barthes. Ellesse cites the protest demonstrations through metonymy, adding megaphones and gas masks; Antoine poses as a star, wearing a military shirt. *edc*

Jeff Wall, *Dead Troops Talk*
(A Vision After an Ambush
of a Red Army Patrol Near Moqor,
Afghanistan, Winter 1986), 1992.
Lightbox, 229 x 417 cm.
Courtesy David Pincus Collection, Philadelphia.

HEATER OF FASHION
TOGRAPHED BY STEVEN MEISEL

In the Nineties, even before Baudrillard and Forrest Gump noticed, war and violence had become the greatest television show on earth: captured in Hollywood freeze-frames, transformed into complicated choreography coated with a thin, shiny, vacuum-packed patina; more or less recent battles were transformed into hyper-realistic images, in which the characters move like sculpted wax figures in stylized poses, halfway between Gericault and Noh Theater. Have no fear: it isn't blood, just tomato juice, as Godard used to say.

As real war seeks refuge in the realm of the invisible with intelligent bombs, neutralized targets, surgical attacks and other CNN euphemisms, culture invents new expressive modules with which to give the battle an image. The reaction to war's disappearance is a surplus of visibility: the representation blunders in the dark, barely illuminated by the flares over Baghdad, and reality retreats when faced with the force of spectacle. *mg*

"Theater of Fashion," in *Vogue Italia,*
n. 578, October 1998, p. 534.
Photo Steven Meisel.

"Fashion is Hell," in *Arena,*
n. 101, August 2000, pp. 118/135.
Photo Carter Smith, fashion editor Paul Stura.

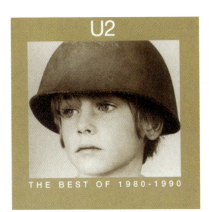

Preceding pages
Pino Pascali with the Bella Ciao cannon,
Rome, 1965.
Courtesy Fabio Sargentini, Roma.

From top to bottom
U2, *The Best of 1980/1990*,
Polygram, 1998.

The Smiths, *Meat is Murder*,
Warner Music, 1985.

Iggy Pop, *Naughty Little Doggie*,
Virgin, 1996.

naug

Chile, 1978.
Photo Miguel, Roma. Agenzia Grazia Neri.

Jonathan Meese in Erwin Kneihsl, *Jonathan Meese*, Gesinnungsbuch, 1999.
Walter König, Köln, 1999. Courtesy Contemporary Fine Arts, Berlin.

"Haight Street," in Gene Anthony,
The Summer of Love, Berkeley, California:
Celestial Arts, 1980, p. 132.

14/5/69. Early Black Panther members
in front of Chicago City Hall.
Photo Hiroji Kubota. Magnum/Agenzia Contrasto.

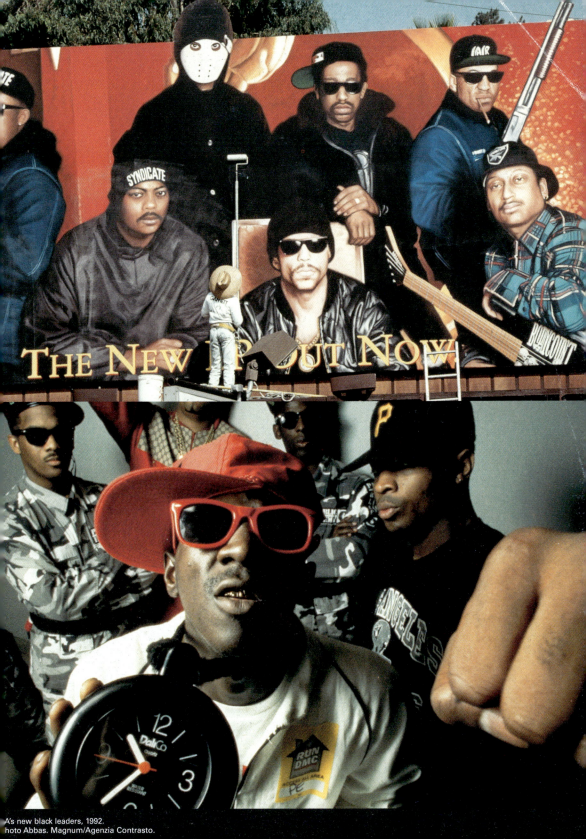

THE NEW [...]OUT NOW

A's new black leaders, 1992.
hoto Abbas. Magnum/Agenzia Contrasto.

ublic Enemy, 1988.
hoto Chris Buck. Visages/Agenzia Grazia Neri.

In an American essay at the end of the Seventies, Michael Selzer borrows the term "terrorism chic" from Tom Wolfe and applies it to the linguistic similarities he sees in the intrinsic violence of advertising language and real terrorism. "Terrorist chic is the extreme limit that can be reached by society in the expression of fantasies that the terrorists themselves make explicit through behavior...." The shared objective of these two systems is to amaze and provoke an emotional reaction in the spectator. In the recent anthology *Fashion-Social Aspects*, Cheryll Herr analyzes the way of dressing and the style of the members of the IRA, applying Selzer's definition to the context of Northern Ireland. The reasoning begins with the statement that the dominant atmosphere in some parts of the country is marked by a pervasive presence of control systems, with cameras ready to record, without any regard for privacy, the development of hotbeds of subversion. Therefore the militants of the IRA are accustomed to living in a condition that simultaneously imposes the need to be hidden and the need to be recognized. This leads to the need to conceal oneself behind a mask, the use of a true uniform that permits the birth of a collective body: the loss of individuality is accompanied by the fact that this anonymity becomes highly visible and reflects, not coincidentally, the symbols and behaviors of the official army. This alternation, in symbolic terms, also produces a short-circuit on the level of relations of power. The same dynamic can be seen in other counter-armies, such as the Black Panthers. In effect, one of the most frequent dynamics in relations between those who hold power and those who are subjected to it and fight against it is the similarity that is produced in the poses of the two opposing sides. *edc*

Black Muslim Army, 1961.
© Eve Arnold/Magnum/Agenzia Contrasto.

Panther, 1995.
Directed by Mario Van Peebles.
© R. Zuckerman/Gramercy. Pic/Shooting Star.
Agenzia Grazia Neri.

Repubblican funeral on Falls Road.
Belfast, 1979.
© Steele Perkins, Magnum/Agenzia Contrasto.

CLOCKWISE
FROM BOTTOM
LEFT

ANDY (18)
JUDE (17)
DEAN (17)
GREG (18)

"Chillin (not Illin),"
in *The Face,* n. 87, July 1987, pp. 62/63.
Photo Derek Ridgers, Sheila Rock.

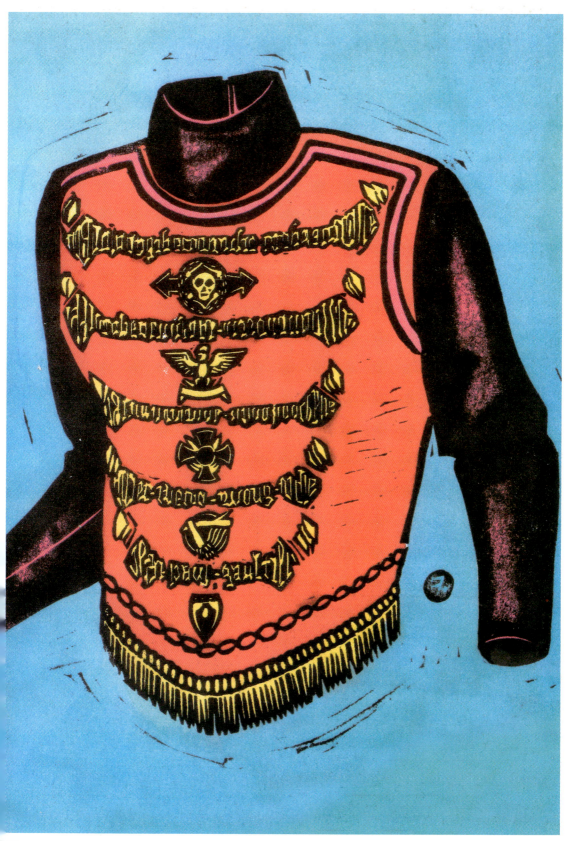

Pet Shop Boys,
Concert, Palavobis, Milan, 24 December1999.
© London Features International/
Agenzia Grazia Neri.

Taiwan, Taipei, 1987.
A celebration organized by the Kuomintang party
in honor of the Taiwanese police force.
© Patrick Zachmann/Magnum.

Leonid Brežnev salutes during the parade
in Red Square in Moscow for the anniversary
of the Russian Revolution, 10 November 1970.
Hulton Getty. Agenzia Grazia Neri.

Preceding pages
Stalin at a session of the Central Committee of the
Communist Party.
Photo Publifoto/Olympia.

Evil is more elegant than goodness: in the most tragic reality and the collective imagination, treachery wears affected clothing of exemplary beauty, as if to conceal its merciless nature behind the perfection of gestures and manners. Actually this is not a mere disguise, but the expression of a need to impose a distance, to utilize beauty as a way of legitimizing presumed superiority. This is how horror selects its clothing: finery, decorations, boots, hats and helmets, but above all gloves and capes, references to an idea of beauty derived from the imagery of the Romantics, from Byron and Bram Stoker.

It was precisely during the 1800s that evil changed its visage and its look: the witches of Shakespeare vanish, leaving room for Count Dracula, wrapped in his cape.

This passage reflects a profound psychological change that is not limited to the world of literature: horror abandons the damp, miry territory of the forest and takes up residence in the palace, in the decadent luxury of a castle in the Carpathians. In other words, terror continues to celebrate its distance, but it no longer dwells in the centerless space of the forest: it now prefers the hierarchical and perspective detachment of power and nobility, transformed into a terrifying, monstrous caricature. The beauty of terror, in fact, is molded around the desires and anxieties of its subjects: that timeless elegance reflects the imagination of a bourgeoisie that tries to escape itself, bridging the gap that separates it from the dream of nobility. *mg*

Chile's military junta twelve years
after the coup, 1985.
Photo Carlos Sarrion/SYGMA.
Agenzia Grazia Neri.

Raf Simons,
autumn/winter 1999/2000 show.
Photo Marleen Daniels and Carl Bruyndonckx.

In the years of Communist China the uniform took on a central significance both in the definition of social norms – the dream of uniformity and absolute functional efficiency, the cardinal element of modernity – and in the definition of gender identity. In particular, the uniform played a role in the nationalist construction of the modern woman or "new woman," focusing attention on class struggle and rejecting anything that could be considered an expression of subjective desire. In the Sixties and Seventies the Cultural Revolution praised the "girl of iron," effectively erasing all differences between the sexes. The green uniform of the army, worn by the Red Guards and representatives of the party, including Mao Zedong, became an ideological instrument worn widely by women seeking to occupy a social position of importance. This was observed by western students who protested in Europe and the United States against consumism, pursuing new forms of essential simplicity: in their demonstrations they waved Mao's little red book and wore uniforms similar to those of the Chinese. Without having all been forced to dress alike by the state, the uniform is a choice that signified equality and sharing of ideals with one's peers. In the case of Veruschka, photographed for Vogue Paris dressed up as Mao in an idea hatched by Salvador Dalì, it is an occasion for glamour. With the drift away from the revolutionary spirit and the opening of Chinese markets, prêt-à-porter invaded the country, and fashion – in a cyclical, specular game of meaning in relation to the context – has become an essential vehicle for the declaration of individuality. *edc*

Preceding pages
Angela Wilde and Serguei,
in *Impec espion de Mugler*,
Moskva, July 1986.
in *Thierry Mugler Photographe*,
Paris: Ed. du Regard, 1988.

Mao.
© Agenzia Grazia Neri.

"Veruschka come Mao:
un'idea di Salvador Dalí per *Vogue Paris*,"
January 1971.
© Alex Chatelain.
Reprinted in *Vogue Italia*,
n. 559, March 1997, p. 519.

VERUSCHKA
COME MAO: UN'IDEA
DI SALVADOR
DALÍ PER "VOGUE
PARIS", GEN.
1971. FOTO
ALEX CHATELAIN.

Power always keeps its distance, in a stance of solemn detachment from reality: it is ready to strike, to burst onto life's scene, but always from a secret refuge. For this reason power requires images and signs that maintain a level of caution while preserving the force and the violence in the realm of imagery. Were the chief a person in flesh and blood here beside us, his power would be enormously reduced: we could attack him, smash him, destroy him. Were it immediately reachable power wouldn't be frightening. It's no coincidence that the images of mercenary commanders, dictators and revolutionaries always maintain an abstract tone. They are stylized forms, constructed with few graphic features: they indicate presence, while at the same time reinforcing distance. They preserve power in the secret refuge of the idea. They are icons, similar to divine emanations, shrouds and standards on which to trace the faint imprint of a visage.

But even icons wear out: there is a subtle distinction between the spectral, threatening presence of power and its parody. The wax statues and posters, the t-shirts of Che Guevara and the merchandise for high school revolutionaries set off a process of image inflation, wiping out the distance. Power collapses due to excessive visibility, the icon decays and becomes a mere logo. Just a few days ago the newspapers reported that a trendy brand of vodka wanted to make an advertisement with the famous portrait of "Che." And for several years now, when tourists come back from the East they bring handfuls of badges with portraits of Lenin and Stalin: you can hold them in your hand, wear them on the lapel of your jacket. They are no longer frightening. *mg*

Glimpses of Cuba.
Photo Terry Smith/Camera Press International.
Agenzia Grazia Neri.

May 1968, La Sorbonne, Paris.
J. Niepce/Rapho.

Hiroshi Sugimoto, *Fidel Castro*, 1999.
Photo b/w, ed. of 5,19.6 x 119.3 cm.
Courtesy Sonnabend Gallery, New York.

Preceding pages
Elvis Presley.
Photo Charles Bonnay/Black Star.

Marlon Brando,
in *The Young Lions*, 1958.
Archives GBB.
Agenzia Grazia Neri.

Piotr Uklanski,
The Nazis (detail),1998.
C-Print, 35.5 x 25.4 cm each.
Courtesy Gavin Brown Enterprises, New York.

For Anselm Kiefer, as for Joyce in
Finnegan's Wake, history is a nightmare
from which we are trying to awake. In
the series of photographs gathered in
the book entitled *Occupations* (1969),
Kiefer portrays himself in the pose of a
Nazi soldier, right arm extended high,
wearing garments that immediately
remind us of the terrorizing uniform of
the Reich.

The liturgy of the Roman salute is
reenacted in the most painful places
of German history, on the traces of
monuments and landscapes that,
according to Hitler, contained the
origins of the Germanic race: the
Colosseum appears beside the sea of
fog painted by Caspar David Friedrich,
the Brandenburg Gate beside an
equestrian monument in Montpellier.
History and geography are defeated,
overwhelmed and bent to the purpose
of the madness of Nazism, in which
the romantic tradition of Wagner is
forced to coexist alongside the myth
of Rome, in a syncretism of signs and
symbols that is simultaneously
ridiculous and merciless, emptying
them of their original meaning and
charging them with pure violence.
Kiefer's procession is a visit to the
scene of the perfect crime: a reverse
pilgrimage into the guts of history,
which returns in its images with the
force of a repressed and, if possible,
even more anguishing past. *mg*

Anselm Kiefer,
from the *Besetzungen* (*Occupations*)
series, 1969.
Courtesy Lia Rumma, Napoli.

Marlon Brando, Elizabeth Taylor,
in *Reflections in a Golden Eye*, 1967.
Directed by John Houston.
Snap Photo/JR. Agenzia Grazia Neri.

The Night Porter, 1972.
Directed by Liliana Cavani.
© Sunset Boulevard, SYGMA.
Agenzia Grazia Neri.

Two women rushed over to serve them: Culculine and
Alexine, charming from head to toe. They were dressed
like Russian soldiers and wore aprons with lacework
over full trousers tucked into their boots: their bosoms
and buttocks swelled pleasantly, rounding the contours
of the uniform. A cap worn crosswise completed the
charm of this military garb. They looked like two little
extras in an operetta.

Guillaume Apollinaire,
Les onze mille verges, 1907

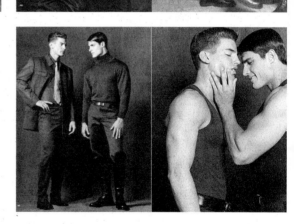

Istante, Versace advertising,
autumn/winter 1996/1997.
Photo Bruce Weber, stylist Joe McKenna.

a class apart

istante

Paris, 14 July 1992. Military parade.
© Giry/Rea. Agenzia Contrasto.

Paris, 14 July 1992. Military parade.
© Mario Fourmy/Rea. Agenzia Contrasto.

Paris, 14 July 1992. Military parade.
© Giry/Rea. Agenzia Contrasto.

Soldiers in the 80th Battalion "Roma."
Photo Eligio Paoni. Agenzia Contrasto.

Artane Boys Band.

Magic Stars Majorettes, Amsterdam.

Mirabelle Gospel Choir, Birmingham.

St. John's Ambulance.

rankendael Group, Amsterdam.

rass Band, Ballington.

Irish Catholic Girl Guides, Dublin.

Dutch Marching Band, Birmingham.
© Steve Pyke, Agenzia Contrasto.

43

**On my honor I will do my best
To do my duty to God and my country
And to obey the Scout Law:
To help other people at all times;
To keep myself physically strong,
Mentally awake and morally straight.**

Scout Oath

Toni Matelli, *Lost and Sick*, 1996.
Epoxy, plaster, paint, 78 x 102 x 96 cm.

SOCIAL IDENTITY, MILITARY IDENTITY

LORENZO GRECO

Towards a sociology of military communications. Every society depends upon the fact that its members agree upon rules and principles to a sufficient extent to guarantee an acceptable level of functioning. While this is true at the more general level of institutions and laws, Erving Goffman[1] has also spoken – regarding any social order – of tacit agreement and consensus that are expressed even in the most banal, everyday personal interactions. Goffman uses the example of pedestrian traffic on sidewalks, describing it as a scenario (though a minimal one) in which reciprocal trust among strangers is a matter of routine: no one would dream, for example, while walking on a crowded street in a city center, of suddenly turning around and starting to kick passersby. Were this to happen, the culprit would immediately be faced with a prompt reaction from the other pedestrians. But it is not the reaction, or the fear of punishment, that keeps the river of pedestrians moving; it is the importance such an orderly flow has for each of the individuals inside it.

Francesco Alberoni has written, "Our entire civil life, our security, is based on this pattern of regularity. In traffic we keep to the right, we cross streets on sidewalks, we greet acquaintances, at Christmas we send cards to our friends, we knock before entering a room, we ask permission, we beg pardon, we respect the rules of sports. . . ."[2]

For the individuals that are part of it, the sense of social reality is defined, specified and made concrete by the acceptance of similar codes of behavior: the social order transforms behavior into conduct, and physical coexistence becomes the proving ground for the character of individuals, a true cornerstone of the mutual trust attributed by one individual to another regarding the very possibility of collective coexistence, the concrete evidence of a mutually declared social morality. It is no coincidence that sudden revelations or discoveries of even minimal shortcomings in the behavior of those around us lead – due to the fact that they threaten this delicate system of mutual trust – to immediate sanctionary measures among peers.

Trust betrayed, good faith deceived and broken promises threaten our entire system of interactions: complete faith in our counterpart is the necessary condition for mutually advantageous interaction. These are the very pillars of coexistence.

Military society is also based on a contract. The crucial moment of entry in military life is a solemn oath, in which the subject publicly commits himself to fulfill the duties related to his new status, which also include the most solemn duty a society can ask of one of its members, the most onerous of all duties: that of being ready to sacrifice, if necessary, one's own life. And yet, within this general framework that involves such a dramatic responsibility, Alberoni demonstrates that there are numberless little, apparently gratuitous duties, or at least duties that don't appear to be particularly justifiable: "In military service great importance is attributed to physical cleanliness, an impeccable uniform, the way of saluting and greeting, the tone of voice when speaking to superiors, alignment when marching, all details which, with respect to the performance of a soldier in battle, appear rather frivolous or uselessly fastidious. But which are actually essential to create that rigorous sense of order and discipline that makes the army a component of a democratic state, and not a band of highwaymen and plunderers, as happened in the past."[3]

In relation to the conventional, codified nature of the social contract established in military life, one important theme is that of faith in others. The appearance of normality which a scenario of military life can – and must – present in moments that are absolutely not normal (in battle, first of all, but also in many other, more frequent situations that are potentially dangerous for individual safety) is the result of a type of systematically constructed trust among all the members.

In the very delicate system of military life, which due to its hierarchical structure is full of situations of potential interpersonal conflict, it is absolutely necessary to rely on an unquestioned mutual trust based on a strong sentiment of consensus and therefore of morality. Trust and morality, therefore, seem to be the crucial values in the type of relation that sustains any social interchange, and especially those of the military context.

As a social and cultural world that is part of an entire, more complex society that contains and encloses it, the military world obviously features analogies of functioning and systems of rules that do not differ from those of the society as a whole. Nevertheless, it also has some characteristics of discontinuity, which are more or less vivid depending upon the historical era and the society in question, but are always quite unmistakable and particular.

How can people tell I'm in the military? The military individual becomes such in a special space and time, in particular social relations, governed by principles – familiar to the entire society, but particularly stringent here – such as hierarchy and subordination (hierarchy is important everywhere, but it is even more essential in the military).[4] Individuality, once inside the military system, is strongly conditioned by this state of belonging. A military man is recognizable (must be recognizable) at first glance. A number of signs make this possible.

Based only on this observation, we can already state that this is a world in which signs constitute a very complex and fundamental system. And here we refer to those exterior or even aesthetic signs par excellence that take on such importance as to approach a condition of paradox: in fact, it is not coincidental that the term "military form" is applied to a wide range of external manifestations, including details which – to the untrained observer – are unimaginable.

To begin with, the military person's way of dressing must (apart from special cases) be semiotically explicit:

1) The individual must communicate his belonging to the military world in his dress. In Italy the specific signs are the stars, two small stars with the same design for all the different branches of the armed forces and all the ranks, worn on the points of the shirt collar or the jacket lapels. An old barracks song for recruits declares: "The stars we wear / are the soldier's discipline." Thanks to the stars, at a glance it is possible to distinguish a military man from a civilian.

2) The uniform must indicate belonging to a particular service (Navy, Army, Carabinieri . . .). This is done with very general signals such as color and shape of the uniform, and with other particular signs like insignia, buttons, badges and other aesthetic details, even very small ones, but always regulated. The meaning of each detail is precisely defined.

3) The uniform must also indicate rank, or the precise position in the hierarchical order. The difference must be evident between a plain soldier and a superior officer.

4) In some of the services, professional specializations or roles must also be visibly indicated. For example, in the Navy, petty

officers and seamen wear the symbols of their respective jobs on their sleeve (engineer, electrician, paymaster, etc.). But the officers are also distinguished according to the corps to which they belong, by the color that forms the background for the symbols of their rank (black for the General Staff, red for the Commissariat corps, etc.). Other services indicate the corps to which an individual belongs not with colors but with small signs, often recognized only by those who know the code (an eagle, a laurel wreath . . .).

So the complex semiotic function of the uniform is evident, with its rich variety of signs and symbols that communicate, for those who know the code, highly detailed information, while providing more limited data, in an eloquent way, even for non-initiates. Even if the observer knows absolutely nothing of that world, at least one essential datum reaches him: the military uniform indicates the fact that its wearer belongs to the particular social group entrusted by the rest of society with the responsibility of using weapons. A social group, therefore, upon which an authority and a power such as those that can only be attained through the control of powerful weaponry, subject to greater restrictions and duties than other citizens. The first restriction has to do (though it might seem banal) precisely with the uniform: here everything is codified, nothing is left up to personal initiative.

In today's society the norms and customs regarding civilian dress have lost much of their traditional statutory force. Not so long ago the cut and color of a garment indicated that its wearer belonged to a certain social class or even a certain profession, offering a very precise definition of social rank. In the life of an aristocratic family, there was a precise garment for every occasion and for every moment of the day. In the society of the not-so-distant past, the codes of dress were well-regulated: it would have been unthinkable for a peasant to wear a hat similar to that of the estate agent, or for the steward to wear the same hat as the proprietor. Forms, colors and ornaments provided detailed differentiation on the social scale with such prescriptive force that no one would have dreamed of upsetting the order. Only at Carnival time could a young peasant boy dare, wearing clothing abandoned by the proprietor's family, to imitate the son of the master, who may well have been his friend or playmate.

Today dress is certainly still a language, but the main function – especially among young people – of the cut, the colors and accessories is to externally manifest one's psychological and ideological personality: for a young man to wear a leather jacket and a belt with metal studs has a different meaning than a French beret and a red wool scarf. In the face of all this subjective liberty, the military standard of the uniform stands out even more sharply today, with its codified rules and precisely defined signs: so much so that a syntagm often used to indicate military life – synonymous with a life without subjective freedoms (both large and small) – is still "to wear the uniform." It is interesting to note that the Italian term for uniform, *divisa*, comes from the French *dévise*, meaning mission or purpose. To wear a uniform, therefore, means displaying, in one's garb, a choice, a status, a condition.

The inversion of sense. In certain ways we seem to be looking at an analogous situation: both the civilian and the soldier display a choice of life in their dress. But there is an evident inversion of sense between the two ways of dressing. The civilian manifests a totally subjective, individual choice. He wears what he wants to, as he wants to. Every morning as he dresses, he creates a small but complex semiotic system, valid perhaps for that day only.

The military man, on the other hand, dons his uniform (which, as we have seen, is a preorganized system of signs established by others), and with it the signs of his belonging to a society that does not tolerate (except in very minor ways) personal differences and individual choices.

The cases in which there is a sort of swap of the two codes are interesting, i.e., when military people wear civilian clothes, and vice versa, when civilians wear parts of military uniforms (a trend today, but also in the past). The regulations regarding the possibility to wear civilian clothing for military staff have recently been drastically updated and, in substance, relaxed. Historical paintings show that military men always, on all occasions, wore their uniforms (without privileges of rank: in fact, it was unthinkable for a high-ranking officer to dress any other way). The use of the uniform in non-military situations today is obligatory only for certain types of students, who need to reinforce on all occasions, including their free time, their as yet fragile sense of institutional belonging. And even their civilian outfits, if permitted, are highly controlled, so much so that it is still easy to recognize their status. In a certain sense their "street clothes," during the brief period in which they are students, represent a uniform.

But in substance, today a demarcation has been achieved that would once have been thought impossible: the uniform is worn only on military time and in military space, while when off duty and outside the military facilities any type of civilian clothing is allowed. Each individual then reclaims the freedom to express himself by means of dress.

The hypergrammar of military form. In a hypercodified system, or one that is minutely regulated and, we might say, hyper-semiotic, other signs related to the body – such as gestures – also become relevant.

Soldiers don't walk, they march. They advance in tight ranks, but also in more ordinary circumstances, must respond to requirements of order, self-control, performance, defined in every minimum pose.

The sense of satisfaction provoked by the sight of a platoon of soldiers marching with precision, with perfect synchronized movements, is part of our perception of the reliability, readiness and security of the use of a military instrument. The order and perfect, regulated formation seem to be the external expression of an achieved, confident discipline. The aim of parades, in fact, is to demonstrate to superiors and to society in general the level of military training achieved. This is why the external part – even the aesthetic part – of military form is so important: because it is what "others" in general can see, constituting an important moment of communication for the entire society. This may appear strange to those who cannot grasp the need for such an elaborate form of communication. In other words, this linguistic behavior is similar to that of someone who wants to prove that he can express himself properly, and does so not only by displaying his knowledge of the rules, but also a marked (or even exaggerated) respect for grammatical norms. Therefore, in this sense military life is connoted by a sort of hypergrammar.

Semiotics of the body. The hypergrammar principle can also be seen in individual details. Where hair is concerned, specific standardizing traditions exist: it has to be short, and cut in a non-eccentric way. The historical reasons for short hair are many: hygiene, first of all. But the ritual regulations of many religions have taught us that even when they appear to be for purely hygienic purposes, they also entail other spiritual and symbolic reasons. This is especially true for hair, which has always been the focus of norms, prohibitions and beliefs in all societies.

The biblical story of Samson tells us that long hair means strength, and therefore autonomy, independence. No less important is the fact that long hair in the human race is a feminine attribute, and military life must effect a precise separation from the feminine world (leading, by the way, to certain difficulties caused by the integration of women into the armed forces). As a result of this complex symbolic value, the first thing that happens to a new recruit is the haircut – a rite of passage and subjection to new rules. A uniform haircut for both military men and women is the first sign of subjection to a discipline that is equal for all. But the hair mustn't simply be short, it has to be cut with a certain uniform style, defined by the regulations.

There are also rules for the posture and position of parts of the body, the head, chest, stomach, feet and arms – especially when standing at attention or saluting – rules that every good drill sergeant makes sure he drills into the recruits, usually with a fair share of shouting and insults.

Attention! The position of standing at attention/at ease is an interesting one: the order *attention!* (to assume a precise, rigid posture), indicates the correct attitude when in the presence of superiors. This is a highly codified position (typical of soldiers in every era and place) full of implicit meanings, which only an explicit counter-order (*at ease!*, a sort of response and completion) permits it to be transformed into another, more relaxed but still thoroughly codified position, that of standing "at ease." Not even the greenest of new recruits would think of sitting down comfortably after hearing the order *at ease!* (Such things happen only in comedy films.)

Just why must soldiers stand "at attention"? Many animals, when faced with danger, or in situations of great alertness, assume a rigid, immobile position, which is very unnatural for humans. Precisely because it is unnatural, the assumption in front of men of higher rank of the position "at attention" – a sort of instantaneous balancing point amidst flight, defense and counterattack – means controlling one's will, and therefore subordinating to a superior will, or manifestating a readiness for such subordination. One renounces (one expresses the readiness to renounce) one's own vitality and any manifestation of autonomy as a sign of subordination and respect. *Perinde ac cadaver*, precisely like a corpse: was this not the motto of the Jesuits, the most military of all religious orders, to indicate the extreme choice of obedience and fidelity?

Standing at attention, alternated with standing at ease, is a form of salute, a segment of a ritual that recurs very frequently. Rituals are successions of movements, separate and distinct, articulated together just as orthographic signs articulate the parts of a discourse. In certain spheres and cultures, a ritual was punctuated – consider Eastern traditions, but also the etiquette required in our royal courts or high society – by many bows. Bowing was part of a ritual; its moral meaning was to make gestures of submission, as a manifestation of homage and respect. In the military ritual –

consider the conduction of any military ceremony, where the arrayed troops do little more than alternate the two positions – the rhythm and pace is marked by the alternation "attention/ease." Two very rigid postures, it is true, whose moral significance is made clear by the contrast with bowing: the soldier never bows; he may do so spontaneously only when greeting a lady and kissing her hand, but he never bows to another military man, no matter how high in rank. In short, "attention/ease" is a linguistic feature belonging to a precise social language, expressing a *sociative* function of that language.

Therefore the code of gesture and body position has the same value as the code of the uniform. From the variegated multiplicity of the signs we all have available in life every day with which to express the individual richness of our sentiments and emotions, we pass to the simplification and reduction of the signs codified in the military universe. But the resulting uniformity of the military world does not possess anything less in terms of semiotic richness. Instead, the use of signs, symbols and rituals meets with extraordinary stimulus. And their value is greater than in the rest of society, because while their "sociative" function is inevitably the same, the fundamental rule of the military world is different and even opposite, with a severe predominance (thus the code of discipline) of the social norm over individual interests and needs.

1. Erving Goffman, *The Presentation of Self in Everyday Life* (Garden City, N.Y.: Doubleday, 1959).
2. "Pubblico&Privato," *Corriere della Sera* (Milan), 3 July 2000, weekly column.
3. Ibid.
4. I take the liberty of referring readers to my *Homo militaris. Letteratura e antropologia della vita militare* (Milan: Franco Angeli, 1999), in which I have attempted to describe the salient aspects of the military world seen as a cultural system (from macroscopic to apparently less important aspects, such as certain details of uniforms, for example).

MILITARY DRESS, MODERN DRESS

STEFANO TONCHI

"Uniforms are the sportswear of the twentieth century," Diane Vreeland said. Strolling through the streets of any metropolis in the world today one gets the impression that they will be an important part of dress in the twentieth-first century, as well. Youths in cargo pants, men in flight jackets and parkas, fashion victims in safari jackets and sailor cabans are common sights on the everyday scene. Fashion runways feature periodic flurries of camouflage-print chiffon evening gowns, haversack vests in multicolored satin, military greatcoats in cashmere with gilded buttons where, more than ever before, the initials of stylists are taking the place of the insignias of royal families, empires and dictators.

In the distant aftermath of the great wars, as real soldiers begin to look more and more like civilians – just consider the consumption of the Hollywood icon of the soldier in khaki trousers, shirt and tie – "the imitation of the military uniform has triumphed over the original prototype." This was the comment of Holly Brubach a few years ago in the *New York Times* on the decision of the American Navy to eliminate the bell-bottomed "sailor" trousers just when the fashion designers and street kids were starting to wear them again.

The postmodern era has witnessed the proliferation of camouflage prints, cargo pants and backpacks, indicative of the sensation that war is remote and, paradoxically, nostalgia for more heroic days is on the increase. At the same time, some observers have noticed that conflicts and dangers seem to be rapidly finding their way from war zones to our cities. The modern city has become a battlefield, a trench, a society of continuous risk.

Fifty years ago the fashion shows in the Sala Bianca of Palazzo Pitti in Florence marked the birth of prêt-à-porter. But the first ready-to-wear garments, with standardized sizes and proportions to adapt to men and women with different physiques, were military uniforms. The history of uniforms is the heritage and obsession of collectors and scholars far from the world of fashion design and expert trendsetters. But at this point it has become, above all, a voyage back to the roots of what we wear each and every day.

The formal and technological evolution of uniforms lies at the origin of modern dress, because standard military issue consists of a system of industrially-produced garments in different sizes and qualities, which change according to social and weather conditions, and communicate belonging, rejection, values and hopes. It is therefore not surprising that military uniforms and civilian dress become nearly inseparable until the military and civilian societies become separate entities, often in conflict with each other. It is no coincidence that the golden age of the uniform begins with the Napoleonic Wars, the birth of the modern state, the rise of the middle classes, and the emergence of nationalism. During the seventeenth century the first signals were the militaresque organization of Gustavus Adolphus in Sweden and the military teachings of Wallenstein, but it was only with Napoleon and Frederick of Prussia that even civilians were put into uniform, from the postman to the elementary school teacher.

In Antiquity and throughout the Middle Ages and the Renaissance, monarchs and emperors financed and clothed armies; but in these cases the clothing for mercenary soldiers was everyday dress, to which particular signs were added during battle – sashes, cockades, plumes of different colors, down to the red cross on a white field worn by the crusaders.

It was only with the beginning of true industrial production and of long-distance transport for the supply of large quantities of inexpensive materials and dyes from the East that modern states could afford to dress immense multitudes of men in the same uniform, with the same fabric and color, for the specific aim of war. This clothing was studied even in its smallest detail with the aim of making the individual conform to a general idea and a series of precise rules to be unquestioningly obeyed; the cut and construction of each garment represented the final evolution of the male wardrobe. From the outset, the military uniform has had a dual nature: theater and function. Over time these two elements have alternated, with one or the other getting the upper hand, depending upon the society in question and the given historical moment.

On one hand, the uniform responds to the need to create simi-

larity, a sense of belonging to an idea and nation, and to celebrate its strength and traditions while striking fear into the heart
of the enemy. Thus the use of symbolic colors: the red coats of
the English, the blue of the Americans; the assumption of ances-
tral values and ethnic traditions: the kilts of the Scots within the
British armed forces, the gilded braiding of the Slavic cavalry
assimilated in the Russian imperial army; the mythologizing of
leather: the shiny boots, large belts at the waist or crossed over
the chest, and armor-like jackets, so precise in the Bavarian and
Prussian iconography as to become an integral part of Nazi
dress. Not to mention the headwear in all forms and materials,
decorated with crosses, eagles, coats of arms, plumes and
panaches, with the sole aim of creating a theatrical effect.

On the other hand, the uniform as clothing for combat responds
to completely different and often opposing requirements: to
blend into the environment and even resemble the enemy himself; to be agile in one's movements, capable of adapting to different climates and situations; to be capable of constantly
evolving in order to respond to the new techniques and technologies of war.

These are the characteristics that best define the modern military
uniform. The dualism intrinsic to the uniform reflects the dualism
implied by the idea of fashion itself, aimed simultaneously at
conformity and distinction, at celebrating the past and the security of tradition while continuously adapting to the technologies
of the future. During the twentieth century, both in military uniforms and civilian dress, practicality and functional factors have
inexorably – apart from certain exceptions along the way – dominated the values of theatricality and tradition. Just as in fashion
certain garments are now relegated almost exclusively to movies
or costume balls, so certain uniforms are utilized only in particular situations, parades or ceremonies, or by special units without
any actively bellicose responsibilities, like the royal guards at
Buckingham Palace or the Swiss guards at the Vatican. The characteristics that for centuries so precisely defined the man in uniform have become increasingly rare. Already at the start of the
1900s the color khaki had begun to replace the red of the English
army, the white of the French and the blue of the Americans,
while the Russians and Germans had begun to utilize different
shadings of gray-green or green-gray, which were not so different from khaki. Color definitively vanished, except for the ribbons and details, with the sole exception of camouflage patterns
and high-visibility fabrics.

Starting with World War I, leather – that intrinsic symbol in the iconography of the warrior – also began to be replaced by more practical and resistant materials like hemp, and later by the new synthetic materials for belts, straps, cartridge belts, backpacks, haversacks and even footwear. Prada nylon backpacks were just around the corner.

In a continuous process of osmosis, military uniforms and civilian dress have influenced each other over the years. Beginning with the French Revolution, when the legwear of the *sansculottes* in revolt against the monarchy became the model for the practical, clinging trousers worn by Napoleon. The same thing happens with the new fashion of the century: the practicality of civilian clothing is continuously incorporated into military uniforms. And the garments perfected and idealized in military iconography make a triumphant return in everyday civilian dress.

The hunting dress of English gentleman – the Norfolk suit – forms the prototype for combat gear, with deep, convenient pockets and a reversible collar. The khaki color – from the Persian word *khak*, meaning dust, earth, mud – of uniforms all over the world was borrowed from the personal wardrobe of Indian soldiers who dyed their clothing with natural pigments to disguise dirt.

But perhaps the most telling of all examples is the continuous and repeated passage of the trench coat from the military to the civil sphere. Created in England, probably by the manufacturer Burberry as a garment for shepherds, farmers and country gentlemen for protection from rain and wind, this coat became such a common feature among soldiers in the trenches during World War I that it took on the name "trench coat" and became a standard feature in the uniforms of many armies around the world. The practicality of this overcoat/raincoat in certain weather conditions justified its utilization even before it became a part of the uniform. Between the two world wars the trench coat returned to everyday closets, and became the uniform of the adventurer, spy and rebel without a country, perfectly personified by Humphrey Bogart in *Casablanca*. After being worn by generals and colonels during World War II, the trench coat returned as the uniform of intellectuals, writers and journalists all over the world. Later it wound up in alternating phases on fashion runways, from Yves Saint Laurent to Giorgio Armani, down to the monogrammed GG, LV or CC versions of this last season.

Dozens of familiar, common items in our everyday wardrobe have shared a similar fate: the blue wool caban jacket of sailors, the leather or shearling jacket of pilots, the parka with the fur-edged hood, safari jackets and cargo pants, vests with many pockets, sports backpacks and Eisenhower jackets. The latter is a perfect example of the way national borders become useless against the power of fashion. This article – Wool Field Jacket M1944 – (originally a combat jacket cut short at the waist for practicality and to save on fabric) first worn by the English troops during the war, was so admired by General Eisenhower, the head of the Allied Forces in Europe and future president of the United States, and so popular among American soldiers that it became Eisenhower's uniform, the uniform of the US Army, and the most common piece of sportswear in the male wardrobe. In the modern version the buttons have been replaced by zippers, and the logo of Ralph Lauren or Tomy Hilfiger has taken the place of the decorations, but the proportions remain the same: ample around the chest, and narrow at the sides with broad shoulders. Soldiers in every war have come back from the front with new experiences and terrifying tales, but also with military garments that silently became a part of everyday dress.

In the United States at the end of World War II, the continued production of uniforms, although not in military fabrics, even became an economic necessity and later the source of great wealth as the garments were sold to re-clothe an entire planet. The functional quality and practicality tested in combat, the technology used to create new, more resistant fibers and fabrics, and the economy of resources and materials represented a legacy which the clothing industry ably transferred from military to civilian production.

While the more theatrical characteristics of uniforms are just a memory in the technologically advanced equipment issued to the modern soldier, over the last fifty years we have seen an increase and refinement of the political, revolutionary, counter-revolutionary, or simply spectacular use of those same details. In the uniforms of the fascists and Nazis of the Thirties, taken as models by all the subsequent dictatorial regimes of the world, and in the costumes of rockstars or the most extreme creations of fashion designers, shiny black leather boots, riding pants, jackets with hussar braiding, coats with epaulettes decorated with gilded fringe, capes and mantles, coats of arms, decorations, metal eagles and gold buttons are all decisive elements. Freed of their practical function – the epaulette, for example, was created as protection against blows of the sword – these elements have assumed a symbolic and at times ideological value, but to an increasing extent they are merely decorative, to the point of becoming simply the surface on which to place a logo or a set of initials: the Armani eagle, the crossed C's of Chanel, or Versace's medusa.

The simplicity of the shirt decorated with coat of arms or insignia on the collar, is the same as that of Boy Scout and school uniforms: it expresses the purity of youthful sentiments, far from political calculations. The cap with visor and leather boots are a memory of the Austro-Hungarian and Prussian armies: they express the value of tradition. The color black and the skull come from the uniforms of the Russian counter-revolutionaries: they express national values to be protected. It is no coincidence that the creators of these uniforms were theatrical costume or fashion designers.

The contrast between the modern functionalism of the American armed forces and the romantic traditionalism of the uniforms of Eastern armies, directly inherited from the czars and the Nazis, is thoroughly illustrated in the films of the Cold War era. On one side, the soldier who fights for freedom and democracy in simple, semi-civilian clothes – khaki shirt and trousers – on the other, the dark, rigid, decorated, almost nineteenth-century uniform of the enemy. The victory of the American aesthetic didn't happen only on the battlefields of Europe and Asia, or only in the arena of political strategy, but also in the everyday wardrobe. In the Fifties and Sixties, Americans sold four million military objects in the world, from jeeps to khaki trousers, permanently transforming the world's way of dressing. The charisma and sex appeal of the American GI – always relaxed but ready for action, comfortable but clean and well-groomed – undermined the idea of elegance previously embodied by the man rigidly garbed in jacket and tie, and laid the groundwork for the casual revolution of the last few decades.

Fashion, with its continuous reprises, has translated these contradictions into civilian dress, unabashedly celebrating the purity and simplicity of the victorious American soldier and, at the same time, allowing itself to be seduced by the dark, often ambiguous charm of the S&M accents of formal uniforms. In like manner cinema, advertising and communications have alternated their use of the seductive powers of the uniform to create blockbusters, to sell all kinds of products – from the simple flight jacket to after-shave – and to promote concerts or shock parents. Over the last fifty years it is hard to find a single actor or musician who has managed to escape the charms of the military uniform, and certainly not out of a sense of duty. From Marlon Brando to Tom Cruise, Montgomery Clift to Richard Gere, Jodie Foster to Demi Moore, American cinema has put and continues

THE POWER
OF THE UNIFORM

AMY SPINDLER

Here's a story that was circulating when I first started working in fashion magazines: an editor-in-chief was asked by the male owner of the company she worked for to don a maid's uniform and serve dinner to some of her magazine's most prominent advertisers. This urban legend of fashion publishing was repeated regularly to illustrate just how misogynist the boy's club of women's fashion can be. And fashion people (especially in the retelling and embellishment of exactly what kind of maid's uniform the editor had worn – French? No, Benny Hill British satire-style with the ruffled panties) understood precisely what made it so horrible.

Part of the horror is obvious, a woman at the top of her field demeaned in such a way. But is the story as awful if she's asked to wear, say, a police uniform instead? What if she were asked to wear judge's robes? A chef's toque, plaid pants, and white jacket? What if she were asked to wear a an IBM salesman's classic wing tip shoes, pinstripe double breasted suit and white shirt?

The message that the mythical magazine owner was trying to get across – we're here to serve our advertisers – isn't lost if she's wearing any other uniform while presenting them with their dishes. But turning her into a dish by putting her into a maid's uniform was really, pardon the expression, the icing on the cake. Even if serving the dinner was only part of the humiliation of the story, it was the power of the uniform that pushed the tale of the evening over the edge.

I've become an accidental expert in the power of uniforms, not by having spent time around orange jumpsuited prison inmates or being rescued by firemen from burning buildings, but sheerly because they've been so in fashion in the ten years I've been writing about clothes. I've written a dozen articles about uniforms for the *New York Times* or the *New York Times Magazine* over the course the past decade. Uniforms have become such a powerful to put men and women in uniform with great success. The generalissimos of rock'n'roll have endlessly flirted with the romantic imagery implied in the use of uniforms. How can we forget the hussar cavalry jacket of Jimi Hendrix, the gilded braid of the Beatles and Adam Ant, the perfect officers' uniforms of David Bowie and Brian Ferry, and the combat suits and camouflage of The Clash, U2 and the Eurythmics?

reference point that today we don't even acknowledge them; they've become part of the vocabulary of designer fashion, which is fascinating because designer fashion is supposed to offer the antithesis of everything that uniforms give. But, as Richard Martin, the recently deceased fashion director of the Costume Insitute once noted, "Inevitably, any fashion by the 1990s, is going to have aspects of immense uniformity to it. We're looking to a small group of suppliers for design ideas." In other words, the more certain designers succeed, the more homogenous and uniform our culture will become.

As the spring 2001 season opened in New York in September, cutting-edge Miguel Andovar and a young design team called Imitations of Christ both used military uniforms and Boy Scout references as the basis for their collections. It looks like 1996 all over again, recycled only four years later.

New York City, a place that prides itself on individual style, is a fascinating place to read the message of a uniform. The same uniform, transported twenty blocks, can mean different things. Sailors in their dress whites on a ship in the harbor look heroic and pure, but turn into Jack Nicholson in *The Last Detail* when on shore leave, wandering through Times Square. Movies like *Detail* and *On the Town* have changed our understanding of that uniform in those places. That's why a policeman in uniform on a solitary menacing street earns our sympathy as a lone man doing a tough job, but a group of such uniforms in a pack can seem menacing. Or why a uniformed officer on our street can fill us with a sense of safety, but that same uniform by the highway when we're driving a new Porsche full throttle can fill us with dread.

Designers love to work within strict parameters, and sometimes just the unbelievably strict parameter of fabric and wearability isn't enough. Every so often they get asked to do uniforms for a restaurant, an airline, or meter maids, and they rise to the occasion. There need to be pockets, for instance. The uniforms have to be washable. They have to think of where pens must go, or keys, or money and change, or guns. Somehow it's hard to believe that designers don't make the clothes we wear every day with such concerns in mind. But given the unavoidable demand for pockets, wearability, washability and comfort, designers have come up with some striking industrial design.

Those attributes are part of the reason why in the past ten years military uniforms with epaulettes, Air Force bomber jackets, UPS uniforms, stewardess uniforms, Boys Scout and school uniforms have all been inspirations to designers for collections.

But designers, so limited on methods of getting their message out there, depend on uniform indicators to do a lot of the work for them. A designer who has a history of run-ins with the police may rip up the uniform and use it like a punk rocker would, to suggest undermining authority. Another designer might use the same uniform to reference the Village People, and a moment of gay liberation and pre-AIDS freedom.

The uniform is so powerful that it means different things to different people.

In 1996, there was an overwhelming use by important designers like Miuccia Prada and Tom Ford for Gucci of indicators of fascist and military uniforms. Prada had also cited the influence of the uniforms of "modern service" workers, "nutritionists, light-and-sound therapists, biologists and micro-chip technicians."

Her Miu Miu collection called uniforms "the most reassuring and elegant dictatorship," adding, "Miu Miu likes discipline and cleanliness of uniforms and she wears them on and off duty in her fantasy world of modern services." Prada herself was a young rebel against this type of authority, so it doesn't take Freud to see her calling for discipline in her adult life.

Young designers were also using uniforms as a source. Laura Whitcomb started several crazes in her short career, first with Adidas sweats turned into dresses, then with Playboy logo clothes, and finally with UPS uniforms converted to sexy dresses in 1994.

At a time of enormous personal freedoms, a moment when George Orwell, Fritz Lang and Aldous Huxley had all forseen that a world of uniforms would be the ultimate sign of oppression, designers asking us to voluntarily dress in uniforms seemed curious. And the fact that the uniform-derived clothes became wildly popular and copied seemed even more curious.

President Bill Clinton's State of the Union address called for school uniforms that year, and John F. Kennedy Jr. asked designers to create school uniforms to publish in his magazine, *George*. In an article I wrote at the time, designers were articulate and pointed about the controversy surrounding uniforms. For children, clearly, uniforms wipe out economic and social indicators of dress, ostensibly causing less hostility – although children seem unerringly able to suss out the rich and the poor whether everyone's dressed the same or not. And while uniforms for children take away rebellious creativity, kids still seem able to find ways of expressing themselves, shortening the skirts, adding emblems, or tightening sweaters.

But what did the uniform craze say about adults, and more specifically, about the fashion industry?

Prada defended her obsession: "I think if you dress in a uniform you feel very comfortable and neutral, your personality is hidden beneath the uniform." A few seasons later, she introduced Outsider art prints and hand-stenciled and cut-out emblems, like those a person being treated by uniformed workers in a psychiatric ward might have created. "You only show what you want to show," she said of uniforms. "You don't have to worry about how to dress. You don't have to think about fashion. So in a way, it's the idea of refusing fashion."

That idea of refusing fashion is a curious one for designers who make their living by embracing it. But Prada wasn't the first fashion insider to suggest such a thing. It was something the legendary creative genius Alexander Liberman believed in strongly. He wore the same style suit every day, gray flannel for winter and gray Brooks Brothers for summer, with a pale blue shirt and knit tie, and his closet was full of them. "I found it easy," he once said, "I don't have to think about what to wear."

Vogue's talented Hamish Bowles settled on his look as a way to focus more on his work. And other big creative brains have used a uniform – a signature piece of fashion – to cement their individuality. Jean Paul Gaultier's Breton fisherman suit. Swifty Lazar and Carrie Donovan's goggly-eyed black glasses. Tom Wolfe's white suit. Halston's black turtleneck, black wool pants, black loafers, black socks and big black sunglasses.

Giorgio Armani, responsible for revolutionizing men's suits, almost exclusively wears navy T-shirts and slim trousers. "As someone who thinks all day about how to dress people, I have decided, perhaps unconsciously, to create a uniform for myself that is above suspicion," he told *Esquire* magazine a few years ago.

Personal and personalized uniforms were a far cry from the epaulette-style military ones that designers were trying to foist on people in the early Nineties.

"It's very 'tomorrow belongs to me' – you know what I mean?" Marc Jacobs said at the time of the *George* article. "Excuse me, but I do remember somewhere in history and someone tried to make this happen, and unfortunately a lot of people died from it. I don't consider this an encouraging view of the future."

Yet it's impossible to ignore the fact that within the fashion community, the only successful designers are the ones who, like Mr. Jacobs, have been able to create a uniform look instantly identifiable as their own. And the packs of editors who wear the looks of the season can hardly avoid cringing a little as they see themselves across the runway in the same garb as everyone else. Yet they still toe the line. There is, each season, one Manolo Blahnik shoe that is approved by a raised eyebrow or a kind word; there is one silhouette or two that is determined to be chic. There is now one haircut: *Vogue* magazine has declared the bob as in. An industry that is supposed to support and celebrate personal expression increasingly asks the members of its corps to, like politicians, stay on message.

"It is a dream for a designer to invent a uniform," Gianni Versace said when I interviewed him about uniforms. "That happens when something becomes a must. Chanel is a uniform. A Versace shirt is a uniform. But a uniform should never become too safe. You can lose your individuality if you don't put your things together in a certain way. That's what scares me about any uniform."

What's amazing is that the most subversive and transgressive forms of dress eventually become uniforms, serving as uniforms do to instantly identify someone as part of a certain group, eliminate individuality, and let insiders and outsiders know where the person stands. The current fashionista obsession with studded rockstar T-shirts, for example, is at once an attempt to, through a fashion message, flag that the wearer is wild and avant-garde. Yet when everyone has them and wears them, isn't the message diluted?

The men's look of the Nineties was recently summed up by a men's magazine as being the Liam Gallagher (of Oasis) uniform: big jackets, directional knitwear, designer jeans, desert boots, dirty shirts. No look indicates cutting edge more easily than an appropriated rockstar or hip-hop look. And yet like the grunge anti-fashion popularized by Nirvana, it lost its message once it went mass. The uniform of the disenfranchised is as dehumanizing as the uniform of the military.

One of the most innovative and experimental designers alive, Stephen Sprouse, confessed to his uniform at the time of the craze: "I take off the same Dickie pants, pocket T-shirt and pea-coat, and put it on the next day. It's easy and I'm lazy. People are so inundated by fashion and style changing that there is something attractive about the ease of some kind of uniform. You have to figure out your own uniform." He went on to design the uniforms for the Rock and Roll Hall of Fame.

His personal uniform, peacoats and Dickie pants, are military based, but they were appropriated through their presence in Army Navy surplus and second-hand stores by hippies in the Sixties, punks in the Seventies and then hip-hop artists in the Eighties. This dress, dedicated to authority, securing the status quo and discipline, was commandeered by three generations of rebels to subvert those things.

It's futile in fact, to try to reject labeling yourself with a uniform. Valerie Steele, who is now the head of the Fashion Institute of Technology's costume museum, wrote an article for the April 1991 *Lingua Franca*, which has been an enduring example, for me, of the power of fashion and the inability for anyone to avoid its codes. Her piece was about how her esteemed intellectual academic colleagues had refused to address the topic of fashion, feeling that even commenting on the subject was beneath them. Yet their studious efforts to ignore fashion was in itself a type of fashion. Dressing studiously as academics do, to look like they don't care about fashion trends, is itself a kind of uniform. The dress code of the professor is as much an identifiable uniform as that of a doctor or a cowboy. A professor could easily have been one of the Village People's characters. Dr. Steele humorously called fashion "the F-Word" in her essay, because academics found it such an obscene topic.

The only danger in uniforms, of course, is that designers allow the message of the uniform to overwhelm the creativity they might otherwise display. The same way that uniforms endanger the professionals who wear them. A policeman, for instance, sees himself more as an enforcer than as a fellow human being. Or a kid dressed up as a punk every day becomes embittered by the hostility shown him by a society that judges such dress codes.

Ralph Kramden of *The Honeymooners*, became famous for his bus driver uniform, and his character became the stereotype of the blue collar bus driver in New York. But his wife Alice always reminded the audience of the humanity beneath. "To think," she'd say, when he'd behaved particularly well by the end of an episode, "I fell in love with the uniform."

FROM WOODSTOCK TO HOLLYWOOD

STEFANO PISTOLINI

A lot of things happened during those three days at Woodstock in 1969, smack between the moon landing of Neil Armstrong and company and the Bel Air massacre in which the disciples of Charles Manson butchered Sharon Tate and her friends, casting the first boulder to smash the technicolor dreams of the Sixties. Among the many seminal events of those seventy-two incredibly symbolic hours, one of the most lasting impressions is that of the song performed by Country Joe & the Fish, diligently captured by the cameras of Mike Wadleigh and immortalized in the film that was to transform a continental musical exploit into an extraordinary planetary and generational attraction.

Country Joe McDonald – folksinger, far left ultrapacifist, influenced in equal doses by Bob Dylan, Woody Guthrie and the warblers of Nashville. Before Woodstock he was a cult artist, known above all on the radical university circuit, famous for his concert-rallies on campus at the University of California at Berkeley and Kent State University, which became an emblematic site when police opened fire on youthful protestors there. Country Joe had a right to speak his piece on the subject of war and peace: before becoming a "minstrel in a Marine uniform," he served four years on a military ship, quitting in 1965, the year of the escalation of the war in Vietnam. The chorus of the tune he sang on the stage at Woodstock that famous afternoon is one of those hooks that stick in your head, and five minutes later you find yourself strumming it on your guitar: "And it's one two three, what are we fightin' for?" goes the chorus – though the actual title of the song is the "I-Feel-Like-I'm-Fixin'-To-Die Rag," and the most famous verse exhorts: "Yeah, come on all of you big strong men / Uncle Sam needs your help again / He's got himself in a terrible jam / Way down yonder in Vietnam / So put down your books and pick up a gun / We're gonna have a whole lotta fun / And it's one, two, three, four / What are we fighting for? / Don't ask me, I don't give a damn / Next stop is Vietnam / And it's five, six, seven / Open up the pearly gates / Well there ain't no time to wonder why / Whoopee! we're all gonna die." A vaguely populistic but absolutely effective act of accusal against the devastating debacle of Vietnam, which caused many messy problems, including the effect of getting about half the world's young people very mad at America. In short, that little blond guy with a big moustache and long hair, with his squeaky nasal voice, got half a million people to sing along with his rhymes on Max Yasgur's farm, and a few months later thousands of Italian kids were getting enthused about the same show in the second-run movie theaters of Rome and Milan. But apart from the very catchy tune of the "Rag," what was striking about Country Joe was his appearance: gray-green and dusty, and yet mysteriously, naturally effective, functional, charismatic and timely. His songs were protests against the slimy dishonesty of the war on the Mekong, but his performance was for voice, guitar and uniform. As if he were a crazed Marine up there on the stage, a deserter, a roaming shell-shocked bum. Harbinger of the desolate Conradian warriors immortalized by Francis Ford Coppola in *Apocalypse Now*, parody of the idea that only the *physique du rôle* of a John Wayne or a Clint Eastwood is suitable to be a real horseback-riding soldier. Country Joe, a dropout from the American dream, artistic castaway, leftover of the great civil causes, used his body as a message, sticking it right inside the object-symbol of his exemplary crusade: that absurd war in camouflage uniforms that hundreds of thousands of his contemporaries were fighting in the name of no-one-knows-what.

Of course Country Joe wasn't the only one who had understood the impact of the reutilization of the uniform. In the Sixties and Seventies the counterculture legions literally pullulated with provocateurs who understood the power of that image of schizoid veteran and refugee from dashed illusions. And in 1968-1969, war was still happening, just around the corner. Death sparks were flashing in the four corners of the globe, and for American youth the sound of automatic weapon fire seemed like the inevitable drumbeat of that world domination their politicians so ardently desired ... Normandy ... Korea ... Saigon. For young Italians, too – the same youths who in the wake of 1968 felt authorized, without shame, to look for any possible means of avoiding the ordeal of military service – the clothes of the soldier and the uniforms of all nations and colors became a part of everyday life. But this was anything but an absolute novelty. Throughout the Fifties, Italy was a poor nation getting over a lost war, a place where nothing gets thrown away, including the strong fabrics used for uniforms. From *Sciuscià* onward, in short, military garments had a long life as a source of material, as narrated by Pasolini in *Ragazzi di vita*, a way of covering the body and shielding it from the elements, although commonly seen as something just short of humiliating. But the canvas was strong, the woolen cloth was heavy, and keeping warm in those years was a concrete priority, even in the midst of the first stirrings of youth culture and street culture.

So it is best to remember that Country Joe should be praised for one thing only in this context, a thing that recurs constantly in the history of pop music: he was in the right place at the right time with the right idea. And the idea was to combine that song with that look. That pacifist message thus expressed becomes pithy, potent, even sexy, with its trappings of bandanas and colorful beads that stand out to such effect against the shadings of gray-green. The following spring *Woodstock*, the film, found its way into our movie theaters, and the Senigallia market in Milan, the market on Via Sannio in Rome, the "mercatino" in Livorno, and the Forcelle in Naples took a giant step in the estimation of teenagers: for just a few lire you could buy a bagful of military surplus and put it on, feeling a strange shiver but also an awareness of becoming a vehicle for a forceful political message. Frankly this deal was just too good to pass up.

But this was just the "dress" rehearsal for the renewal of codes that was to lead to the gray-green wave that covered the bright, chaotic colors of the youth universe of the Sixties. We are now in the Seventies, and the scenario is quite different indeed: the outbursts are more extreme, the violent flash of liberation ("we want the world and we want it now!") turned into a collective case of bad nerves, as no tangible, or immediately recognizable results appeared after so many hard-fought battles; and the results that were evident didn't seem to bring even a small part of the promised satisfaction and bliss. The word "struggle" took the place of the word "cause." Rather than protesting, people began to fight. There is no need to dust off the old rancors here. Even the external generational image underwent a process of decolorization. The message was clear: there is nothing to celebrate. Leave the flowers in the fields. Anger, instead, was the order of the day, seething to the point where many couldn't even remember why they were so angry. City streets and suburban crossroads become places of clashes and contrasts, anything but "common places." Anyone wearing a uniform was seen as an equivalent of repression. And yet, thanks to that absurd echo that happens in extreme moments and extreme visions, the uniform itself also took on the role (desired ... denied ...) of the "father": the repressor, the enemy, but also the indissoluble link with history.

People were ready to hit the streets to do battle with the uniforms – the army, the police, the authorities – while admitting that their existence represented a necessary negative, an organic part of the modern world. The collective dream lost its overtones of pacifism, and for a brief moment drifted towards the vague hypothesis of a revolution, only then to tumble pessimistically into the awareness of an unbridgeable diversity, a distance between reality and daydreams, between (for example) Western society and a youth culture steeped in Eastern paraphrasing, moral metaphors and global utopias. Against this backdrop, uniforms reappeared on the scene, worn by twentysomethings, but this time the irony of the Woodstock era was gone.

Contemporary to the fatuous flames of the angry youth of Italy in 1977, a curious stylistic coincidence took form. On one hand, the radicalization of the confrontation with the system reached its historical peak, marked by an absolute refusal of any compromise. On the other, certain inevitably typical mechanisms of the system itself, starting with the merchandising and symbolic functions of fashion, managed to worm their way into the ranks of the rebels. In a context in which obedience to an aesthetic and exterior code that went beyond pure functionalization of intellectual roles and use as an instrument for the missions of agents of the alternative was forbidden, clandestine scriveners were busy secretly rewriting some of the most interesting (precisely due to this secrecy) pages of modern youth fashion and subculture. Once again the uniform is a central focus. Because the uniform is the manifestation of the enemy and, as a consequence, his materialization. In order to effectively combat the enemy – according to a sort of compliance with conventional laws – it becomes necessary to use another uniform (or even the same uniform, but with an antithetical interpretation and meaning). Only then, in a situation of parity of codes, of mutual recognizability, can the battlefield be defined and the clash finally take place. In other words, since this was to be a take-no-prisoners war, uniforms were legitimate, meaningful. Their symbolism was perverted, their hierarchical meanings were ridiculed, everything was twisted into the language of confrontation. Infantry boots and haversacks, parkas with endless pockets (renamed "eskimos" by the Italians due to that trend of meteorological exaggeration that inevitably emerged in a Mediterranean land), marching trousers and navy jerseys. The battle against the preppy aesthetic of the counter-revolutionary normaloids (displayed, for example, in the total refusal of any member of the "movement" to wear a tie or a "normal" shirt, leading to the widespread fashion of wearing a pullover directly on top of a T-shirt) assumed the solemn overtones of a generation at war, a Western Europe in its twenties that declared its own form of community long before Maastricht, brandishing slogans and – in iconic terms – a sea of dull hues, and a pale, skinny physique. Take a look at the documentary films or photos from that period: these kids communicate a sense of electrifying restlessness and mobility.

In the three intense years before the onset of the Eighties, the centrifugal and centripetal tensions were already hard at work. Wherever the concentration on the private put the public on hold, wherever distrust developed regarding all things "collective," wherever ideological certainties began to lose their force, unexpected tensions arose, and unprecedented temptations. In London, for example, punk culture spread like wildfire. In Italy the "committed" youth rushed to accuse the punks of being sellouts, fascists, counter-revolutionaries. Nevertheless, that atomic, spontaneous movement contained a force that could only be envied by the weary assemblies of the "politicos." Punk radicalized the refusal to integrate, disgust for the family and institutions, fascination with extreme artistic gesture and display of the body as a nihilistic object – an effigy to be carelessly tossed onto the bonfire of indolence. Apathy was a form of protest that shoved the revolution aside in favor of an immediate path to self-destruction. But not before having left a mark on the wall – blood red, powder white, leather black, sadomasichistic. The punk epidemic spread to the capitals, snubbing the provinces: black flowers grew in Berlin, Paris, New York and Milan. Punk was afraid of nothing by definition, because it had nothing to lose. Its macabre obsession with the signs of suffering that have punctuated human history couldn't help but latch onto the signs of Nazism. This led to a mixture of the other typical accessories of the movement – porno fallout, garbage bags, safety pins – with SS jackets, swastikas, thick belts, gloves and other horrible reminders of death. Below the spiky hair petrified with dry grease, bony faces, self-inflicted wounds and scratches and exhibited bruises, the most putrid excrescence of the Third Reich appeared, spreading out into the corners of the city, rendered ridiculous as never before, humiliated, twisted and exterminated by that purifying power of punk – based on innocence – which was the movement's most lucid value. The swastika on Siouxsie Sioux's arm-band or Sid Vicious's T-shirt is light years away from the one on the gear of the Hell's Angels in California, the first who were bold enough to dig that icon out of its grave of horror. "The collective worldview of the Angels has always been typically fascist," in the typically frank opinion of "gonzo" reporter Hunter Thompson. But the sociologist Dick Hebdige makes haste to define the differences with respect to Punk: "Now," he writes, "the signifier, the swastika, is intentionally separated from the concept it usually represents, namely Nazism. Its primary value and attraction lie precisely in its lack of meaning: in its capacity to deceive. It is exploited as an empty effect." The symbol, therefore, is just as mute as the anger it provokes. And its aim is to shock those who observe it. Drawing their attention to the effects of the authoritarianism embodied by the uniforms, and certainly not to their charm or mystique.

And there's more. Something else is happening a few blocks further on and a few months later, but still in the climate of that restless London governed by youth and organized as a non-stop workshop. In the nursery of extremes that at this point characterize the creative exploits that straddle the categories of music, visual arts, environmental design and omnipresent fashion, the "new romantic" notion is born. No less intransigent than punk, in spite of its posturing as an opposite extreme, and united to punk by a shared sense of alienation, a glimpse of the absolute uselessness of gestures beyond their aesthetic flash. So here we have the short-lived afflatus of the last, die-hard romantics, populating Sloane Square (the "Sloaners") and then Place de la Concorde in Paris and Shinjuku in Tokyo with dandies dressed up like Barry Lyndon, imaginary Hussar officers, fusiliers of a virtual Alsace, gentlemen of arms and unrequited love stories in a reproduction inspired by the most ephemeral form of hedonism. Here again the game is overcharged with negativity, although in this case it is not displayed, but dissembled with lace and braided trim. To make merry of everyday life, to transform the night into a masquerade, pulling the wool over reality's eyes. It all happens in discotheques, clubs, hang-outs, passageways, alleys and crevices, in the gloom of moonlight colored by flashing neon – just another way to use up a futile juvenile period of existence. Just one of the ways, because many different uniforms can be seen in this contorted moment of youthful sensation. Extreme, tense, without light. Lots of uniforms for lots of irregular tribes. All of them ephemeral, all losers, all glorious.

But the youth wave continues to move through the seas of the end of the twentieth century. Just as soon as the entertainment industry gobbles up a youthful intuition, spitting it back out in the form of merchandise on display in department stores, the idea has already progressed and moved on, dazzled by new totems. And so, as the absolute alienation of punk, the self-destructive mental short-circuit of Sid Vicious and Jimmy Pursey come into contact and fraternize with the breezy self-absorption of the new romantics, the two intellectual currents combine, and the new style assumes the name "dark" – dark thought, gothicism contaminated with electronic temptations and the first stirrings of hyper-tech. And once again, when the time comes for a uniform, uniforms are the source. After all, what could be more gothic than a garment created to host weapons, pain, dignity and death? What could be more appropriate than those wan, easily camouflaged tones? In Florence a shop appears, and its reputation soon spreads throughout the peninsula. Its name is Ultra. At first glance it is just a pair of unassuming shop windows, an austere interior, uncrowded shelves. But this is the place that spread the word about "dark" to all of Italy (to the soundtrack of the productions of IRA and Kindergarten): pure trendiness and melancholy decadence. Uniforms from all over the world, with the exception of American uniforms, excluded due to their unbearable odor of chewing gum. Instead, we find New Zealand lead gray, West German forest ranger jackets, Belgian paratrooper pullovers. Gritty chic, with mind-boggling prices. Uniforms for nocturnal interiors.

European youth at the end of the Seventies is, therefore, a puzzle of malaise, marked by tough, grotesque fashions that implode and drag the look into their desire for a rapid demise and total erasure. Post-punk, post-dark: the leftovers are stripped of flesh, cadaverous. All that is left is a certain sense of the absurd and near-nausea at the very idea of the appearance of the umpteenth vision in black. The normalization of the early Eighties, which assumes the label "backlash," cancels out any depraved insistence upon the reutilization of the military code, annulling any "artistic" decontextualization of uniforms. The phenomenon is swept away by the new habits and consumption patterns of the dominant youth tribes: once the warriors of the revolution have been reduced the status of a depressed minority, while the disciples of the absolute styles of the preceding decade have become species threatened by extinction (punk and dark, but also mod, rockabilly and prog), the remote control (and therefore the attention of the media) is passed on to a generation that wants to re-establish clear roles: fathers are fathers, sons are sons, and there's a time for education, a time for work, a time for play. At the end of the line, there is the voracious desire to pull up a chair at the table of consumption, without recriminations, without guilt. The paraphernalia of a very recent yet very distant past wind up in the attic. The consumeristic hedonism of a yuppie who works in the city is about as far as you can get from the perspective of a punk sitting on the sidewalk at the corner of Fulham Road. Uniforms suddenly vanish from the wardrobes of all the juvenile tribes, replaced by a creed that previously belonged to the enemy, to the adult world of power and status symbols: the creed of the "signature," the trademark, the designer label. Instantly the uniform and all of its transgressive, second-hand remanaging seem to be the mere vestiges of a fanciful past. Now is the time for material things, statistics, numbers, lives measured on the basis of annual income. Very little space is left for the rule of mutual recognition connected to the use of uniforms, except outside of their natural context. But these reduced spaces are still quite noteworthy and charged with a certain glamour. Take the case of the gay phenomenon that spreads out from the discos of New York across the rest of the globe: the use of uniforms – preferably those of the police, the Marines and even the cruel Nazi persecutors – as an explicit S&M bondage icon starts in the world of disco music and then contaminates the entire homosexual side of street culture. Doffed by The Clash, Spandau Ballet and Ultravox, uniforms become the sign of recognition of the Village People and their millions of followers. Mixed with lurex tights, spangled suspenders and perfumed brilliantine, uniforms become the favorite game in town in the liberating ritual of nocturnal disco-delirium and the related, frenetic cruising scene. Deprived of any coefficient of socio-political aggression, recovered precisely in that zone where, in theory, there would seem to be an obvious obstacle. (While the Village People were chanting "In the Navy," episodes of persecution of homosexuals in the US armed forces were on the increase. Amazingly enough, the recruiting office of the US Navy actually considered using this song for its advertising, unaware of the original context!) In the end, the uniform is all but forgotten in the world of juvenile styles and trends.

The last pocket of utilization of the uniform happens where the transgressive theoretical legacy of non-regulation uniforms is utterly ignored. The uniform is worn once again, but with blatantly self-consolatory aims, fully accepting its significance of standardization, the appeal of order and discipline, and an environmental setting permeated by machismo. In times of slackerism, of extreme individualism, grunge perplexities, widespread environmentalism, uniforms become the territory of skinheads, who don them in the hopes of amplifying, multiplying, exalting their meaning. But in the skinhead lexicon the uniform (or its extreme surrogates, like the bomber jacket) loses any superstructural meaning, it is the opposite of an aesthetic urge, a mere sign of recognition and appreciation of the accessories of force, even the force controlled by a military army. Moreover, the use of military elements in the dress of skinheads, given the low cost of such clothing, fits right in with the essentially lumpen proletarian matrix of this youth tribe, especially in its English and German versions (but much less so in the United States, as in the latest tragic example of the massacre in Littleton, Colorado, whose youthful perpetrators belonged to well-off families, and were sympathizers of white power militias, collecting weapons and uniforms as an expression of their racism, anti-Semitism and anti-gay sentiment).

The present: in today's situation of chaos and mingling which Ted Polhemus has called the "supermarket of style," but which we prefer to define as the "pulverization of subcultures," an object such as the uniform, one of primary recognition and definite attribution of belonging, has trouble finding a stable sphere of utilization. Perhaps its message is just too explicit, the ironic content of its reutilization is worn-out, its symbolic weight is excessive after decades of stratification of protest against its repressive role. Of course its aesthetic appeal remains, the charisma of its forms and colors, the authority of its appearance. But it appears to have been deprived of its potential for extreme, grotesque yet romantic, disheveled and provocative use. It is still possible to see a military jacket on some traveler wandering through a big city. Trousers with multiple pockets have become the most obvious among the accessories used for trekking. Camouflage T-shirts are worn by people who spend time in health clubs. And the famous lace-up boots? Nowadays you can see them on youngsters garbed in T-shirts and knee-length baggy shorts. They wear them unlaced, enough to make a grown Marine cry. But they are always well-shined, if only because Mom takes care of that, after lining them up neatly beside Dad's loafers. A tragic, fashion-victim feature.

In the midst of all this sloppy decontextualization, all that remains is a trip to the movies for a look at the last possible heroes: the ones on celluloid. To feast our eyes on the tanned, sweaty bodies of the *Thin Red Line,* or the drenched, wasted bodies of *Saving Private Ryan*. Admitting that at the end of a process of expropriation, chaos must return. And that nobody, not even Johnny Rotten, can wear an unbuttoned green shirt with the same kind of class as the soldiers of cinema. The ultimate charm of the uniform. Strictly in the Hollywood version, of course.

THE NINETIES UTILITY MOVEMENT: PRIME SUSPECT IN THE DEATH OF DESIGNER FASHION

JAMES SHERWOOD

London. "What have international designers learned from London street style? Well, they have seen the future and it is utility chic. They have drawn inspiration for the spring/summer 1999 collections from khaki, Velcro, hip holster bags, combat pants pockets and trophy trainers. Utility is high fashion's spin on the urban street uniform. There is only one problem. Utility is an imposter."

Thus the *International Herald Tribune* closed my case for the prosecution of the Nineties utility movement. As a London-based journalist for the *Independent on Sunday*, I had mapped the rise of utility for the best part of a decade. It was my supposition that the sidewalk's influence on catwalk design had gone too far. Just as history blamed the excesses of the rococo court for the French Revolution, I blamed high fashion's decline and fall in the Nineties on designers becoming too reliant on street style for inspiration. The *International Herald Tribune* presented my evidence in the following spring 1999 commentary:

(Utility) is the Nineties take on Marie-Antoinette playing milkmaids in the Trianon. Sportswear (and utility) was a street uniform born in the dark ages of early Nineties Grunge. The puffa jacket, combat pants and trophy trainer were adopted by a generation of DJs, dealers, skate kids and underground clubbers. It signified the disillusionment of generation X. These were cruel world clothes: wind, bullet and knife repellant fabrics cut into streamlined urban armor-plating. It was a don't touch, Teflon-coated declaration of independence from the chi-chi fashion labels.

In its eight-year reign as a Nineties fashion icon, army surplus combat pants traveled from East London underground sweatbox techno clubs to Paris haute couture runways. This social-climbing street style finally stormed the Bastille of haute couture in fall 1998.

It was Donatella Versace's first couture show as design director of the house since the murder of her brother Gianni in July 1997. Versace took cotton combat pants and translated them into beige moire satin with spattered patch pockets with rhinestones. A regiment of four combat pockets circled a black faille column dress. The utility detail stood out, as Raymond Chandler would have it, "Like a tarantula on a piece of angel food."

"Couture exists in a parallel universe, a charmed place where nothing really matters except the abstract power of a designer's imagination," wrote Sarah Mower in the fall 2000 debut issue of London's latest style bible, *The Fashion*. "You're in for one of the most spectacular entertainments the modern world ever laid on exclusively for the enjoyment of womankind."

Combat pants were designed for neither womankind nor entertainment/enjoyment. Born on the battlefield, the combat pocket looked as inappropriate on the Versace runway at the Paris Ritz as Che Guevara at a cocktail party. In retrospect, combat couture was a final nail in the coffin for Nineties utility.

Combats were originally utilized in their correct context: a period of conflict and dissent. London's generation X men were style renegades on the attack. High fashion was the enemy. To put early Nineties London street culture into perspective, we have to analyze the collective mood of generation X.

Generation X, which came of age at the turn of the decade, missed the affluent "greed is good" times of the Eighties. When British Prime Minister Margaret Thatcher was ousted in 1992, the country nose-dived into a recession. So not only did generation X turn-up two years too late for the party, they also had to clear up and pay for damages. Teenagers and twentysomethings in the Nineties were suffering a hangover by proxy.

Rewind to spring/summer 1990. Fashion's old guard – Gianni Versace, Thierry Mugler, Claude Montana and Azzedine Alaïa – didn't speak to generation X. Young Turk Rifat Ozbek's all-white collection literally wiped the slate clean and erased Eighties ancien regime excess. Fashion was going back to the drawing board. We looked forward to a radical new movement to take us into the Nineties. But designer fashion never accelerated. Instead it remained stuck in Ozbek's minimalist first gear.

"At one point, in the early Nineties, people wanted only simple clothing to cancel everything out," Miuccia Prada told US *Vogue* in her retrospective of the Nineties. "After Lacroix zero. So there was minimal: Calvin Klein, Jil Sander. But after zero, we have to go on, to do something else." Miuccia Prada was one of the few who knew where to go. She released the first black nylon rucksack in 1992. It will be remembered as the first piece of high fashion utility design. More later on Miuccia Prada's utility chic. By and large, fashion didn't actually know where to go from zero. Minimalism literally made fashion disappear and generation X dismissed it as the Emperor's New Clothes. Minimalism was apologetic, anonymous no-label design for a society made to feel uncomfortable with consumerism and guilty of past excesses.

If generation X style was subjected to the psychiatrist's couch, it would be diagnosed passive-aggressive. Their disappointment, disillusionment and anger pulled fashion design off its pedestal – the catwalk – and dragged it down to street level. Grunge was the first wave of anti-fashion street style: a hybrid of Seventies slash-and-burn punk, ragged thriftshop seconds and army surplus. Kurt Cobain and Courtney Love, the Sid & Nancy of the Nineties, were king and queen of grunge. Hollywood's lost boy, River Phoenix, was its crown prince. The suicide of Cobain and the death by accidental overdose of Phoenix signified the nihilism underlying grunge.

At first high fashion resisted grunge. In 1990, then British *Vogue* editor, the late Liz Tilberis, put the five reigning supermodels (Linda Evangelista, Christy Turlington, Naomi Campbell, Tatjana Patitz and Cindy Crawford) on her January 1990 cover. By 1994 the Eighties were proclaimed officially dead when Corrine Day shot superwaif Kate Moss in grubby underwear and a council estate mise-en-scène for British *Vogue*. For the older generation, Kate Moss was a personification of Nineties teenage angst; a totem for heroin chic, anorexia and Lolita-like youth corrupted. Grunge infiltrating *Vogue* was an acknowledgement that high fashion in the early Nineties was in crisis.

It is fashion's role to reflect society, but the mirror *Vogue* held up to the world showed a generation openly hostile to high fashion. Don't for a second think the fashion industry sat back and applauded grunge. When Marc Jacobs, then designer for Perry Ellis, tried to elevate grunge to the catwalk in 1993, his collection was booed and roundly condemned.

Grunge inadvertently gave birth to deconstruction. Cultural backwater Belgium emerged as the melting pot of the new deconstruction movement as Martin Margiela and Ann Demeulemeester took Paris by storm in 1993. Deconstruction was nothing more than an autopsy on designer fashion: turning garments inside out, cutting open the body of the silhouette and spilling its guts out on the catwalk. Exposed seams, raw edges and unfinished stitching was a way of tearing down impenetrable Eighties tailoring. Demeulemeester and Margiela put fashion under the microscope, and there was little sign of life for deconstruction outside a very small avante-garde clique of fashion mavericks.

Utility appeared as a kind of coup d'etat against high fashion. The early Nineties recession that gripped London made high fashion not only inaccessible for generation X, but also superfluous to requirement. When the economy bombs, fashion is invariably the first casualty. The Tory administration that followed Thatcher's fall in 1992 sliced student loans and effectively rendered the UK student population penniless. Necessity – being the mother of invention – and poverty pushed generation X to find a new style aesthetic.

Army surplus addressed the needs of a generation who felt they'd been abandoned by the establishment. London was a bleak, depressed wasteland for teenagers in the early Nineties. The search for a style aesthetic that matched this mood was solved in some part by the Gulf War. As the first interactive, televised war, it was little more than an extension of PlayStation for generation X. The Gulf War was received with nothing but apathy by generation X. But images of combat struck a chord for teenage guerillas trying to survive an increasingly hostile urban jungle. Uniforms also address the dual obsessions of teenagers from time immemorial: sex and death. By assuming the uniform of urban foot soldiers, Nineties London lads were playing with imagery of aggressive sexuality and danger.

Club culture has always dictated the street style of a decade. In the Seventies disco decade, Studio 54 spread the words "Halston, Gucci and Fiorucci" to the masses. Disco glamour reflected the champagne, cocaine and casual sex pre-AIDS clubber. Ecstasy and the monotonous hammer blow of techno were the mind-numbing means of escapism for generation X. Techno and hard house were made to make you sweat. Suits were not only inappropriate, they were banned. Techno sweatboxes made clothes – designer or otherwise – superfluous, and the gym-toned body was the only accessory required.

Combat pants first appeared on the London club scene around 1993. They met the practical requirements of E culture and the aggression of the beat. Multi-pocket pants were a mobile medicine chest for a night's drug cocktail: a wrap of speed in one, a couple of tabs in another, a bottle of Evian in the last. Also, multi-patch pockets made drugs easier to conceal and get past security.

Trade, East London's hard house temple, was a Dante's inferno for London's gay techno scene. Boys naked from the waist up favored combat pants with tight white Calvins riding the groin. Trade's operating hours, from 3AM Saturday morning to noon the following Sunday, demonstrate the energy induced by E. Nine hours of techno demanded practical footwear, and the trainer met the challenge.

The gay scene arguably was first to embrace combat pants for clubbing. The leather scene was deemed too Seventies, and combats – as well as concealing E – also left room for condoms, lube and a spare pair of Calvins. London's gay boys rediscovered army surplus store Lawrence Corner, and made combat pants the techno club uniform.

Trade and the East London fetish club The LA (London Apprentice) were still relatively underground in the early Nineties. But the location of The LA on Old Street is crucial for mapping the rise of combat pants. By 1995, Hoxton had already been colonized by London's contemporary art, fashion and music industry renegades: all priced out of the West End and looking to establish a new Soho. Hoxton, a depressed, industrial quarter of London's East End, was rich in derelict warehouse spaces, cheap loft apartments and new generation creativity.

At the (now defunct) Blue Note club on Hoxton Square, Talvin Singh was establishing the second generation Asian underground music scene. London's new generation fashion designers, Alexander McQueen, Tristan Webber, Andrew Groves, Sonja Nuttall and Antonio Berardi, all established East London studios. Generation X style bible, *Dazed & Confused,* (the name says it all) opened editorial offices on Old Street.

The Old Street underground posse patented a uniform that would eventually dominate mainstream fashion: khaki combats, old school Adidas white leather trainers, sleeveless puffa jackets and plain white T's. A new school of utility labels launched to meet the needs of a new generation: YMC (You Must Create), Maharishi, Griffin Laundry and Acupuncture, to name only those who survive in 2000.

Fast forward to 2000, and YMC has a flagship store in London's West End. The label is in good company on Conduit Street, standing alongside Vivienne Westwood, Issey Miyake, Yohji Yamamoto and Alexander McQueen. Maharishi's iconic snopant – a variation on combats with rip-chord at the waist and ankle, but elaborately embroidered with the Maharishi opium den dragon – are worn by Madonna. Having dropped the Laundry tag, Griffin (designed by Jeff Griffin) has a presence in high design emporium Jones, and Acupuncture is acknowledged as the trainer trainspotter's Mecca.

When Hardy Blechman launched Maharishi in 1994 from a warehouse in Hoxton, his camouflage pants were the uniform of the East End underground alone. Accupuncture opened in a Soho back alley opposite a sex club, selling vintage Adidas trainers and accessories. Jeff Griffin's military-inspired survival clothes in hard wearing, warfare fabrics were the choice of the few who knew. As yet, utility hadn't made it into the mainstream.

When Hardy Blechman won the British Fashion Award in 1999 for street style, he launched into an expletive-heavy rant against High Street monoliths who he said were "ripping-off truly creative people." By 1999, Maharishi's snopant was arguably the most copied piece of original utility design in its six-year history. Monserrat Mukherjee, then buyer for directional young design boutique Browns Focus, was an early supporter and buyer of Maharishi. When I interviewed her in 1997 for the *Independent on Sunday* "Style Police" column, she reported that the major fashion monoliths – including Calvin Klein, Donna Karan and Ralph Lauren – had all sent scouts to buy Maharishi for "inspiration." "How do I know?" she laughed, "they pay with their corporate cards."

By 1994, elements of army surplus had already started to creep into the biannual catwalk collections outside London. For fall 1994, Prada's military collection was the first to absorb military references. It was dubbed utility chic. Monserrat Mukherjee was justifiably angry on behalf of the Old Street school designers who initiated the utility movement. "In my opinion, Prada is copying styles that have been worn by the really cool people for years," she was quoted as saying in the *International Herald Tribune* 1999 commentary.

"You saw them in the streets with cross shoulder bags from Manhattan Portage, wearing the original camouflage, army surplus stock and knife-proof hooded jackets designed and made in dodgy Soho stores. The street uniform came from a creative bunch of stylists, DJs and students; all of whom didn't have a regular income. They made their own fashion identity. It is the kids who are the real survivors of urban life. They are the ones who make real use of streetwear simply because they are the ones who take the tube, get soaked when they are touting their portfolios around London in the rain and live the life."

Sportswear, albeit vintage from Acupuncture, was a strong element of the Old Street uniform. Inevitably, the mainstream sportswear companies capitalized on its street style status and started reissuing old school styles for the mainstream. The British High Street had been invaded by The Gap, and Donna,

Calvin and Ralph launched spin-off sport labels DKNY, CK1 and Polo Sport. Gap khakis and combat pants capitalized on army surplus underground cool. Thus the boom in utility and sports-wear chic was unleashed on the general public. Gap's jingoistic ad campaign, "Everyone in Khaki," proved prophetic.

We in the fashion industry look to designers to deliver us from uniform. As soon as the mainstream absorbed underground street style, designer fashion should have left the building. Instead, London looked on as the US fashion industry caught up with techno club culture five years too late. It was no secret that Chanel's Karl Lagerfeld sent minions onto London's club scene as inspiration ambassadors. Where else did the forgettable Chanel double-C trainer or gilt chain Evian-holder for spring/summer 1998 come from? Designers who actually did shake a tail feather in clubland, such as Galliano, Gaultier and Berardi, were wise enough to leave hooded tops, sleeveless puffas and combat pants on the street where they belong.

In their January 1998 issue, US *Vogue* published a "Techno Couture" portfolio shoot by Steven Meisel. In *Vogue*'s accompa-nying editorial, Marc Jacobs explained that his $800 fleece hooded tops and $3,500 mink puffa jackets were "not holding a mirror up to the streets, just taking a look at those proportions and colors and trying to interpret them in a very sophisticated way." Utility deluxe, however, merely smacked of creative redundancy. US *Vogue* declared, "Rockstar style is dead. Is America ready for the techno revolution?" It was like Boris Yeltsin saying, "The Tsar is dead. Are we ready for Communism?"

"Any kind of sub-culture is so quickly sanitized by the media," said London club bible *Sleaze Nation* editor Steve Beale, in response to the US *Vogue* shoot. "Club culture is so fragmented now. I hate the urban warrior uniform. Club style is fickle and individual. We're going back to more dressy, wild, rock'n'roll style. You can't dip into one club, water down individual style and flog it as high fashion uniform. If you want to know what's happening at street level, you have to be in the clubs every night."

"Sportswear is just a victim of its own popularity," said Soho boutique Shop co-director Max Karie in 1999. Everyone on the British High Street is bumping out copies of khaki Helmut Lang combats. And if big designers are copying street style, then it is disastrous: a vicious circle. Face it, nobody is going to buy labeled combat pants at Miu Miu when they can go to the source at London army surplus store Lawrence Corner, or New York's

Old Navy. It's a depressing thought that we will all be approaching the millennium wearing fleece.

Prada, after playing with Seventies retro in 1996, seemed to come down on the side of sportswear. 1999 saw the launch of Prada Sport and another broadside from the *Independent on Sunday*'s "Style Police."

When Miuccia Prada declared sport the way forward, we wondered what took her so long. Call it sport, utility, easywear or practical chic, spring (1999) is selling London style repackaged for the millennium. The elements of designer sport were so easy to absorb: Velcro fastening, man-made fibers like Jil Sander's trainer mesh top, drawstrings (and toggles) on every extremity and aerodynamic streamlined shapes. Techno sportswear is as much a part of our lives today as PlayStation and South Park. It would be naive to think fashion would not reinterpret what it is seeing on the street. But it never pays to be too literal. If high fashion has a hope of survival past 2000, it will not pay to get too populist.

Like a deadly virus, utility culture had developed in Old Street, and then spread to designer fashion, High Street and even haute couture. Within a season of writing the *Herald Tribune* case against utility in spring/summer 1999, combat pants on the streets of London looked as passé as a whalebone corset. We have the designer fashion resistance movement to thank for the timely death of utility.

As far back as 1995, Tom Ford presented his debut collection as creative director of Gucci. Leaning heavily on Halston's Seventies disco glitz aesthetic, Ford gave designer fashion the shot in the arm it craved. A year later Tyler Brule launched *Wallpaper** magazine, with Ford's Halstonesque white jersey keyhole dress on the cover. *Wallpaper** magazine was the Gucci of fashion publishing: a retro sexy, kitsch and luxe style bible for fashionistas starved for glamour. As techno gave way to trip-hop, garage and kitsch cocktail tunes on the London club scene, Gucci's clothes seemed to make sense. London clubbers now lived to lounge, not pop pills and endure nosebleed-inducing hard house.

The first two seasons of 2000 were a wild, eclectic maelstrom of maximalism, vintage chic, retro reinterpretations and avante-garde conceptualist fashion. Utility was dead. Uniqueness ruled. The sheer diversity of designer fashion was celebrated. The alarm bells began to ring at Matthew Williamson's spring/summer 2001 London show when the designer sent out white leather utility hip holsters loaded not with bullets but lipstick.

The designer then cut flirty crêpe-de-chine skirts in combat print but translated into pastels and sequins. Was utility rallying the troops for a new assault on high fashion?

In Milan Tom Ford for Gucci revived combat pants pockets on voluminous electric-blue satin pants with low-slunk skate crotches. These pieces were an acid flashback to Donatella's debut Versace combat couture. True combat prints came through in Paris at Galliano for Dior and Castelbajac, while Marc Jacobs for Louis Vuitton revived the khaki military coat with gold buttons and epaulettes. But the military advance on spring/summer 2001 was resisted by the fashion press. *The Times* fashion editor Lisa Armstrong reported, "Ford heading down a dangerous road," while *The Telegraph*'s Hilary Alexander asked, "Surely it is far too early to bring back baggy combats, even if they are re-done in cobalt satin? All Saints's original pairs haven't worn out yet."

But even if high fashion will inevitably reject utility as the way forward for 2001, there's a strong case for the military influence taking back its rightful territory in menswear and gay club culture. Under the editorship of Fabien Baron, *Arena Homme Plus* fall/winter 2000/2001 stripped David Beckham down to his regulation white cotton boxers on the "David Beckham: Hot & Hard" cover. Fashion editor Karl Templar styled an eighteen-page portfolio of boot boy Beckham in customized khakis, camouflage pants, black boots from military surplus store Rokit and green squaddie vests. His hair is shaved into a turfstrip buzz cut.

The intro to the Beckham story reads, "David Beckham takes it to a new level in these pictures. What better way to tease? A pop-culture icon turns his back on pretty labels and toughs it out on his own turf." Dolce & Gabbana gasp, "We love him!" Giorgio Armani can "understand his magnetism," and Tom Ford calls Beckham "A macho role model who is not afraid of fashion, or of being attractive and showing off his body." The world knows he's married to Posh, yet the story is unashamedly homoerotic. Beckham looks and poses like an extra from a hardcore gay porn movie like *Military Ass-Spankers*. These images are not a fashion statement: rather a stylist's in-joke about sexuality in the millennium. The military references are subverted and David Beckham is clearly in on the subtext of the story. Ultimately it's more high camp than high fashion.

When we try to crack high fashion's own enigma code, what makes designer clothing desirable? The pleasure principle will always be paramount. Utility was and is ugly, aggressive, practical and anti-fashion. We didn't wear the army surplus urban guerilla look for pleasure. They were lifestyle essentials which suited the social climate of the Nineties. But when designers sell out to street style – as they did in the last decade – fashion goes into remission. We look to designers for inspiration not imitation.

STALIN'S UNIFORM, OR THE INCARNATION OF THE SUBLIME

GIUSI FERRÉ

After a certain night hour only bad news arrives. Levitan, the most famous Moscow radio announcer, spoke in more serious and solemn tones than usual. It was four in the morning on 6 March 1953 when the radio spoke: "Attention, attention! This is Moscow," and in a slow, deliberate tone, carefully pronouncing each syllable, Levitan read the text of the announcement of the death of Stalin, which took place on 5 March at 9:50PM in his quarters at the Kremlin. The Bliznaja, the dacha in Kuntsevo where the leader usually resided, had been sealed off; bodyguards, secretaries, servants had been sent away. Some were later tried and exiled to the far eastern regions. The long agony suffered in that small villa outside the city by the Vodz – the master, as he was called – was revealed to the world in some detail only years later, in 1966. But his daughter Svetlana, who sat beside her father for three days, holding his hand, kissing it and squeezing it although Stalin, half-paralyzed by a cerebral hemorrhage, didn't show any signs of recognizing her, kept her counsel until 1991, well aware of the obscure circumstances of his demise.

But in those days of mourning "for the immense calamity that has struck the Soviet Union and the civilized world," Josif Vissarionovic Dzugasvili – who became Stalin, the man of steel – lay in rest in the Hall of Columns of the Palace of the Trade Unions, where he had once taken part in the honor guard for the other great fallen leaders of Bolshevism: Lenin, Kirov, Ordzonikidze. In the cold of Russian March, he lies there surrounded by palms and flowers, below flags at half-mast bearing the shining gold inscription: "Workers of the world, unite!" By his tomb the workers, united, walk two by two, in such profound silence that the shuffling of their feet is audible. An endless line, sixteen kilometers long, of people waiting their turn in the streets: in four days of national mourning, over five million people paid homage to the "little father of the people," the "man of victory," the "savior of civilization," as he lay at the center of the hall on a pedestal, beneath the spotlights.

"Death has not changed the features of the face familiar and dear to the entire world," wrote *Avanti!* on 8 March. In contrast with the portraits, that face was pockmarked by the smallpox he had had at the age of six, but the big mustache and the violet-black Georgian hair were the same, like the uniform that had always accompanied him in both private and public life. "When Stalin died," recalls Molotov, the People's Commissar of Foreign Affairs who signed the famous pact of non-aggression with Ribbentrop on 23 August 1939, "there was nothing available to dress him presentably. His jacket was worn out at the cuffs: it was necessary to mend it, and wash it . . ."

Austere to the point of heedlessness, although his quarters at the Kremlin occupied the entire first floor of a fine eighteenth-century building, for every season Stalin had just one outfit, always the same, the fur-lined military greatcoat he had worn at the front during the civil war, his marshal's uniform. Symbol of the party and the state, eternal combatant on the internal front more than the external, interested in nothing other than power, Stalin is a unique case in the modern history of terror. All dictators, born as revolutionaries, appear in uniform to represent the idea of permanent mobilization and authority conquered in battle, but Stalin *is* the uniform: no portrait exists of him wearing civilian clothes, and in fact he owned no clothing for recreation or relaxation.

We are tempted to say that the leader is only public, always visible in his function, although he is actually distant and invisible. "Precisely for this reason, attempts have been made to associate artistic modernism and political Stalinism as contemporary phenomena: in the Stalinian elevation of the 'wise leader,' the void that separates the object from its place is taken to an extreme, and nevertheless well considered," Slavoj Zizek remarks. In a key essay dated 1950 and entitled *On the Problem of the Beautiful in Soviet Art*, the Soviet critic G. Nedoshivin wrote: "Of all the beautiful things in life, the first place should be occupied by the images of our great leaders. . . . The sublime beauty of the leaders is the foundation for the simultaneity of the beautiful and the true in the art of social realism."

Of course no one would define Stalin or Malokov or Krusciov as examples of male beauty. The point is that they represent the function of beauty. In this sense the word sublime must be taken literally: the renowned wisdom, generosity and humanity are pure representations embodied by the leader who "pays the price of total alienation for this transfiguration. Thus the true person is treated as a mere appendix of this political image to be celebrated and worshipped. It is no surprise that the technique of retouching was so prevalently used in official photos, often with such obvious clumsiness that one wonders if it may not have been intentional, as if to indicate that the *true person* had to be entirely replaced by his effigy."

There is no difference between the portraits of Viktor Dresnikov or Dimitri Nalbandjan and the official photographs of Stalin with the members of the political directorate facing the mausoleum of Lenin as they watch a parade, or as he embraces little Svetlana or poses at the Yalta summit between Churchill and Roosevelt. Everything that might appear personal is public, and that which is public is personal. Only those who had known him in the days of Batum (1901) – the Black Sea port where the still social-democratic Stalin in his twenties reawakened the class consciousness of the workers of the Roschild refineries and the Mantaev factories – can recall him dressed in traditional Russian clothing: the blue satin shirt fastened at the side, a tight jacket and Turkish-style skullcap. (Like much of the personal information, this comes from the precious Fund 558, containing one of the most important Stalin archives.)

According to the identification profile of the Ochrana, the Czar's secret police, he was "an intellectual, of less than average height, medium build, olive skin, regular nose, clean-shaven, small black cap and overcoat with collar." Actually he was 1.67 meters tall, and due to an accident at the age of ten his left elbow was rigid, which exempted him from military service. But he was slim and had good posture, giving him a certain presence.

It was in the summer of 1918 that he began to dress and walk in a different way. Sent first to the southern front as director of provisioning (with an armored train and a Red Army detachment in order to be more persuasive), then involved in repressing the terrorism of the socialist revolutionaries ("You can be certain that my hand will not tremble," wrote Stalin to Lenin), he realized that although he was considered Lenin's right-hand man, for the professional soldiers he was nothing more than a politician. Therefore, beginning in the civil war period, he began to use a semi-military salute and bearing, and wore boots.

In April 1918, a provisional commission was formed for the creation of the uniform of the Red Army, and shortly thereafter a competition was announced, whose results were presented to the Revolutionary Military Council. Approval went to a pointed cap, which was substantially a reproduction of the steel helmet of the

Russian warriors of the fourteenth century, but with earflaps for the cold, and, in April 1919, to the military greatcoat, shirt and "lapti" (the typical leather shoes of poor peasants). We know that first prize went to the painter S. Arkad'evskij, but the final uniform was probably the result of a collective creation, combining traditional decorative elements with formal needs based more on image than on practicality. The long greatcoat in heavy gray or camouflage cloth made rapid movements difficult, impeding the legs, but it made a heroic, monumental impression.

Stalin, who often forgot to dress appropriately for the season, preferred to toss a topcoat over his shoulders, and there is an unforgettable photograph in which he is shown with a light-colored summer uniform and a dark coat against the lively backdrop of a square. In all the official images from the war on, he appears in the marshal's uniform. After all, he possessed almost no other clothing. When an inventory was made of the Vodz's personal effects, they found only some cheap furniture, a few old armchairs. No antiques. On the walls of the Bliznaja there were only reproductions on paper in old wooden frames. Two carpets on the floor. On Stalin's bed, a military blanket.

He who weakens, even slightly, the iron discipline of the party of the proletariat (especially during its rule) is actually helping the bourgeoisie against the proletariat.

Lenin, *Extremism, the Childhood Disease of Communism*, 1920

Fatally connected as they were to the figure of Stalin, his boots are the subject of a curious legend narrated by Victor Zavlasky in his story entitled *Stalin's Boots*. In its desriptions of life at the time of the Vodz and "destalinization," it contains accents worthy of the finest tradition of Russian satire. "In a city in Georgia the authorities, after a telephone call from Moscow, dynamited a colossal bronze statue of the Master. By some strange chance, after the explosion, only the gigantic boots remained atop the pedestal. It was absolutely impossible to remove them. Tourists got into the habit of having their picture taken with the boots. It is said that on the night in which Stalin was removed from the mausoleum (in 1961), the boots walked by themselves through the city, returning to their place on the pedestal at dawn."

DESTROY

MARIA LUISA FRISA

Almost no human activity is so essentially social as modern war. When a military unit loses its internal cohesion and its members start to go into combat as individuals there is such a drastic increase in casualties that it is almost always decisive for the outcome of the battle. Ever since 1914 everyone knows that in modern war the courage of the individual is just about as important as his good looks.

Leo Cawley, Vietnam veteran, in James G. Ballard, *A User's Guide to the Millennium*, 1996

When the snipers, as happens in Sarajevo, shoot not at those who cross the street quickly, carefully avoiding their aim, but at those who walk calmly, denying the authority of their treacherous fire, reality has become so grotesque as to defy the imagination.

Claudio Magris, introduction to Paolo Rumiz, *Maschere per un massacro*, 2000

A gang of uniformed men cruelly leads an unlucky group of young women and young men on leashes, accompanied by the rhythm of the atrocious ditties of the regime, mixed with offensive, lewdly shouted orders. The victims are naked, forced to walk on all fours and to bark like dogs. For nourishment they are thrown scraps of food on the ground, or served in dirty bowls. Certain morsels, for the amusement of the villainous tormentors, are filled with nails.
In 1975, precisely from March to May, Pier Paolo Pasolini shot *Salò or the 120 Days of Sodom*. The film follows the absolute, precise order of the construction of the novel by the Marquis de

Sade. Pasolini juxtaposes the Age of Enlightenment with the year 1944 in Salò, during the anarchic experiment of a fascist republic without a people, a pure oligarchic state that survives its own defeat. The poet is disappointed and bitter about events in Italy: "Everyone in Italy feels the degrading urge to be equal to others in consumption, in happiness, in freedom, because this is the order he has unconsciously received and must obey, if he doesn't want to feel 'different.' Never before has diversity been such a terrifying sin as in this period of tolerance. Equality has not, in fact, been attained, it is a false equality, granted by largesse."

In *Salò* the Sade-ian practice dominated by a pervasive idea of order organizes a terrifying closed universe, without exit or escape. The different uniforms indicate the hierarchies and authorize the torment of the bodies of youths who do not have clothing/uniforms, apart from the signs that display their status as slaves, allowing the masters to abuse them as they please. It is precisely the garment, the carapace of the withered, burnt-out bodies of the four monsters worn to declare and to assume power that permits their words to become an instrument of power. In *Salò* order is necessary for lust, i.e., for transgression; order is precisely what separates transgression from protest.

In these images constructed by Pasolini's indignation, the naked, happy bodies of Woodstock seem very far away. The nude body of protest is triumphant. It disarms the gaze with its glimmering splendor. It lets itself be swept away, unhesitating, by the Dionysiac power of the music, dreaming of a different world. Those new bodies have impact because they are aware of their devastating power. Without clothing, false ornament or rules. Courageously they shoulder the task of detouring the gaze and imposing a new viewpoint. "The world is changing," was the refrain of a pop song here in Italy, when we weren't yet in our teens. We dreamed of going to London and settled for buying a flowery shirt outside the legendary Piper Club in Rome. The anomalous wave of the Sixties started on the campuses, in the universities, crossing continents and countries with a new form of nomadism of ideas, no longer the territory of the privileged few, the political establishment, the people who count. It swept away thousands of orderly little figures in suits and ties, skirts and blouses, chemisier and pearls, camelhair coats and beaver furs. All marching in uniform on the road of productivity and profit. Some of them eager to forget history and tradition for the siren song of the factories. The goal: a standard little apartment with cardboard walls in clumsy buildings plunked down on the outskirts of sprawling cities. Others were ready to rapidly discard dreams and utopias in exchange for money and power, like the extraordinary Vittorio Gassman in *We All Loved Each Other So Much*.

Changing the world also means changing one's clothes. Doffing one uniform and donning another. But it also means stripping off one's garments and being naked, as Yoko Ono and John Lennon did to call for peace. "War is over (if you want it)." Clothing is always a uniform. It declares intent, announces a project. You blend into a group, it protects you. The naked body is disarmed, unprotected, it sends no signals. It can only speak of itself. It declares its existence with all its imperfections and weaknesses. It is a recurring, universal nightmare: we awaken in fear because we have dreamed that we were naked. Suddenly nude, forced to walk down a crowded street, in the midst of completely dressed people. Utterly defenseless, exposed to curious eyes, full of scorn and derision.

The dead body of Che was displayed nude by his Bolivian assassins. The head is held up so we can recognize that handsome face. It is 1967, one of the icons of the fight for freedom lies dead, surrounded by his uniformed executioners. They have left him only a pair of old, tattered trousers, and stretched him out on a dismal cement catafalque. As my gaze follows the hand of the soldier who touches his ribs in a desecrating gesture, I reflect that the humiliation of the legend also happens by means of the erasure of his uniform. Che Guevara without his beret and his military jacket.

The fabulous Sixties came to an end in the desert of *Zabriskie Point*, where Daria, the film's protagonist, gives form to her impatience and her aggressive desire for change. Before her eyes the house, overflowing with affluence, explodes to the sounds of Pink Floyd.

At this point the body of Patti Smith photographed nude by Robert Mapplethorpe captures our gaze. "Take me now baby here as I am / Pull me close try and understand / Desire is hunger is the fire I breathe / Love is a banquet on which we feed." The Seventies, a different sensation. There has been endless talk of the revolution of the Sixties, but there was actually no revolution, nothing of the kind. "When you take stock of what happened in those years, you have to realize that nothing really changed, and even the people who participated in the celebration ten years later were back wearing gray suits," John Lennon declared in an interview. Chaos is useful as long as it pays, then it's time to go back to order. Mapplethorpe photographed Patti's skinny, androgynous body with the tenderness of a friend and traveling companion. Sex, drugs and rock'n'roll. Psychedelia means baring the soul. Subverting the rules can be a hellish race that consumes and destroys. The artist's black and white images narrate dazed paths to reach the awareness that baring the soul profanes the body, and they enumerate, as in a catalogue, the various practices regulated by precise rituals that unwind in the darkrooms of sex. Black leather, belts, chains and whips. The atrocious depersonalization of the individual defines the ritual order of the fetish scene. The uniform of the dominated erases identity and freedom, revealing only those parts of the body that serve the pleasure of the dominator.

The body as language is always, therefore, under different guises, on view on the stage of the world, and it is proposed, case by case, in different versions. Triumphant, sacrificed, diffused, propagated, dramatic, tragic; political body, social body, extreme body. Body as the most ancient tool of communication through tattoos, piercings, tribal citations, manipulation of organs – to say what must by said without words, sound or drawing. It's still a way of declaring one's opposition to the dominant culture, but it is also the manner of desperate forms of conformism. "I wanna be Anarchy / You know what I mean? / And I wanna be an anarchist / Get pissed / Destroy!" the Sex Pistols furiously yell. While the violated body expresses the rage of the no future generation. The violent signs borrowed from Nazi mythology, the swastikas and skulls decorating one of the many uniforms of terror become tattoos, brandings and scarification. The skin is imprinted with the terrible belonging to the order of violence and abuse, racism and incomprehension, rancor and hate, in the indelible uniforms of the skinheads. The path of expiation of the agonizing Edward Norton, playing the violent skinhead in *American History X*, won't bring him back into the social order that would mean salvation for him and his family. As often happens in true stories, in the end the disorder of evil demands a sacrifice. The life of his innocent, beloved brother. Norton discards his steel-toe boots and thug uniform, and with "normal" hair, like all the other youths in the squalid houses in his neighborhood, all he can do is scream out his pain.

"Who are you, can't you see the uniform?! The uniform has done a miracle, it has transformed a man into a hero," Totò thunders in an old black and white movie that tells the micro-story of an Italian nobody during World War II, who becomes a hero almost by mistake, thanks to the most profound meaning of the clothing he wears.

And the story continues. Dressed as a warrior in military green and cap with visor, Bono, the singer of U2, on a peace mission meets with the Pope to discuss canceling the debts of the third world nations. Not so far away, I am struck by the image of another naked body, clutched in the fetal position. An unrecognizable male body, faceless because the head is wrapped in a keffiyeh. The universal symbol-uniform not only of the Palestinians, but also of the battle of all peoples for freedom. The photo was taken in a studio together with others for a fashion feature by Matthias Vriens. It conveys the dark foreboding that grips us when we see all the images that speak of repression and violence, images we see every day on television.

Sooner or later everything becomes television. And that is when the paradox explodes. Through the window of the TV screen the sequence of events is so dense that we no longer see it: a massacred body on the news, the face of a desperate woman in a soap opera, the violence of a rave party in a documentary, a multiple rape in a film, or punk citations at the latest fashion show. It all invades and occupies our field of vision, destroying any sense of context, proportion and distance in the spectator. Order and disorder are flattened out on the same bleary surface.

SIGNS OF ORDER, SIGNS OF DISORDER: THE OTHER UNIFORMS

PATRIZIA CALEFATO

The clad body and certainties. In his essay entitled "The Making and Unmaking of Strangers," Zygmunt Baumann introduces an image borrowed from Orwell – a military boot trampling on a human face.[1] The context in which the image is evoked involves the analysis of the procedures with which societies, in particular modern societies and states, produce the figure of the "stranger" defined by Baumann as he who does not adapt to the cognitive, moral or aesthetic maps of the world.[2] Boots, Baumann goes on to say, are a part of uniforms, symbols of the servants of the state, seen as the source of all power, and above all of the coercive power sustained by the legitimate authority of self-acquittal of the charge of inhuman cruelty.[3] The function of the uniform, in this sense, is a guarantee of state power, the watershed between order and disorder. The image of the boots, metonymically connected to the uniform, representing its sign-index, thus establishes a horizon of certainties, an ordered, classifying sphere of existence, with respect to which anything else is construed as the reign of uncertainty and chaos.[4]

A close relationship exists between what we wear – which we can generically call "dress" – and identity, or that socio-cultural construct produced through recurring, constant elements and stereotypes, and through which we achieve what is commonly known as "self-recognition." The history of dress, in fact, is the history of the body, its imagery, discipline, the hierarchies inscribed upon it, the discourses that have constructed its passions and senses, the way in which the difference between the male and female bodies has been socially and culturally processed on the basis of productive and reproductive functions. Thus the "clad body" represents a system of signs through which certain social meanings are uttered and through which their sense is produced and organized.[5] In the language of dress, the signifying value assumed by a garment or a decoration depends upon the positioning of these elements inside a network of paths of meaning, a sort of spiderweb reproducing a cartography of the body, a map in which each sign takes on a precise social value and meaning, according to its positioning and its synchronous or diachronous relation to the other signs. In the case of the uniform, the social subject experiences identification, controlling the overall network of meaning which, through the signs of the body, provides information regarding his status, and therefore creates a high level of adhesion, of certainty in relation to the idea of identity sustained by the garb-uniform. The universe of the uniform, especially in its military expressions, represents a "reservoir of meaning" of which the clad body makes use for the moorings of its certainties regarding identity.

In the history of customs the uniform represents a meaningful instance of the way dress can become a regulatory apparatus for the body, sanctioning a closed system of correspondence between external appearance and social order. It is no coincidence that uniforms, especially but not only in the modern era, are signs of recognition of belonging to those total institutions – from the armed forces to schools, prisons and hospitals – which form the foundation of the most profound guarantees of social order of the discourse, as Foucault put it. The uniform is the emblem of separation between the inside and the outside of a hierarchically ordered culture, between the "upright" world and the "upside-down" world, between familiar and alien, "ours" and "theirs," identity and otherness.

In Italian the term *divisa* (uniform) is also used to indicate a currency, i.e., that generalized equivalent of value in which differences are taken back to the dimension of possible exchange or trade. In this sense, the uniform can be seen as an impersonal sign, separate from the traits that might make it (or its wearer) unique or irreplaceable. While on the one hand it indicates certain established meanings regarding the role of its wearer, on the other it is indifferent to specific individual differences, and fundamentally indifferent to the element of corporeity seen as a material nature resistant to universal interchangeability. Long before the garment industry had invented mass production or prêt-à-porter, military uniforms already had made use of standard sizes. And standard sizing represents a significant infraction in the context of that duality-opposition between dress and custom within which, according to Barthes,[6] garments function as language. The dimensions of a garment tailored to the measurements of the body belong, as Barthes says in the wake of

Trubeckoj, to the realm of dress, or the individual dimension of the language of dress, similar to the Saussurian act of *parole* in verbal language. Numbered sizes, on the other hand, group bodies into standardized categories: in this way, one of the practices or forms from the field of dress finds its way into the realm of custom as a social institution, similar to Saussure's *langue*. And it is no coincidence that it has been precisely the uniform that has led to this sense-producing transformation, a transformation the fashion industry, with prêt-à-porter and its mass-produced reproductive potential, has absorbed and amplified.

Many articles of clothing, terms and habits of normal bourgeois dress have been directly lifted from the culture of uniforms. The universe of the military and of war has represented, above all, a bottomless archive of objects, cuts and forms, which even the most recent fashions and styles continue to explore. One fundamental element in this genealogy is the men's suit, which has a democratic, military origin, as Barthes explains.[7] After the French Revolution, in fact, it was precisely the idea of democracy that led to the concept of a suit – which has remained substantially the same, even throughout the twentieth century – inherited from the uniform and from the values of equality, also reflecting an aesthetic break with the Ancien Régime. Of course, as Barthes also points out, the separation among social classes was not erased after the Revolution, and the dress of upper middle class men of the nineteenth century had to come to terms with the rise of the middle classes: first dandyism and later fashion made it possible to distinguish rank or to blend in, through the rhetoric of detail and the pursuit of distinction. And yet the ideal of certainty in the cartography of the signs of the body, whose highest realization is the uniform, is pursuit in modern menswear, so much so that Virginia Woolf, in her feminist, pacifist essay of 1938, *Three Guineas*, listed the ways in which the fashion of her time managed to provide men with a rigid and, at the same time, grotesque social symbolism. Like the little tags in a shop window, Woolf noted, each sign, color, knot or scarf indicates the social and professional role of the public man: this man is a member of the Bar, this one must be a member of Her Majesty's Order of Merit for Work, the clothing seems to say. But were a woman to advertise her condition of motherhood by placing a tuft of horsehair on her left shoulder, she would not inspire any such veneration.[8] It is a well-known fact that the figure of the soldier in uniform, muscles and camouflage, returns periodically and repeatedly in the imagery of society, deeply forging the male stereotype, and not only in terms of dress.[9]

Semiotics of the uniform. No one is extraneous to uniforms, in the sense that the "signage" characteristics of dress intrinsic to the uniform mark, in the history of customs and lifestyles, an entire series of clothing-specific acts and "declarations" aimed at intentional use of the garment as a sign of recognition or belonging, and as a social regulator. Thus uniforms make bodies into social signals. It is difficult to speak of the body in terms of "signals," given its innate reluctance to closure within a circumscribed taxonomy of meanings. But we cannot help but recognize, even in everyday life, that it is precisely the uniform that serves as an unchallenged indicator of profession or social function. The uniform of a policeman causes a thief to flee, regardless of any considerations regarding which policeman is wearing it. The white coat of a doctor provokes a sense of trust and/or fear in the patient. The vestments or habits of religious figures endow them not only with authority, but also with a specific identity as the representatives of God on earth.

The signal message of the uniform functions on a paradigmatic axis, as expressed in the case of military uniforms, for example, by distinctions of rank indicated by means of small details (insignia, stars, stripes) within the same service; and along a syntagmatic axis expressed in the variety of form of the garment, as in distinctions between different services or the armed forces of different states. In this sense the uniform-clad body displays a certain structure in relation to the three spheres of its functioning as a sign: on the semantic level, each detail has its own precise meaning (just consider the value of colors); on the syntactic level, it is necessary to follow an order and precise sequences when putting on the uniform and its accessories (as in the case of military uniforms, with their rigid rules for correct wear); on the pragmatic level, the wearer of a uniform "does" or "makes others do" something precise, prescribed by a pre-established social code (the doctor, for example, not only "does" his job as a doctor when he dons his white coat, he also "makes others do" their role as patients, with all its implications: undressing, getting into strange positions, making unusual sounds for diagnostic purposes, etc.).

So it would appear that the status of uniforms within a community is based on the fact that the meanings they communicate and the rules they follow are absolutely certain, stable and fixed. But the modes of socio-semiotic functioning of the uniform in relation to the construction of certainties in our present are complex. These modes, in fact, particularly in our time, cannot avoid operations of destructuring, manipulation and irony, through which the certainty of the clad body passes in relation to the construction of its multiple identities. If, in short, the uniform-model continues to exist as a signal element of a social role, the dress-related culture of our era is capable at times of transforming this signal status into a complex semiotic construct. Dress, in fact, is a veritable cultural text that cannot be thought of – even in the case of the uniform – as a closed, consistent, self-sufficient system. It must be analyzed in terms of the modes with which it constantly transforms itself into textual practice, immersed in worldly circulation, open to different gazes and manipulations. The text-uniform has a social life of its own, it is open to multiple possibilities of reworking and recontextualizing within the semiosphere,[10] the semiotic space in which different cultural texts with complex reciprocal relations and different degrees of translatability or untranslatability insert themselves at multiple levels.

The uniform as jargon. Military communications typically make use of the "password," that verbal declaration, possibly accompanied by gestures, which permits mutual recognition, an understanding that leads to the opening of a channel of communication, albeit the transmission of a war dispatch, the gate of a barracks, the fortifications of a bridge, or the gates to a city under siege. The password requires knowledge not only of the word itself, but also, especially in the case of a declaration composed of multiple monemes, of a correct sequence, a predetermined order based on a code whose sense is clear only to the interlocutors, and only if they are the "right" interlocutors. In short, this is the manifestation of a contact, an expression of that "phatic function" of language which, in the linguistic theory of Jakobson,[11] represents the function that focuses on the channel, on the simultaneous presence of at least one sender and one receiver of communication. By means of the phatic function, we ascertain that there are no obstructions in the channel, that the social dimension of our declarations is preserved, apart from their literal significance, apart from the quality, quantity and nature of the information to be transmitted.

In general, the uniform functions something like a password, because its function of social recognition is based on signals that confirm the position, in the same semiotic universe, of two or more interlocutors. And in this sense the password belongs to the communicative realm of jargon, i.e., of a sign-based code inflected on the social plane, with simultaneously restricted, variable and collective characteristics. So restricted as to border on the marginal – so variable and collective that they share some essential traits with style. And jargon, in the linguistic sense, is in fact an idiosyncratic variant of language, albeit verbal or non-verbal, characteristic of social groups that do not identify with the standardized, institutional languages.

Subcultures have their own uniforms, components of a jargon with which the groups make themselves recognizable both inside and outside their circle, and through which they exchange, as in a communications grapevine, their passwords regarding tastes, stylistic twists, everyday practices and forms of behavior. The street uniforms typical of the urban tribes are based, just like institutional uniforms, on a logic of group identification and separation of that group from the others. But in these cases the identification does not involve an institutional social role, anything but: the dress jargon characterizes groups that do not recognize themselves in standardized and conventional languages, and make a destructuring, ironic use of their special uniforms. The twentieth century, especially during its second half, has produced a plethora of street styles and their copies,[12] giving rise to typifications that have, by now, become classics in the history of lifestyles and which, in some cases, have provided inspiration for institutional fashions, "from the sidewalk to the catwalk." The slang nature of the uniforms of street style stands out precisely due to their "marginal"[13] and "subcultural"[14] character. We can trace this phenomenon back, without going beyond Western cultures, to very distant roots: the masks of medieval goliards, the disguises of brigands, the costumes of gypsies.[15]

Today marginality or subcultural characters are not synonymous with separation from the center of culture and social communication, if it is still possible to speak of a center in a context in which the distinction between local and global increasingly tends to vanish in the direction of economic and communicative globalization. Just consider, for example, the constant plundering of subcultural styles on the part of the designer clothing market, which pays very close attention to youthful consumers organized in terms of "tribes."[16] Nevertheless, the slang dimension or, to use a suggestion made by Barthes,[17] the idiolectal dimension of the styles in which bodies are clad with true uniforms as signs of recognition and shared belonging exists in the space of meaning that Lotman[18] would define as "frontier." The Doc Marten's shoes of skinheads in the Sixties, the Edwardian jackets of English teddy boys, the eskimo jackets of Italian students in the protest years, the safety pins and unnatural hair colors of punks, the studded leather jackets of heavy metal fans, the plaid flannel shirts of the grunge movement, the oversized trousers of hip hop

– just to mention of few of the garments and gestures typical of the most famous uniforms of the styles of the twentieth century – contain a guarantee of identification for the members of a shared cultural space, but for an external observer they represent elements of chaos and disorder.

The punk style, as Hebdige noted at the time,[19] represented, in this sense, an exemplary strategy of surrealistic deformation of the nature of the uniform. "If the cap doesn't suit you, wear it!" was the password, as Hebdige himself emphasizes. The contrast between the "artificial" context and the "natural" context had to be clearly visible ("confrontation clothing" was Vivienne Westwood's term for this technique). In the very moment in which a contrast or excess is manifested, a performance is enacted from which its maker stands apart, detached.[20] The game takes place at the frontier, on the borderline, a place that, as Lotman says, functions as a "buffer mechanism" in which information is transformed into a "block of translation sui generis."[21] Rather than an identifying sign, the body that wears the uniform is thus transformed into a translating sign, in which the two languages through which the translation passes are simultaneously evident, along with a "third language" that belongs to the border zone. And it is no coincidence that the body of a punk was a surface without gloss and without limits: every part could be perforated by pins, sliced by blades, associated with the exhibition of an absolutely abnormal object – a truly grotesque body.[22]

Uniform and otherness. In a recent contribution Jean Baudrillard[23] compared the uniform to that universal and utterly democratic garment of our time: jeans. In his view, while the uniform is the reflection of a structured, hierarchical society and seals like an emblem the ideological cohesion of a nation, a class or an institution, jeans, on the other hand, are the reflection of an undifferentiated society.[24] But what the French scholar doesn't seem to include in this reasoning is the fact that on many occasions in our century, even jeans have played the role of emblems or uniforms for unique forms of elitist dress codes, certainly not connected to a hierarchical social differentiation but, on the contrary, to the ideological values of the given situation. For example, in the use of jeans as the garment-ensign of the protest movement of the Sixties, or connected to the worldly, sophisticated image of affluent nations – as in the dream of owning a pair of jeans typical of youth in all of Eastern Europe during the Iron Curtain years.

Today, now that all these ideological investments have been consumed, the puzzle composed on the body starting with jeans, perhaps accompanied by high-tech sneakers and a backpack, is seen by the "adult" world as the planetary image of the uniform of teenagers. And yet the dialectic between standardization and identification with a style of appearance, from which no more or less youthful subject in search of certainties has ever been able to escape in any era, reveals how deceptive such a superficial reading can be. Just as the Pokemon characters, those cartoon creatures that combine something of the elf with something of the robot, all look the same at first glance, but then turn out to be many individuals with an infinity of idiosyncrasies similar to those of humans, so we can observe that just a single detail can destroy the illusion of a disciplined, uniform body. In the multiple ways of presenting the body characteristic of our era, the phenomenology of the uniform reflects, in many ways, the logic of the border zone and of denaturalizing disorientation. Its regulatory function, that through which the body is forced into a hierarchy by means of the visual evidence of its status and the clear separation between order and disorder, is accompanied by procedures of constant manipulation and reassessment-renewal.

To understand certain mechanisms of the present, it is often necessary to make use of models of interpretation and representation from the recent past, especially when these models – in literature, art, film and fields of knowledge – have attempted to forecast a near future, just as in the case of Orwell's *1984*, the source of the initial image of the boot trampling a human face. Cinema, that endless trove of such models, in Fritz Lang's *Metropolis* (1926) has offered an interpretative model that has continued to provide stimuli throughout the twentieth century. In the underground city of Metropolis all the workers wear a uniform, overalls that standardize them and mold them into a Fordist mass. They always hold their heads bowed, in a posture that symbolizes submission. In this case the uniform represents subjection to power and not, as in the case of the military, its exercise, although the society is organized at production and work levels along military lines. The uniform imposes the impossibility for men to set themselves apart from others, and it is accompanied by the impossibility for the workers to look anywhere but downward. The worksuit is an emblem of enclosure in an internal world (the underground city), subordinated to the external world above it. The order of the city above is guaranteed by the rigid discipline of the subterranean city, a discipline that is structurally expressed in the total replaceability and interchangeability of the bodies in uniform, all equal, also because their faces (which would represent their only unique element, an exception to the rule of the standardization of the bodies) are not visible due to the position of their heads. In the film, the symbolic element of disorder and revolt intervenes in the moment in which the robot appears – the vile double of the gentle female protagonist, Maria – whose body is an extreme expression, but also grotesque paradox, of the body in uniform. The robot bursts into the orderly underground world like a creature that is itself a part of that world, given the shared inorganic nature of the uniformed bodies – reduced to mere standardized automata – and the body of the robot. But the latter is to be precisely the body that takes inorganicity to such an extreme as to destroy its functional efficiency.

The imagery of the body and society envisioned in the Fordist era by *Metropolis* points to the fact that the destiny of the uniform is probably that of excess, of dysfunction, of constant contamination between the world it is supposed to contain, and the "other" against which, as a symbol, it is supposed to rally defense. Armies make men uniform, they standardize them within parameters that not only allow them to recognize their reciprocal belonging, just as with ensigns, banners and standards, but at the same time unify and, especially in mass armies, communicate signs on an increasingly vast scale. Therefore military uniforms do produce, on the one hand, order, as in Orwell's image recalled by Baumann; but at the same time they cannot make themselves immune to the disorder and otherness of which they are emblematic reminders. The peace symbol that appears on T-shirts since the time of the war in Vietnam, for example, becomes an anti-uniform in its way, and is transformed into a recognizable, mass-produced sign in the spheres of youthful protest. The camouflage suits sold in used clothing shops become prototypes for fashion houses that copy their designs and colors. The black mourning color of Palestinian women stands out as a strong sign of international pacifism in the movement of "women in black," who through the color of their dress manifest an immediate solidarity with those who suffer the consequences of war. In the meantime, a society that is highly characterized by the everyday use of the "civilian" uniform, such as modern-day Japan, explicitly reveals the paradoxes of this regulatory dress, which is subjected to the reworkings of fashion, the transgressions of teenagers and the translations of the pop culture of manga comics.[25]

The extreme limit of the uniform is the body: those bodies it standardizes and cancels out in its uniqueness, just like garments on the body of a manikin.[26] And yet the body that is inside the military uniform is, by definition, the healthy, athletic, disciplined body trained by marching, calisthenics and exercises. The body of the fashion model – cancelled out by the dress – is at the same time emphasized and brought alive in social discourse, in that constant translation of top-model into pop-model[27] typical of the dress culture and fashion of our time. And in turn, the body of the "other" uniforms is marked, tattooed, pierced, written and inscribed in the social space.

What is left to cancel or erase? What borders are left to mark? What certainties to establish?

1. Zygmunt Baumann, "The Making and Unmaking of Strangers," in *Postmodernity and Its Discontents* (Oxford: Blackwell, 1997): 17-34.
2. *Ibid.*
3. Baumann, 1997: 56.
4. *Ibid.*
5. See Patrizia Calefato, *Moda, corpo, mito* (Rome: Castelvecchi, 1999).
6. Roland Barthes, *Scritti. Società, testo, comunicazione*, ed. G. Marrone (Turin: Einaudi, 1998): 21. See also R. Barthes, *Oeuvres complètes*, Eric Marty, ed. (Paris: Seuil, 1993, 1994, 1995).
7. Barthes, 1998, 76.
8. Virginia Woolf, *Three Guineas* (Richmond: Hogarth Press, 1938).
9. Natalia Aspesi, "Miles gloriosus," in *Uomo oggetto,* G. Malossi, ed. (Milan: Bolis, 1999).
10. Jurij M. Lotman, "O semiosfere," *Trudy po znakovym sistemam* 17 (Tartu, 1984).
11. Roman Jakobson, *Essais de linguistique générale* (Paris: Minuit, 1963).
12. See Ted Polhemus, *Street Style* (London: Thames & Hudson, 1994).
13. See Glauco Sanga, "Gerghi," in *Introduzione all'italiano contemporaneo, La variazione e gli usi,* A.M. Sobrero, ed. (Rome, Bari: Laterza, 1993).
14. See Dick Hebdige, *Subculture* (London: Methuen, 1979). See also Caroline Evans, "Dreams That Only Money Can Buy...Or The Shy Tribe in Flight from Discourse," *Fashion Theory* 1, issue 2 (1997).
15. See Elizabeth Wilson, "Bohemian Dress and the Heroism of Everyday Life," *Fashion Theory* 2, issue 3 (1998).
16. See Alessandro Giancola, *La moda nel consumo giovanile* (Milan: Angeli, 1999).
17. Roland Barthes, *Le bruissement de la langue. Essais critique IV* (Paris: Seuil, 1984).
18. Lotman, 1984.
19. Dick Hebdige, *Subculture*.
20. Patrizia Calefato, *Mass moda* (Genoa: Costa & Nolan, 1996): 22.
21. Lotman, 1984.
22. Calefato, 1996: 21.
23. Jean Baudrillard, "Design e Dasein," *Agalma* 1 (2000).
24. Baudrillard, 2000: 12-13.
25. See Brian McVeigh, "Wearing Ideology: How Uniforms Discipline Minds and Bodies in Japan," *Fashion Theory* 1, issue 2 (1997).
26. Roland Barthes, *Système de la Mode* (Paris: Seuil, 1967).
27. Calefato, 1996: 100-107.

EROS AND UNIFORM

RICHARD BUCKLEY

I always did like a man in uniform,
and that one fits you grand.
Why don't you come up and see me some time?

Mae West, in *She Done Him Wrong*

The erotic appeal of a man in uniform can never be underestimated. By idealizing the masculine form, uniforms represent power, simultaneously inspiring emotions of security, awe, fear, repulsion and desire. Just as the sexual impulse differs with each person, so the erotic potential of uniforms also varies, whether their context is iconic, hardcore or camp. Outlining, and sometimes exaggerating the male physique, uniforms literally and figuratively command attention. Because of their association with authority and force – soldiers, policemen and prison guards – uniforms are related to sexual potency. Affording the wearer with a sense of anonymity, they can intensify or subvert conventional gender role-playing. The erotic nature of uniforms manifests itself throughout contemporary popular culture in fashion layouts, films, photography and art. From Tom of Finland's pornographic drawings of tumescent sailors and highway patrolmen to the undercurrent of repressed sexual tension in Claire Denis' Foreign Legion film, *Beau Travail*, there is a particularly seductive allure to this kind of masculine dress. The sexual significance of uniforms is fundamentally inherent in their construction, which designer Paul Smith says is based on "posture, elegance and cut." Smith learned his craft from a military tailor whose specialty was ceremonial uniforms – apparel fashioned to make a man look as powerful as possible. The jackets, Smith explains, are tailored with heavy inner facings to make the chest look more pronounced, shoulder seams are hidden along the back for a clean shoulder line, and the armhole is shallow to give a slim appearance. The overall cut of the jacket is intended to convey the visual illusion that the man is standing tall and straight. Similarly, the high-waist trousers are hollowed out in back to aid posture. Trouser legs without a side seam and the addition of side stripes are details intended to give a uniform a long, lean elegant look. The garments make the man into a tailored "erection," the sartorial symbol of male phallic power. Uniforms are equalizers, alternatively creating and obliterating identities. There are no distinctions between rich and poor. Military uniforms, for example, neutralize individuality to create a sense of order within a group. In a combat situation, functioning as a unit is often essential for a soldier's survival. Conversely, uniforms can offer the means to invent an alternative identity. In its most extreme form, the French Foreign Legion even goes so far as to give a recruit a new name when he enters the service, effectively erasing his past. "You are no longer African," one soldier says to another in *Beau Travail.* "You are a Legionnaire, understand?" What we wear does not necessarily say who we are, but often who we want to be. "Dress, which is an extension of the body yet not quite part of it," Elizabeth Wilson writes in *Adorned in Dreams*, "not only links that body to the social world, but also more clearly separates the two. Dress is the frontier between the self and the non-self." In Stanley Kubrick's *Full Metal Jacket* (1987), Private Joker refers to Marine basic training as a "college for the phony tough and the crazy brave." It would not be an unfair assumption, therefore, to say that there are a number of men who join the military to learn and prove their masculinity.

"Erotic desire for another person is a desire literally to have that person," Brian Pronger explains in *The Arena of Masculinity*, "to incorporate that person into one's own being." In other words, to emulate what is considered the ideal is to attempt to possess that which we desire to be. This brings us to the inevitable discussion of the man in uniform as being the masculine archetype and therefore being inherently homoerotic. "In our culture, male homosexuality is a violation of masculinity, a denigration of the mythic power of men," Plonger adds. "But because masculinity is the heart of homoerotic desire, homosexuality is essentially a paradox in the myth of gender." Through a series of one-on-one interviews in the books, *Barrack Buddies and Soldier Lovers*, *Sailors and Sexual Identity* and *The Masculine Marine*, service men tell author Steve Zeeland how the conditions in the US military are ripe for homosexual activity. In *Sailors and Sexual Identity*, Zeeland describes how intimate relationships between men who live in close, all-male quarters and initiation rituals involving simulated sexual acts might technically be considered homosexual, "whether or not penetration or ejaculation ever occur," but do not compromise masculine identity. Separated from the possibility of sex with women, Scott, a US soldier based in Germany, tells Zeeland that "in the barracks everything is sex." "Situational" same-sex encounters are not infrequent, but they are not necessarily considered gay because there are no emotional attachments and they are generally just for release. Alone, while cleaning the barracks bathroom in their underwear, Private Joker looks at Private Cowboy in *Full Metal Jacket* and says, "I want to slip my tube steak into your sister, what will you take in trade?" In the military hierarchy, latent homosexuality is built into the relationships between soldiers and their commanding officers. There is the classic dominant/subservient, father/son dynamic between the Marine DI (drill instructor) and his recruits, as in *Full Metal Jacket*, or the shifting power play between the officers and prisoners in Sidney Lumet's *The Hill* (1965). Repressed homosexuality is the theme of John Huston's film *Reflections in a Golden Eye* (1967), where Captain Penderton, played by Marlon Brando, is enamoured, to the point of obsession, with his wife's lover, Private Williams. The psycho-sexual narrative between a military superior who is jealous of, and sets out to destroy, a younger soldier has been explored in films such as Claire Denis' *Beau Travail* (2000) and Marco Risi's *Soldati 365 all'alba* (1987), both interpretations of Herman Melville's novella *Billy Budd*. While most uniforms represent power and authority, there is something boyish, and slightly feminine, about a sailor suit. The V-neck top that stops just below the waist, and the tight cut of the trousers, draw the eye to and focus attention on the man's genitals and backside. Perhaps because they spend so much time at sea away from the company of women, or because when they get to shore they are ready for anything, sailors have always been gay icons. Advertisements for designer Jean Paul Gaultier's scent Le Male features two sailors arm wrestling. While the image can be interpreted as a macho test of strength, it also carries a homoerotic subtext as a prelude to sex, and which one will be the dominant "top" and who will be the submissive "bottom." The ultimate gay sailor film, Rainer Werner Fassbinder's *Querelle* (1982), with Brad Davis in the title role, has been the inspiration for a number of homoerotic fashion layouts from Norman Watson's images for *Arena Hommes Plus* to Bruce Weber's "Showboys" for *L'Uomo Vogue*. Nothing, however, carries the erotic wallop of Jean Cocteau's pornographic drawings for the illustrated version of Jean Genet's original novel.

"All costumes are caricatures," said Oscar Wilde. In the sexual theater, uniforms become costumes of sorts that allow the wearer to experiment with role-playing and gender identity. The military or police force offers the ideal environment to both appropriate and magnify gender stereotypes. In *Rambo* (1985) and *Commando* (1985), the kind of action films that take machismo to its most theatrical extremes, Sylvester Stallone and Arnold Schwarzenegger exaggerate masculinity to the point of parody, becoming "male impersonators." Perhaps the eroticization of men in uniforms unconsciously begins in childhood when we are made to understand that the police and military represent a higher form of authority that is outside the father/mother family unit. As adults, this hierarchy of control and subordination can take on another dimension. In *Fetish: Fashion, Sex & Power*, Valerie Steele writes, "the erotic connotations of military uniforms derive, in part, from the sexual excitement that many people associate with violence and with the relationship between dominance and submission." An element of danger can often make a situation erotically charged, returning to the idea of sex as power. Consider George Michael's entrapment in a public toilet in Los Angeles by an undercover cop, and then the singer's response with two policemen kissing in the video for his single "Outside." Cops in general are revered as sexual icons. They are symbols of force and discipline, which makes them perfect characters for S&M sexual fantasies. While policemen in uniform certainly have their place in gay mythology, the idea of being "disciplined" or taken by force by a policewoman appeals to heterosexual males. Models role-playing in police uniforms are the subject of Bruce Weber's aptly titled "Streetwear or Costume?" photo shoot for *L'Uomo Vogue*. Conversely the biker, in the words of Tom of Finland, "to this day remains a strong symbol of amoral masculinity." The motorcycle jacket and boots are not only elements of the biker's uniform, but fetishistic sexual objects as well, immortalized in such films as Kenneth Anger's *Scorpio Rising* (1963), Sidney Furey's *The Leather Boys* (1964) and Laslo Benedek's *The Wild One* (1953) with Marlon Brando. Although the eroticism of military uniforms is the focus of this essay, in the sexual arena, a person's fantasy can incorporate many different kinds of dress, on to which people can project their fantasies. These include male icons such as soldiers, sailors, policemen, firemen, cadets, Boy Scouts, cowboys or bikers, and for women uniforms of subservience (maids and nurses) or virginal innocence (brides and schoolgirls). The cult of the schoolgirl is so strong in Japan that vending machines reportedly sell their previously worn underpants. Priests and nuns form their own subcategory, as the repression of desire and their renunciation of sexuality make them all the more appealing. What could be more titillating than to go into a confessional and tell sins in the most lascivious details, with the intention of arousing the priest? There are, of course, any of a number of hardcore sex films set in strictly regimented convents with nuns frolicking in and out of habit, such as *The Demons* (1972), *Love Letters of a Portuguese Nun* (1976) and *Immagini Convento* (1979). Films set in women's prisons and boarding schools are camp pseudo-lesbian romps. Classics of the correctional institute genre include *Women in Prison* (1955), *Girls Town* (1959) and *Caged Heat* (1974). Originally banned in Germany and the US, Leontine Sagan's *Madchen in Uniform* (1931) is the story of a young girl who finds herself in the "prison-like confines of a Nazi boarding school." She falls in love with one of the teachers, but when found out, she is subject to the "harsh and cruel punishment" by the head mistress.

Nazi uniforms and paraphernalia have always had strong sexual and fetishistic appeal, from the young Marlon Brando as a Nazi officer in *The Young Lions* (1958), to porno films like *Ilsa, She Wolf of the S.S.* (1974), *Deported Women of the S.S. Special Section* (1975) and *Nazi Love Camp* (1977). Recently, Piotr Uklanski gathered together fetishistic images of actors dressed for film roles for his book *The Nazis* (Scalo).

While uniforms may aid in distinguishing who plays the dominant and subservient roles, a reversal in situation or character sometimes makes the equation more exciting, allowing men and women to escape from the pressures of gender stereotyping. In *L'Avventura di un Soldato*, Nino Manfredi's segment in the film *L'Amore Difficile* (1963) concerns a soldier, Manfredi, who gets in a train compartment with an elderly couple, a little girl and a shapely widow played by Fulvia Franco. In her widow's weeds, another fetishistic uniform, Franco looks more like a model in a Dolce & Gabbana show than she does someone in mourning. The ensuing dance of love between self-control and desire is one of the most erotic scenes ever filmed. Gary Cooper and Marlene Dietrich play an interesting game of gender bending in *Morocco* (1930). Cooper is a womanizing Legionnaire, who has a definite boyish demeanor under his uniform. Dietrich, on the other hand, is the tough-as-nails, world-weary cabaret singer who performs in tailored tails and a top hat. "The most refined form of sexual attractiveness (as well as the most refined form of sexual pleasure)," Susan Sontag writes in *Against Interpretation*, "consists in going against the grain of one's sex. What is most beautiful in virile men is something feminine; what is most beautiful in feminine women is something masculine." For both Cooper and Dietrich, their uniforms define their roles. By the end of the film, however, Dietrich kicks off her pumps (fetish symbols of women's power), and takes the subservient role by joining the women who follow their men into the desert. Perhaps because of its mystery, the French Foreign Legion is the most romantic of any military organization. They are the highlight of every Bastille Day parade, marching down the Champs Elysées looking like one block of testosterone, their virility so potent it almost perfumes the air. Claire Denis' *Beau Travail* just could be the sexiest film on the Legion ever made. What makes Denis' Legionnaires so arousing is not the obvious homoerotic appeal of toned muscular bodies that dominate choreographed training exercises, but the poetic exploration of the male psyche in the microcosm of repression and desire she creates within their garrison world in Djibouti. It is an environment where emotional longing is channeled into masculine ritual, such as the scene of four men at four ironing boards pressing their shirts as if they were on parade. Or the tender male bonding between two soldiers as one teaches another, while they are hanging their laundry out to dry, how to say the names of the various garments in French. There are, of course, strictly pornographic films geared for gay viewers with titles such as *The Private*, *The D.I. & The Lover*, *Berlin Army Knights*, *Below the Decks*, *Das Butt* and *Suck This, Staff Sergeant*. Internet sites like Active Duty Marine Meat (www.MarinesMeat.com), which, through "secret contacts near Marine Corps bases worldwide" offers its members videos of "what it looks like when the dress blues come off and those hot, straight jarheads get real fucking horny." Recently artists and fashion photographers have added their own interpretation to the sexuality attached to men in uniforms. The book *Soldiers: The Nineties* (Verlag der Buchhandlung Walther Konig), by artist Wolfgang Tillmans is a collection of photographs culled from magazines and newspapers. Taken out of context, and isolated as images – the soldier dressed in camouflage leaning in a railway carriage, a swat team lying on their stomachs on a rooftop, or soldiers, arms entwined, consoling each other – are highly suggestive and subtly erotic. Tillmans gives us a voyeuristic look at soldiers through the eyes of other photographers. Another artist, Collier Schorr, has taken a series of pictures that, like *Soldiers Bathing*, *Schwabish Gmund* or *Thomas on Watch*, turns the tables on the perception of a military that trains killers in favor of something far more innocent by capturing images of boys who are learning to become men. Recently military apparel has been transmuted into style in a number of fashion stories. Photographer Carter Smith's *Arena* spread titled "Fashion is Hell?" with the subtitle "This season? khaki is the color to die for," was followed two months later with a similar piece in *TK* with pictures by Victor Yuan, called "Join the Ranks!" The tag line to this spread reads, "All the fun of dressing like GI Joe – without having to enlist." Amid burning tanks and exploding bombs, the idea of "war is hell" is recreated as a battle over designer brands. Models in distressed denim and camouflage cargo pants replace sexual fetishism. Whatever turns you on.

A DEMON ON YOUR SKIN

DANIELE BROLLI

The illustrated man has one appearance only: that of tattoos. He is invisible, behind his decorated skin. The body becomes transparent beneath the indistinct throng of the single designs. Fragments of object-ivity emerge from the symbolic aspect of the depictions, but the image is stronger. The skin is something concrete, the blood is a dramatic living substance, yet the intangible fluid of the narrative overshadows any proposal of reality. The living disappears and the histories rise to the foreground. The story knows the dimensions of time, it clutches at memory in ritual form and prevails. "The most brutish of men," Theophile Gautier writes, "senses that ornament traces an indelible line of demarcation between him and the animal, and when he cannot embroider his clothes, he embroiders his skin."

The narrative, to tell its tale, feeds on immediately recognizable syntheses and contours, and like a freeze-dried substance that resumes it form placed in contact with liquid, it redefines its visible borders to be swallowed up by the user. Stories achieve definition by mingling with the image-bank of those that approach them. They move along that subtle crest between what is immediately recognizable and what is vague and indistinct.

The characters portrayed in narrative form with images are conceived in symbiosis with their dress. This is a signifying integration through which part of their story is told. And because image narratives have a serial aspect shared with other forms of folk narrative, the repetition of the characters and the contexts supports the need for a single, recurring form of dress. A garment which, for any fictional protagonist, functions in the same way as a uniform, making subjects self-equivalent (over time, in spite of the evolution of the sign that portrays them and the succession of different authors), and it extends its domain also to physical aspects, tics, postures, the way the character is depicted, constructing a sphere of implicit categories, never catalogued but nonetheless quite efficient. Recognizability within one's own universe, coupled with differentiation from all the others. The principle of uniformity and difference in comic strips operates on two levels: the first is the evidence of the accessories that make characters and scenarios identifiable, mobile silhouettes of the imagery; the second is the sing, or the type of graphic synthesis chosen by the author: the intersecting of these two elements creates narrative variables for endless sequences of images. Bibì and Bibò, Popeye and Donald Duck wear sailor suits; Buster Brown, Little Nemo, the Kin-der-Kids and Little Orphan Annie have collars closed with a bow; Rip Kirby, Dick Tracy and Secret Agent X9 wear overcoats. These are aspects of dress that become the key element for the recognition of the characters, completed in the variables of the physiognomy and the style of drawing. The body of comic strip characters often doesn't exist apart from their clothes (or makes just a few fleeting appearances), we see only hands, neck and head. Otherwise their physical existence is one and the same as that of their clothing. Apart from certain exceptional cases, there is no time in the economy of a comic strip for the everyday rituals in which characters get dressed and undressed, and any change of garb would only threaten the immediacy of their recognizability. In fact, the specific mechanism of the language of the comic strip interacts with this compactness, making it a fundamental narrative tool. Little Nemo's departure for every trip to Slumberland happens in pajamas, in position under the covers. The uniform is not only a signal of belonging and difference, it is also a propitiatory condition for a rite of passage. The detective has his hat, the astronaut his spacesuit, the bad guy wears a black mask, the lady-killer has his hair slicked back, and the dark lady wears an evening gown. These are just some of the stylemes that also function for other languages, from film to popular novels, but in the economy of the comic strip they take on a summary value that bundles the motivations of the character. There is no sound, no description, no action or real movements. The comic strip lives as a reflection of other languages, so it is forced to call attention to very precise signals. Even the various cats, dogs, mice and rabbits assume a humanized behavior according to rules that reshape physical function and visible appearance. These are bodies that have been revised in their function (a procedure that remains evident when they are transposed into animated cartoons). These animals are similar to one another, in spite of their species, because their principles of movement are shared, along with their forms of transposition from reality to the drawn equivalent. Out of this uniformity certain distinctive traits emerge that make each of them unique (Willy the Coyote and Roadrunner, Tom and Jerry, Mickey Mouse and Goofy have a shared genetic background with variations in the graphic DNA). One of the problems of the early days of film was how to make neophyte viewers understand a new language in which framing and sequence editing were of fundamental importance. What is taken for granted by the contemporary spectator seemed difficult and contrived to the pioneers of movie-going. Apart from problems of interpretation, how would an absolute beginner, someone looking at a comic strip for the first time, manage to distinguish among the different characters? It has to be something like the idea of divine creation: for men to recognize each other as men they need to resemble one another, but for them to be able to interact they must have slight variations. For an alien landing on Earth today from Alpha Centauri without having made any preliminary studies, it would probably be hard, at first glance, even to distinguish a man from an ape, never mind the finer shadings of physiognomy and behavior. After all, for Westerners it can be embarrassingly difficult to distinguish between Koreans, Chinese and Japanese. So we return to the tattooed body, on which differences are inscribed. Writing and mimetics, extreme revision of identity, with an accompaniment of writing and drawing that can be ethnic (through which to intuit origins and roots of the subject) or psychic (communicating character traits and programs). Clothing, hairstyles, expressivity, all in the re-created universe, contribute to give a precise place to the characters. Their past and their destiny are written in the whole of their representation: the Mickey Mouse of the early years, with baggy shorts and suspenders, was a country bumpkin, while today he's a metropolitan yuppie; Tin Tin with his zouave trousers, high-neck jersey and forelock was the son of the Belgian bourgeoisie; Tarzan with his leopard loincloth, long shaggy hair, white skin and aquiline nose is a savage of noble European lineage; Mandrake in his top hat and tails is a magician and a gentleman; Diabolik with his leotards and black mask, his villas and expensive cars, his ingenious gadgets and prosaic dagger is an astute, daring, uncatchable criminal; Charlie Brown with his round face, shorts and T-shirt is a rather slow-witted youngster; Corto Maltese with his seaman's cap, long sideburns, cigarette and earring is an adventurer.

The superheroes are an exception to the rule in the world of comics: they have a uniform that becomes a symbol of their power, and represents an alternative to the clothing they wear in everyday life. The category of the classic superheroes includes ancient warriors like Superman, Batman and Flash Gordon. These are fellows who began their activities back in the Thirties, donning tights with accessories on top (underpants, belts, capes, hoods; poor Flash even had a metal bowl with handles!), whose design was out of style right from the start: homemade costumes with baggy knees, stretching clumsily at the crotch and under the arms, the hero's pajamas. The colors and accessories of the costume were signs of identity, while the trademark printed on the chest set each character apart from the rest of the superhero brigade: S for Superman, a bat for Batman, a lightning bolt for Flash Gordon, the lantern of the Green Lantern, Atom's atom. Female or juvenile counterparts conserved the basic model with slight variations, in keeping with a military logic. The story of the superheroes has changed somewhat with the advent of cinematic special effects, starting with Tim Burton's *Batman*. The protagonists have become heroes of the near future, and have had to radically update their look, much more than over the decades of their earlier careers. Batman and Flash Gordon, for example, have had plastic surgery with silicon injections, and their costumes have been upgraded with latex. To avoid modifying their bodies (and, above all, those of the actors in the films) their uniforms have grown, as if they were biological prostheses. The restyling, including the graphics, of the classic superheroes comes in the wake of the innovations brought by the generation of superheroes born in the Sixties, those of Marvel Comics, whose Spider Man, Devil, Fantastic Four and above all the mutant X-Men revolutionized the idea of comic strip heroes. These are protagonists who have been deviated from their human condition, and the premises of normality and the extraordinary are reversed by their narrative destiny. They are condemned to do battle in the war on crime, exiled from the world of the normal by their own powers. Their bodies are modified and the costume/uniform clings to their skin like a tattoo, canceling out their humanity. Often the heroes and supercriminals assume forms that remind us of animals, things, or the properties of their special powers: the Beast is a man covered with fur, like a bear; the Scorpion has a deadly tail; Octopus has mechanical arms grafted onto the sides of his torso; Molten looks like metal in a liquefied state. The variety is infinite, including individuals who are victims of extraordinary events that have given them special powers; others have artificial prostheses; some are extraordinary beings from other planets, others are the result of genetic mutation. Spider Man, who can be considered the pioneer of this second generation of superheroes, sums up many of the new elements of the genre: his costume is a tight suit designed like a spiderweb, synonymous with his qualities. For a certain period, after a mission to a distant planet, he wore a new black uniform, a parasite that clung to his body, making him look more like a spider (slender and black). But as in the case of the illustrated man, in which the tattoos speak in the place of their wearer, so the new skin is a symbiont that makes decisions in the place of its host. The X-Men, human beings who are the result of a mutant gene, capable of re-producing properties and forms of the human body, are the symbol of a rebellion against the official body of homo sapiens. No longer a uniform worn that declares their belonging, but an appearance that is also substance (the story is no longer fiction for them, it is reality).

The X-Men, or all the altered beings so effectively represented in comics, are the prototype for many of the protagonists in video games. The main reason is the technological essence of the characters of video games. The polygonal substance of the digital image of the bodies set in motion in video games makes them both interior and exterior. For example, a protruding object on an arm is an integral part of its structure, although it belongs to a garment. The method of construction starts with the need to simulate the actions of a human being, but it doesn't operate with the same criteria, because the natural habitat is different. Normality and monstrosity in the realm of the 3-D electronic image have the same origin, and the elements that compose the different characters have to do with a variation of components covered with different colors and accessories. Lara Croft in *Tomb Raider* is not very different from Regina in *Dino Crisis* or Jill Valentine and Claire Redfield in *Resident Evil*. Shoot-it-up, hit-em-hard, survival horror, platform or role-playing games are related to one another by protagonists with a similar basic model and variations that belong to the sphere of behavior in which they adapt to the rules of the game. Their very mission is tattooed: an appearance that is stronger than the substance. Their life is a uniform.

EMANCIPATION AND UNIFORM

REBECCA VOIGHT

What do women want exactly? Looking at the wild extravagance and sheer diversity lavished upon the feminine wardrobe during the twentieth century alone, women seem to be more than amply taken care of in the clothing department. And yet, modern women spend most of their time in men's clothes. One quick glance on any big city street will confirm this. Delete the Manolos and the latest Gucci and Prada dresses from your vision and you will see women in jeans, chinos and trousers, tailored jackets, running shoes and shorts, windbreakers, workshirts and T-shirts, trench coats and cabans, fatigue pants and sweatshirts. At any given moment, over half the feminine population is wearing at least one piece of clothing commonly associated with menswear. And if you dig a bit deeper, it's menswear from the uniform tradition. Just how did men and women come to this uniformity in style at the dawn of the third millennium? Women appear to have slipped into uniform without regrets. Just past mid-century, they grabbed their most feminine tools of seduction, a feather boa, diamond clips and stilettos and stepped right into a man's tuxedo, courtesy of Yves Saint Laurent who put the erotic style spin on androgyny when he introduced *le smoking* in 1966.

A place for everything and everything in its place. Early twentieth-century womenswear looks like a disaster waiting to happen on all levels of the social ladder. Photographs of grande dames, taken before 1920, show how poorly adapted their elaborate clothing was for the new activities which began to fill their leisure time: tennis, cycling and even walking briskly down city streets appeared to be an acrobatic feat considering the fashions of the times. *Women at Work*, a collection of 153 photographs by American social historian Lewis W. Hine (Dover Publications, New York), taken between 1907 to 1938, shows that despite the demands of factory jobs, working class women in the early part of the century joined the assembly line in dresses with lace collars and shoes with a heel. Hine's photos of immigrant laborers in New York City show them balancing huge bundles of piece work on their heads as they headed back to their tenements to slave on sewing, silk flower assembly and even shelling walnuts with their children. They were dressed like babushkas in dirty long flowing skirts, aprons and headscarves. They looked miserable. Although it was obvious women were seeking a place outside the home, they still lacked the appropriate clothing for it. Women's clothes weren't suited for work or play, and they looked like a frustrated bunch of outdated objects before World War I. By the end of the war, the world was moving faster. That's when young women began sporting copies of the long, lean men's chesterfield coat with a velvet collar, which gave them a taste of tailoring early in the century, as well as feminine versions of the American-made Arrow detachable starched white shirt collar, which had a less frilly look than the blouses of the past. With the war, women got their first taste of the austere, practical dressing based on work practicality and they took to it. Military styles like Aquascutum's trench coat were adopted by men after its use in the trenches during World War I, and it wasn't long before women were borrowing the look.

Saying no to the corset with Coco Chanel. After centuries of laborious feminine dressing, waists and bosoms squeezed to the point of suffocation by corsets, legs hobbled by hobble skirts, and shoulders weighted down with enough passementerie to overload a Victorian parlor, women at the start of the twentieth century were ripe for a revolution in dress. The old lace, restrictive undergarments and hoop skirts were stashed in the attic and in their place stepped Gabrielle Chanel, a French woman who had different ideas for herself and all women. Chanel, more than any other designer in fashion history, liberated women through clothes. And almost all of her bold, successful ideas were inspired by classic menswear, which in turn was derived from uniforms. Chanel's desire for change was based on the restrictions she experienced herself. Born in 1883, she began her career dressed in the style of the past century even as she was dreaming up the concepts that would revolutionize the new one. She wanted to be a chanteuse, she ended up a courtesan, and because she loved her independence more than anything else, it wasn't long before she launched a business doing the one thing she knew best: dressing herself and by extension other women.

Chanel opened a hat shop in 1910, but her activity soon extended to clothes in a resort spirit with shops in Deauville and Biarritz where people of leisure congregated. The cardigan jacket was Chanel's first coup and in time it became her house signature. According to Thames and Hudson's *Dictionary of Fashion and Fashion Designers*, the cardigan was originally "a long-sleeved military jacket in knitted worsted, trimmed with fur or braid and buttoned down the front, made for British Army officers during the Crimean War and named after the 7th Earl of Cardigan, Thomas Brudenell (1797-1868), who led the Charge of the Light Brigade." In Chanel's hands, the cardigan became a twinset in inexpensive jersey, a knit fabric previously used only for underwear. Eventually it morphed into a three-piece suit with a boat-neck top in patterned knit; and finally it became the most feminine of twentieth-century suits in the house's signature bouclé tweeds, trimmed in braid with smart gold blazer buttons. Chanel promoted this suit throughout her career and Karl Lagerfeld has continued it at Chanel to this day. But the cardigan was only the beginning. Chanel based her creativity in feminizing menswear standards. In 1920 she brought out trousers, inspired by wide-legged sailor's bellbottoms which prefigured the hippie styles of the early 1970s. These she called "yachting pants," and they were followed closely by beach pajamas, which in satin became a sort of negligé cocktail ensemble and one of the uniforms of 1920s chic. Chanel championed trousers for women, open-necked shirts, berets, soft-belted raincoats and chemise dresses designed like big shirts. Her tweed skirts were tailored like trousers. She was the first to adapt the sailor's pea jacket to womenswear, paving the way for Yves Saint Laurent's chic caban years later. More than anything Chanel rejected the corset and put women in suits, which was their first step to entering the work force in the twentieth century. Chanel would not have been so successful at introducing these men's standards for women and a sense of uniformity in a woman's wardrobe if women hadn't been more than ready for it. The signs were everywhere.

From rational dress theory to *La Garçonne*. The Rational Dress Society was the first. Founded in 1881 in London by a certain Mrs. Bloomer, the group actively promoted utilitarian fashion for women and an end to clothes which "deformed" the body. Based on Mrs. Bloomer's concern for women's health, the RDS members wore harem-style Turkish pants and boneless stays the group had devised – a departure from the radical S-bend corsets popular at the time. They condemned high heels and prescribed wearing "no more than seven pounds" of underwear, which indicates the confining style of women's clothes at the time. In the Paris of 1922 it was a novelty that turned heads and helped change women's fashion. The fact that Victor Margueritte's novel *La Garçonne* was considered sexually daring only added to its appeal. The heroine, a student at the Sorbonne with an illegitimate child, cuts her hair boyishly short and wears a shirt, jacket, tie and other masculine classics. The character was emulated by a generation of daring young French women in the Twenties for whom *garçonne* style, and the long, slim-hipped body that went with it, became the height of seduction. Androgyny as a fashion statement had begun and it would come back in force in the swinging Sixties. And so, the feminine wardrobe loosened up, borrowed increasingly from menswear and became less individualistic and more uniform in the Twenties. It was more than just borrowing from menswear and discarding contrivances that brought women to a more rational style of dress. The spirit of uniformity shows in the way women rejected the dressmaker and began to buy clothes produced in series. Although the real ready-to-wear revolution wouldn't arrive until well after the end of World War II, women's dress had already simplified. The little black cocktail dress, pajama suits, and Chanel's cardigan suit put women in a common uniform that they'd never had before. Paris's young *garçonnes* looked like an elegant army ready to shape a new place for themselves in the world.

Women at war. World War II was the clincher. In Paris, the couture houses closed and women in England and the US went to work in munitions factories and shipyards. The prevailing atmosphere was military and utilitarian. It was time to put the tea frocks in moth balls and get behind the war effort, which women did with elan. The boiler suit or overalls – put in effect by the military – became the official work uniform for factory women involved in war work. Precious high heels were saved for special occasions and women kitted up in work boots even at the office. Stockings were scarce, so they took to ankle socks. Without any designers to push ahead new fashion ideas, women relied on their own devices to come up with a feminine look that met all the requirements of the time and bypassed the shortages. The short and simple bias skirt, wedge heel sandals, hair tied up in a scarf and a sexy little twinset were perfect for riding a bicycle. After the war, the shortages continued, but women gradually regained the diversity and femininity that had been missing in their wardrobe. The Paris couturiers were back and so were stockings and frills, but women had changed. It was time for a new generation of designers, for the introduction of ready-to-wear, and the giant social and youth movements which would usher in radical styles from mod, to unisex to hippie looks in the Sixties and Seventies. All of this would radically alter both men's and women's approach to clothes. Men and women would in fact begin to dress increasingly alike.

Navy surplus and the jeans revolution. The notion of surplus was born out of World War II. The stacks of clothes left by the GI's in French shipyards after the war did not gather dust. Military style was an emblem for power and efficiency, and so civilians of both sexes began incorporating the jeans, T-shirts and bomber jackets left behind after the war into their civilian wardrobe. In the United States, GI's took part of their uniform home with them. In a celebrated Norman Rockwell cover for *The Saturday Evening Post*, which was analyzed recently in an extraordinary article in *Vanity Fair*, a man in a military bomber jacket sits alone on a soda fountain stool. Although he's wearing a bomber, he's not in a military cap – so he's probably a war vet taking a break from his job as a delivery man or other post-war labor job. Not far from him sits a fresh-faced teenaged couple staring into each other's eyes, on what one imagines is their first date. He's wearing a white jacket and is pinning a corsage on her evening dress. And the soda jerk behind the counter is beaming. The situation on the counter is a reflection of everything that was going on in America at the time: post-war home-coming and renewal. The fact that war changes men and can even make them stronger, and the realization that when war is over it's time to rebuild is communicated in the clothes of Rockwell's subjects. It also shows how the mix of uniforms and civilian dress was launched in the middle of the twentieth century. Clothing has never been the same since. James Dean and Marlon Brando were the archetypes for tough teens in many Fifties films from *Giant* to *The Misfits*. The personification of rebels without a cause, they were joined by Marilyn Monroe as symbols of everything that was glamorous and a bit lost about teenagers at the start of the second half of the twentieth century. They dressed in Levi's jeans or chinos, tight white T-shirts, high top sneakers and bomber jackets; all essentially military surplus gear. That the boys were wearing these clothes was logical; the radical difference was that teenage women were dressing the same way and that the effect was powerfully sexy. Military surplus, workwear and western classics became the teenage uniforms in the Fifties and they still are.

The androgynous Sixties, hippie Seventies and power Eighties. Women would never have come to look so much like young men in the Sixties, if men hadn't become so feminine. Fashionable young men were poured into tight, darted floral shirts, velvet blazers and hip-hugging pants with their hair long and flowing by the end of the Sixties. On their arm, young women sported a spaced out version of the old Twenties *garçonne* style, their hair cut in a geometric bob like Mary Quant and attired in a micro-mini dress, more like a tunic or long shirt, preferably in paper. The clothes weren't meant to last and everybody was switching roles so quickly that it was hard to tell the boys from the girls. Nobody seemed to care. This was before women were trying to prove anything. All these young people wanted to do was look gorgeous and they succeeded. Hippie chic followed and women mixed country peasant blouses with overalls. Bellbottoms put women in pants and their practicality won out over skirts fairly quickly. Women began working in increasing numbers. Feminists appeared on the scene, and to show they meant business burned bras and adopted an unflattering, masculine-style work uniform, which fortunately didn't last long. What women retained from this period was the desire for comfortable clothes and the establishment of a business-like, albeit seductive, system for work. This culminated in the Eighties with the power suit, a man's suit, with extra-large shoulders for women who wanted to dress for success.

YSL – the designer who gave women everything they had always wanted. The chic mastermind Yves Saint Laurent was the man women had been waiting for, although they didn't know it. The social movements gave a direction for women's clothes, but with the dawn of Saint Laurent's influence on fashion in the Sixties, women discovered that it was possible to borrow men's clothes and still be a femme fatale. Saint Laurent showed women that they could have their cake and eat it, too. They fell in love with him. With a more romantic, dramatic and elegant style than Chanel, YSL– the tall, timid and delicate French couturier – transformed men's classics for women. Unlike Chanel, YSL had no personal stake in the clothing he designed. He was not his own guinea pig and women had already adopted men's classics years before. He had nothing to prove, just an incredible vision. With a view of women only a man can have, his aim from the Sixties on was to elevate feminine seduction. This he did, by pairing down excess details to a minimum. For his first collection in 1962, YSL came out with the caban, his souped up version of a man's classic peacoat that Chanel had inaugurated in the Twenties. His was much sexier than hers, especially in black satin. He gave women thigh-high boots in 1963, velvet knickerbockers in 1967, and in 1968 put his ladies in see-through blouses and safari suits. It wasn't really scandalous, it was triumphant. Never content, YSL forged ahead with trouser suits, blazers, fur-edged cardigans, Russian-inspired cossack jackets in 1976 – a seemingly endless parade of hits, many of them inspired by military uniforms and menswear – that made women look better, bolder, more elegant and powerful. The fact that he was universally copied created a tidal wave of high style to carry women wherever they wanted to go. What Yves Saint Laurent has proposed since the Sixties is not a uniform per se, but rather the freedom to play with the entire arsenal of feminine seduction – there is always satin, lace and bias draping in his collection – while at the same time adopt from a man's wardrobe the pieces which are most practical and elegant.

Dressed-down for the third millennium. And so women found themselves at the end of the century with a wardrobe bursting at the seams. The choice was theirs in terms of length, color and cut. Trends were designed to be broken in the search for one's personal style and comfort. Hardly any trace remains from the old battle of how to dress for work and play that began the last century. Women know how to do that, they know how to dress for men and most importantly they know how to dress to please themselves. The uniform spirit in clothing now comes from the desire to look good and feel good on an equal basis. The boundaries between what is considered formal and casual attire, or dressed-up and dressed-down occasions have been blurred slightly. A sexy cashmere T-shirt doesn't look out of place worn with a billowy taffeta ball skirt. Today's jeans are in snakeskin, and Prada retails its Sport collection right next to the most elegant, refined and delicate clothes from its main line. Women have learned to edit their own personal look and the days when they were constricted and hobbled by narrow-minded dress conventions are long gone.

ARMY DREAMERS

NICK SULLIVAN

In search of authenticity. I have a Swedish army greatcoat. I bought it when I was a student for £20 at a Camden Market army surplus stall. A major investment then, it has served me well ever since. According to the washed-out purple date rubber-stamped on the cotton lining, it was made in 1957 by GKA of Gothenburg. It is a nondescript sort of green, not quite khaki. Its rough wool – like the felted stuff you put under carpets – has kept me warm across Europe, in Morocco and in Colorado. The lapels button high across the chest, and a tab hidden under the expansive collar closes the neck right up – a function designed presumably with Sweden's blistering Baltic winds in mind. On the occasions when I wear it now my friends say I look like an escaped prisoner of war or a U-boat commander. I don't particularly mind this. Rough as it is, to me it's as fine a piece of sartorial engineering as any Savile Row suit. I am proud to say that even now every detail is original and authentic. These things are important. It is unlikely that when William P. Yarborough finished the specification drawings for his cargo pants sometime in 1942, that he knew he was the creator of the most lasting bit of military inspired fashion ever to hit the catwalks.

He mounted nine-inch square pockets on the side of each leg – not with Notting Hill or Milan in mind, but to carry two packs of K-rations – the daily food portion for US paratroopers on the battlefield. Now they carry mobile phones and MP3's. But it is precisely from such mundane functional beginnings that military fashion was born.

Military clothing was already playing a crucial role in male style well before Yarborough put his US Government issue pencil to paper. As far back as the seventeenth century, a regiment of Croatian cavalry mercenaries served King Louis XIII of France in the Thirty Years War. In the great melee of European warfare they were noticed not – to their undoubted chagrin – for great martial prowess, but for the thin slivers of colored cloth they used to tie the collars of their shirts together. (Croat or *Hrvat* in their own language in turn coined the word "cravat.") When non-combatant courtiers began to wear the cravat as a bit of military affectation – heroism by association perhaps – the tie was born – a classic bit of army chic that had crossed over forever onto civvy street.

We may like to think that the military and the civilian are distinct worlds – that the military only encroaches in our lives at difficult or auspicious moments in our country's history. But in men's fashion the military is there all the time, even when you can't see it. It's one of the more trivial side-effects of humanity's penchant for mutual destruction, but throughout the twentieth century, war and its aftermath provided almost all the impetus in the transformation of male style from the fundamentally formal to the fundamentally casual. We may still – in spite of dressed-down-Friday – wear our suits to work, but in all else our wardrobes have been transformed beyond all recognition.

Military influence quite naturally pushed menswear towards the casual – since uniforms are made to be comparatively cheap, but also to perform and be comfortable in exacting situations. So not only was fashion's performance sportswear founded on military experience, trial and error, in the thick of the action, so to speak – but the whole concept of dressing down came with it, too.

In World War II the casual demeanor of American troops serving with Allied forces was a regular source of irritation to their hidebound opposite numbers (and a delight to bored British women). But their uniforms were more effectively purpose-built in general than those of their British counterparts. This goes a long way to explaining the dominance of American style in fashion in the postwar period, as well. The explosion of army surplus in the ten years following the war also made denim jeans widely available in Europe for the first time. Of course, it's pushing it to distill a century and more of suffering down to a few details on a catwalk. Military matters are hardly something to make light of. But the appropriation of militaristic imagery has been part and parcel of Western culture for generations. If we can use it to sell pop records and sandwich spreads, it can hardly be out of place in fashion.

But what is that vital element – what makes military design so alluring to a whole swathe of fashion designers and their customers? Military functionalism exerts an immense gravitational pull for acknowledged fashion experts. Fashion designers have long been hypnotized by military clothing for two primary reasons. First, the obvious heroic associations for men with military exploits, a way of thinking that we men never really grow out of. But designers are also obsessed by the way military clothing is actually made, meticulously reproducing the zips, buttons, closures, seams and stitching, even whole garments straight our of the quartermaster's store. These are details borne out of necessity, clothing designed to perform very specific functions. Increasingly the differences between men's and women's fashion – even the way we approach fashion – are being eroded. The kind of looks seen on the catwalks of Florence, Milan, Paris, London and New York are less about detail and more about impact. But menswear at its most trangressive is still fundamentally conformist in a way that womenswear is not. Deep down we seek consensus – safety in numbers. And therein lies our obsession for military detail. We want to belong, be part of the gang. To a generation of designers like Moreno Ferrari at CP Company, Paul Harvey at Stone Island, and the legendary Massimo Osti, military detailing is the life blood of modern male style. In their hands, menswear has become a discipline easily as rigorous as architecture. As modern men in a largely peaceful environment, we lack heroic possibility – ways to prove ourselves. You don't get medals for going to the shops or cleaning the car, do you? But clothing such as this equips us for an imaginary daily battle.

In the absence then of real life-or-death struggles, we tend to make war on day-to-day adversity. Stress, pollution, congestion and even time are our enemies now. We think we deserve a gong for just getting out of bed. But if we do manage to get out of bed it's because we're armed by specialists – the likes of CP Company – our arsenals filled with clever functionality. For if we men are anything, we are definitely gear freaks – a fact that has made many a gadget-maker rich in the past. It's a battlefield out there – and modern man is in a constant war of attrition against the rush hour, the elements and the city.

Our clothing is armor not against bullets but against life itself. To designers such as Osti, Harvey and Ferrari, this is an aesthetic argument that allows for no frippery, clothing with nothing extra, just the essential fulfilment of a desired function. Because original military clothing is often created in conditions of austerity – even in peace time uniforms are usually made to strict government budgets – that can only emphasize its pared-down symbolism. Like workwear, it is the ultimate expression of design driven not by something as nebulous as "fashion," but by necessity. Indeed if anything, military functionalism is an argument against fashion. If we look for authenticity in the tiniest detail, we do it to focus on anything but the overall impact. Fans of Stone Island over the years know the subtle differences between a jacket made last week and one from five years ago. But the differences are not self-evident. And that's precisely the point. You have to be a bit of a trainspotter to pick up on everything that's going on. This is boy's stuff.

If Ferrari and Harvey approach their work like scientists, that does not mean that military inspired fashion exists only in a test tube. Far from it, because style has just as big a part to play in the appropriation of military imagery in fashion.

In the late Seventies and early Eighties – Ferrari's and Harvey's formative years, no doubt – military clothing in street fashion was at its height. Inspired by bands like The Clash and combined with a Perfecto leather biker jacket, combat pants were a staple item in the youth wardrobe some fifteen years before the Nineties explosion of sportswear into high fashion. What fueled it was pop. Since the early Sixties, we've had mods, hippies, punks, post-punks, mods (again), even new romantics – cult after cult that turned the trappings of militarism into symbols of organized teen revolution. Back then, army surplus was worn with hefty dollops of irony by a generation pitting itself against the forces of conservatism, against rules, against parents – against anything really.

Battledress – even on pop programmes – clearly suggests power, strength in numbers, that there are more of us, more of us with the same message, even if the message consists of little more than an edgy guitar riff, some spiky hair and a song, like Sting's about a girl called Roxanne. Back then, for fans it was an easy (and cheap enough) look to emulate. In cold war Europe and post-Vietnam, army surplus was everywhere. But even then it was essential to get it absolutely right. Just any old jumpsuit would hardly cut the mustard when you were after Sting's Royal Air Force version. And no self-respecting Clash fan would settle for the wrong pockets on combat trousers. We are clearly schooled to authenticity from an early age.

During my three weeks (or was it four?) as a committed mod during the 1979-1980 revival, I scoured the local surplus shops looking for a parka. At sixteen – too young and too broke to ride a Lambretta – a parka would at least keep me warm on the windy promenade in Bournemouth. But instead of the authentic US-issue fishtail parka, all I could get was a kind of gray cotton anorak with West German flag flashes on each shoulder. It was okay, but it was all wrong for my purposes; it might as well have been a wetsuit. Combat pants and MA1 flight jackets were also put to use by bands whose declared political intent amounted to rather more than sound bites and sleeve notes. Before their "ironic" period, Irish rockers U2 were rather more earnest individuals preaching left of center, charging round a disused American airforce base in a Willy's jeep in World War II bomber crew outfits. Few went as far as packing weapons as well – but in the late Eighties, Public Enemy's uzi-toting "urban night" camouflaged cronies only served to underline the political message in Flava Flav's black power raps. Politics (and royalties) aside, there is clearly something deep-rooted in the male psyche that conditions him to seek out the authentic in his clothing. And it's a facet of our interest in the military, which has found rich expression lately. Nothing back in the Eighties could match the sportswear explosion of the mid-Nineties for sheer breadth. A wholesale reinvention of casual style that incorporated the modern military functionalism of groundbreakers like Stone Island and CP Company, blending it with technical sportswear (itself rich with military detailing) and a high fashion sensibility.

Gradually that modernism pervaded the whole of fashion from the highest designer to the most accessible street store, to a point now where fashion is moving in a different direction. It had to happen of course. When you see seventy-year-old men in fashion combat trousers, you know it's time to put on a suit. But even if fashion is now moving away from that anorak-and-blousons-with-everything mentality, the advances made in terms of comfort and functionality are unlikely to recede entirely. Many tailoring firms have incorporated technical details into their jackets, and show performance rainwear with their suits. We're demanding as much performance from our smart gear now. The war goes on.

I now have a rather bewildering array of military/sportswear in my wardrobe at home, anoraks boasting more or less everything but built-in TV and a fully functioning shower. "How many anoraks does a man actually need," asks my wife when she catches me pensively fingering a new style or some army surplus in a boutique. The answer, of course, is always just one more. With my ever growing collection I feel prepared for anything London can throw at me. But for all that modern technicality, I do hope it gets cold enough soon to wear my Swedish Army coat.

SOLDIER'S STUFF

CRISTINA LUCCHINI

Introduction. The history of military uniforms has given us materials, fabrics and colors that have become irreplaceable constants in modern menswear. The implicit functional and aesthetic-communicative value of the uniform is closely connected to research in the fields of textiles and technology. The last fifty years are marked by continuing products, like felt, gray-green cloth, ribbed twill, khaki, and by the imperative of the "anti" prefix or the "proof" suffix in the area of experimentation and development of materials. The postulates of performance evolve from simplicity of use to the very survival of the soldier-individual. Characteristics like strength, comfort and thermal regulation are almost taken for granted. Evolution focuses on the quality of materials and treatments to make materials chill-proof, waterproof, wind-proof, fire-proof, anti-bacterial, anti-radiation, etc. High-tech safety features find their way from the original military context to wider applications in the fields of work clothes, sporting gear, designer leisurewear and urban protection styles. Just consider all the treatments of waterproofing, rubberizing, coating, silicon treatments, oilcloth, polished fabrics, parachute nylon, Gore-tex® and camouflage patterns to get an idea of the continuing transfer of fabrics and finishes developed for military applications into the fashion world.

Typologies and structures. The world of textiles for military uses is by definition quite uniform and rigid, closely connected to the need for mass production and standardization, but variegated by high-tech innovations in the garments for the special forces. The official iconography and the rare textile archives regarding the first half of the twentieth century limit the fibers and typologies to the wool industry and the use of linen and cotton for warm climates. The traditional gray-green cloth is the very emblem of the

Italian army. The regulation jacket of World War II was the Baistrocchi model: four pleated patch pockets and smooth shoulder loops, again in gray-green (a low-visibility color in the field). Lined with linen cloth, it is the epitome of uniformity, in which only the collar – and the related insignia – indicate order, rank and grouping. Before 1940 officers and marshals were issued a made-to-measure jacket in ribbed twill (a refined gabardine) with a velvet collar: austerity measures led to jackets that were the same as those of the troops. The fabrics for the military world always have a diagonal weave, which is more compact and therefore more resistant. The range of felts is joined by beaver cloth, still used today for regulation overcoats, the above-mentioned ribbed twill, and *orbace*. The latter is a rough Sardinian traditional woolen cloth, made with thick, raw wool, spun by the women of the island and colored with vegetable dyes (usually in black, but also in red for the costumes for local folk celebrations). During the two decades of Mussolini's rule, in keeping with the policy of autarchy, it became the fabric of the uniforms of the fascist party officials and notables. Updated in a lighter version, it was the object of a lukewarm revival in the Seventies, as an alternative for capes and coats.

Cotton fabrics in twentieth-century military history include, apart from the famous troupe khaki, Massaua fabric (a heavy cotton weave with a compact diagonal structure, rough to the touch and with a twill weave). These fabrics were launched during the campaign in Ethiopia in 1935-1936 for colonial uniforms and work garments, in imitation of the jackets of the German Africa Korps. There have also been many military uses for linen, both for tropical uniforms (in light cloth, heavier weaves and jute) and for pillowcases and sheets. Special gear and protection uniforms deserve a separate chapter.

Non-color colors. With the exception of camouflage gear, modern military clothing is substantially monochromatic. Somewhat similar to what happened in the area of men's civilian dress (deprived of brocades, velvets, damasks, tunics, stoles, jewelry and lace in the wake of the French Revolution and the subsequent triumph of the bourgeoisie), the decorative and multicolor images of uniforms vanished into radical banishment, in favor of monochrome solid colors. The only concession to decorative impulses (as the hierarchical order can thrive only on communication and recognition) remains the medals, insignia, ribbons and decorations. The choice of the colors for the fabrics, in any case, is also closely connected to the concept of camouflage. The gray-green of the army blends with the earth; the gray-blue of the air force with the sky; khaki with the sand; the white of alpine ski troops with the snow. Even the English gave up their traditional "redcoats" (the symbol of the identity of the Union since 1707), using them only for official ceremonies. From function to communication: the dual identity of the uniform is also revealed in its chromatic choices. This is the case, for example, of the black utilized by the Third Reich – in both cloth and leather – and in the Italian fascist's *orbace*: striking examples of skillfully coordinated communication designed to create a climate of terror.

The chameleon garment. The high point of mimetic dress was achieved with the creation of camouflage patterns. Their origin dates back to World War I, when they were developed as a way of concealing artillery against attack from the air. Soon enough tanks, airplanes and other vehicles were concealed under camouflage covers simulating trees, leaves and bushes. The first example of the camouflage jacket is the one painted by hand in 1915 by the French soldier Guingot. But it was not until after World War I that the camouflage uniform achieved its position as a protagonist. After the French, the second army to make use of camouflage fabric was the Italian army. First it was applied only on oilcloths used to cover weapons and vehicles, but soon the tents of the troops were also patterned. The motif – known as "model 1929" – was extremely repetitive and not really very effective. But in any case this was the first time that an army had created and utilized a mimetic fabric to defend both men and machines. The "model 1929" opened the way for the use of camouflage in battle uniforms. A series of green-brown patterns, based on trees, were used by the Waffen-SS: their function was further enhanced by the symbolic significance of the German nature mystique. Use of such fabrics was still rather limited in World War II, but it continued to grow during the postwar and Cold War periods among NATO forces and in Vietnam. Between 1970 and 1985 we can count more than 300 different types, and many countries diversified their camouflage uniforms for different specialized applications.

From wartime invasions to fashion runways. No printed fabric has ever met with such continuing success among young people as camouflage. And the most interesting thing is that it manages to be simultaneously fashion and anti-fashion. The stylists send it out on the runways, making high fashion statements or aesthetic provocations. Street style made it a favorite fabric in the

1990s, in second-hand and vintage versions. Its success is comparable to that of denim, and its symbolic impact is very strong. The camouflage uniform seems to contain, on its own, the mythology of the ancient warriors, the primordial ancestors who battled for the survival of the species. The new generations have made it into a sign of rebellion, against the system, against the gray of office uniforms, against social and wardrobe dictates. Like the jeans of the Sixties and Seventies, it has been raised to the status of a banner against the conformism of the nine-to-five suit, with accentuated overtones of tribal mimesis, group uniformity, return to nature. A choice that was also born as a war on fashion, but has wound up serving as a stimulus for fashion creativity.

Cuirass-caresses. One of the biggest problems in military dress is the reconciling of protective strength and comfort in a single garment, standardized by definition, that needs to offer the same performance levels in any climate, in any part of the world. The uniforms of the Western armies do not appear to have changed much since 1945. And yet there has been a silent, radical revolution in the world of materials and their treatments. In the early Eighties the American army replaced the traditional steel helmets with helmets in Kevlar, a synthetic material invented in 1971 by Du Pont, which is five times more resistant than steel, but much lighter and more comfortable. With progress in the area of synthetic fibers, there has also been a comeback of the concept of the protective cuirass or breastplate.

These new protective shields have the same function as the heavy armor of the Middle Ages, but they are much less heavy and uncomfortable. The pioneers of the new cuirass-caresses were the Americans in Vietnam, with the use of bullet-proof vests, which since 1980 have become a standard part of regulation combat gear.

There are two principle types of bulletproof garments: one is made in Kevlar, while the other incorporates special ceramic plaques that disperse the kinetic energy of the bullets. Courtaulds Aerospace has developed a special sandwich-composite known as Ceramid, used in the bulletproof vests of the British army. All these garments have velcro fasteners, another recent invention that has taken the place of buckles and laces.

ANTI and PROOF. The need for rapid movements from one climate or geographical area to another leads to the use of thermo-regulating fabrics and layered garments. A veritable systems wardrobe permitting a soldier to adapt to tropical humidity and arctic chill. Fibers like wool, cotton and linen have an innately high level of hygroscopicity: they allow the body to breathe and perspire, while avoiding the sauna effect. But in order to combine transpiration-ventilation and total waterproofing (although they are compact, felts and traditional types of cloth are not impermeable to external agents) we had to wait for the birth of Gore-tex®, a special membrane invented in 1976, which has revolutionized not only the military world, but also that of active-sports-wear and fashion. Protection from atmospheric agents – wind, rain or snow – is total, just as the maintenance of the body's microclimate inside the garments or footwear is complete. While Gore-tex® is now a household word, only sector professionals are aware of the infinite range of high-tech articles produced by the colossal W.L.Gore & Associates Inc. One specific division of the company supplies only the army, and is bound to the rules of military secrecy. It makes some fabrics that are also used in sportswear, like Gore-tex Best Defense® or Windstopper®, but also fabrics for nuclear and bacteriological shields. Over the last fifty years the needs of the military in terms of garments have changed drastically, in functional rather than aesthetic terms. And the world of textiles has made giant steps forward, creating fabrics and fibers that are flame-proof, anti-infrared, fire-proof, anti-radiation, anti-bacterial, anti-static (today the enemy is technology?) and anti-magnetic. The flame-resistant X-Fires® (30% Kevlar and 70% preoxidized carbon) is the showcase example, along with Janotex®, by the Neapolitan firm Q2Roma. As opposed to the other flame-retardant fabrics, it doesn't char, liquefy or become ash: it remains practically intact, while generating a minimum quantity of fumes. It is also anti-static, anti-micro-bial, anti-bacterial and hypoallergenic. The protective mission of many materials developed for bellicose uses has also invaded the world of leisurewear, ever since the Seventies. A military framework lies behind the identity of two leading trademarks like CP Company and Stone Island (produced and distributed by the Sportswear Company of Carlo and Cristina Rivetti). In constant dialogue with the uniforms of the military tradition and the world of work clothes, CP Company has made "urban protection" its stylistic trademark, going so far as to design veritable garment-dwellings. Stone Island, in turn, has been an actor in the history of technological innovation since its birth at the beginning of the Eighties, marking the passage toward non-woven fabrics. Examples: the thermo-sensitive Ice Jacket (a camouflage parka designed by Massimo Osti that changes color in keeping with temperature variations); the camouflage canvases; the topcoats in 100% stainless steel and bronze, developing the concept of contemporary armor; the jackets in Kevlar or in the so-called Exploded Radial (the rubber used for gas masks) or in Nylana (a nylon chevron used for the coverings of the seats and interiors of Israeli tanks), with highly flame-retardant and wear-proof characteristics. Another successful trademark openly based on military borrowings is Mason's (produced by the Foster company of Carrara): from the trousers of Comandante Che Guevara, in that particular, very strong Colombian ripstop windproof cotton known as Libertador, to the garments of the German army of the Forties and Fifties; from the ceramic finishes that guarantee a high level of protection against temperature changes, to thermo-sensitive iridescent signal fabrics; from the multipocket garments of the Colombian army to the two-in-one of Operation Desert Storm; from the flight jackets of the office personnel of the American Air Force to the jackets of the Marines. A wardrobe based on a selection from the archives of military history and the work clothes of the past, interpreting garments as symbiotic objects.

Visibility and invisibility. In the military world the visibility of a uniform is connected with the communication aesthetic, while invisibility is a vital requirement for survival and functional quality. The design of the material itself must respond to two different imperatives: the institutional-social imperative and the tactical-strategic imperative. In the first case the uniform, in all its versions, establishes and communicates differences of role, hierarchy and organization within the armed forces. But the soldier, or the public servant, must also be recognizable as a person who ensures public safety, the guardian of law and order: a person who necessarily must be distinguishable within the context of the everyday world.
So the public lawman must be visible and recognizable. Finishings, decorations and insignias can do the trick. In recent times a second concept of high visibility has emerged, based on the use of materials. Substances capable of emitting their own light in conditions of total darkness guarantee visibility for law enforcement officers in their work during a nocturnal roadblock; firemen and civil defense personnel also make use of such materials. In such cases, the material used becomes the signage element. The first such applications were in the field of aviation, but then they spread to contaminate public spheres, and the garment industry itself. From an anti-aircraft deck at an airport to the uniforms of highway police to the jumpsuits of highway workers,

and then to all kinds of sportswear with reflector patches, fluorescent inserts and batteries for light.

In a more technical military context (i.e., in war) rather than visibility the accent shifts to invisibility. Survival depends upon not being seen or discovered. Once upon a time it was sufficient to be concealed from the naked human eye. Today there are radar, sensors, rays and probes that can perceive human presence thanks to body heat. Blending in is no longer sufficient: soldiers need to be truly invisible. This has led to an evolution in camouflage. In the beginning, the mimesis of reality was limited to the reproduction of the colors of the context; then came the textures, patterns and forms of the vegetation of the place in question; next came the simulation of climate conditions, in rain, snow or wind. But all this wasn't sufficient. Today a perfectly camouflaged soldier in the underbrush of a forest can be seen with infrared sensors. So now manufacturers have invented special anti-infrared finishes. The soldier is safe from infrared sensors, and his camouflage uniform, apparently the equivalent of the version without this new finish, is even more effective, precisely because it is the summa of the aesthetic and technical performance features that are the very soul of the uniform.

UNIFORMS AND SIGNS. ART AS DESERTION

FRANCESCO BONAMI

We wear Uniforms. Now, the wearing of uniforms simultaneously humiliates and exalts us. We look like unfree people, and that is possibly a disgrace, but we also look nice in our uniforms, and that sets us apart from the deep disgrace of those people who walk around in their very own clothes but in torn and dirty ones. To me, for instance, wearing a uniform is very pleasant because I never did know, before, what clothes to put on. But in this, too, I am a mystery to myself for the time being.

Robert Walser, *Jakob von Gunten,* 1908

Laurent Kabila, president of the Congo, wears a grape pomace colored jacket with gold buttons. Behind him stands a young officer and a soldier. In front of him, in this photo by Hoslet Olivier for *The New Yorker*, a bodyguard in a double-breasted jacket and blue necktie. Kabila is the most elegant of the group, the least sinister looking man in the image. He is actually the most dangerous, but this hybrid jacket – part fashion, part army, part dictatorship and part vegetarian sect – makes him charismatic, transforming his sneer into a benevolent smile.

For the acceptance of his Nobel prize for literature, Gabriel Garcia Marquez wore a fantastic white jacket, rejecting the official, conventional, bourgeois uniform of the morning suit. Nevertheless, his jacket was a military jacket of a cultural emperor. Rejecting the morning suit, Marquez was not rejecting a convention, but establishing a distance between the intellectual and the common man, underlining the power of ideas over the power of deeds.

By forcing the Chinese people to wear a uniform, Mao did not manage to make everyone equal, but only to make them all resemble him. Looking at the last of all Chinamen, anyone in the world would have thought of him – the great helmsman. The uniform worn by the people became the symbol of an idea.

If Pinochet had insisted upon wearing a uniform, he would never have lasted as long as he did in England before extradition. The image of an elderly gentleman in a jacket and tie seemed to contrast the image of that cruel, callous dictator we all remembered. No one had forgotten that Pinochet was a war criminal, but the doubt arose that those two images, the grandfather and the butcher, might not belong to the same person.

The uniformity of the dress of the world's largest democracy, India, exports a pacific, generalized idea of the people there, although much of the continent is torn by violence. Another stereotype is the image of the Islamic world, composed of women in chadors and men with beards and turbans, an image that calls to mind only abuses and violence, leading us to forget that behind these images lie a culture, a philosophy and a religion of great complexity.

In the Seventies, the tundra jacket was the anti-system uniform that, snatched from its military "rightist" reality, became the symbol of the army of the "left," while Lacoste shirts and RayBan sunglasses became the accessories of the neo-fascist forces. Today the armies in the pacific West are no longer formed around ideas but around economics. Their uniforms no longer reflect utopian visions or battles, but goals achieved in work and in everyday life. The streets of the West are invaded by tin soldiers of affluence, washed and ironed, not out of discipline, but only out of obsession. Observed from any angle, the idea of the uniform in fashion, army or subculture, is evident in its nature as a threat for any contemporary society.

Even the advantages offered by the traditional uniform are portents of concern and temptation. When I was in school children wore aprons. The idea was to conceal class differences: a noble aim, were it not for the fact that it was intended to hide the signs of poverty that the clothing of certain children would inevitably have displayed. Poor children could avoid feeling humiliated, and rich ones could avoid feeling guilty. The uniform in school was a merciful veil. Now that this veil is no longer there, things haven't improved much, because the fear of inequality has been replaced by the fear of difference: we must all dress alike, all belong to the army of opulence.

While the political revolution was supposed to bring the individual to identify totally, even in terms of dress, with an idea, today's economic revolution urges the individual, the adult or the child, to identify with consumption. The work of the Polish artist

Piotr Uklanski brings out precisely this idea of consumption, not in terms of clothing, in this case, but of images. The parade of actors dressed as Nazis has the troubling result of exalting the elegance of these characters, and the fact that this elegance is produced by the symbol of one of the greatest tragedies of history takes a back seat. It is hard to find an argument with which to counter the claims of those who insist that boots and a black shirt are elegant, because objectively they are elegant. But if these two elements were to come back into vogue, not ideologically but commercially, society would have to establish the limits of elegance in order to remain a civil society. If the violence of dress transformed into uniform – leather jackets, boots, bowler hats (as in *Clockwork Orange*) and hoods – also generates new consumption and new products, it is important that the limits of a bourgeois society, i.e., a non-militarized society, be decisively defended.

The hedonism any uniform implies can thrust the individual into a very dangerous historical oblivion. If certain people have dressed in a certain way to do certain things, ugly things, horrible things, then no fashion or elegance can constitute an excuse to revive that same way of dressing, those signs. Kabila is elegant, but his elegance conceals a terrible reality for which Kabila is responsible: therefore it is not possible to dress like Kabila.

While, on the other hand, it is legitimate to dress like Joseph Beuys, the charismatic German artist who transformed the "uniform" of the sports fisherman into his own uniform as he transformed himself into an icon of contemporary creativity, a symbol of the revolutionary force of art. To be truthful, it is not possible to dress like Beuys without seeming stupid: in fact Beuys's uniform, like his felt suit, represent the uniqueness of an individual, an army of one. If Mao's suit reflected the idea of equality, Beuys's way of dressing underlines that each of us is independent, different from the others. If repeated, Beuys' uniform becomes a costume, like that of Zorro or Superman.

We might say that the difference between uniform/costume and uniform/dress is what generates disorder and order. While the costume underlines the uniqueness of the individual, bringing out his characteristics – which are often virtues, often transforming the individual into a hero – the uniform conceals the characteristics of its wearer, which are often defects, and transforms him into a symbol of violence, be he a dictator or a mere soldier, a member of the Ku Klux Klan or a Taliban guerrilla. Beuys, Zorro, Superman, Punchinello, in their immense diversity, are symbols of Good; Stalin, Mao, Kabila, Pinochet, in the similarity of their uniforms, today represent Evil. It is interesting to note that key religious figures like Jesus, Mohammed, Abraham or Buddha have never needed to wear, or to be represented wearing a garment/uniform that identifies them, as if they were above the dualism of Good and Evil. Only the religions these figures have spawned have felt the necessity to create armies and uniforms: the Catholic Church, the Buddhist monks, the Iranian mullahs. If diversity of dress conceals the seeds of weakness for religions and ideologies, the uniform is the instrument that reinforces a society, a thought or a creed.

Today, in our increasingly secular society, the fashion system has become the vehicle through which the weakness of diversity is channeled into the strength of many little armies created by designers. The immense archipelago of fashion functions so that no one army can get the upper hand, allowing diversity to exist among the various armies, rather than among their individual recruits. A single army of fortune, without ranks or flags, remains that of artists, never really able to get organized, never really capable of sacrificing their diversity to a sign as precise as that of the uniform. This doesn't mean that in the art world power doesn't find other clear channels for self-representation through signs of dress that are just as precise as a star or a stripe. Sarah Lucas, in her self-portraits, gives ordinary garments, a pair of jeans or a motorcycle jacket, the authority of a uniform through the irreverent, aggressive posture of her body. Paul McCarthy and Mike Kelle y, by sullying and debasing the uniform in the cruelest of ways, manage to extract its subversive dignity, also manifested in the cruelest of defeats, such as that of the veterans of Vietnam. The ski masks of Rosemarie Trockel speak of an ordered disorder in the hands of fate, like the Tania/Patricia Hearst of Cady Noland, elegant, spoiled revolutionary, forgotten by true history, whose style, however, resurfaced on the cover of a recent *Harper's Bazar*, impersonated by the actress Winona Ryder.

Artists, in contrast with fashion, have always had an ambiguous relationship with the charm of the uniform; even those war-mongering Futurists opted for the flexibility of dandyism over the rigidity of military garb. After all, the concept of the uniform is linked to a personality, and often a weak one, in search of recognition, and weak personalities are a rarity among artists. We could conclude that art looks to the uniform in the moment in which it is emptied and ceases to be a hedonistic instrument, in the moment in which it remains an empty shell of a power that is consumed in its own self-representation. The mannequins of Do-ho Suh tell a story of failed discipline, and the soldiers of

Vanessa Beecroft speak of discipline as eroticism, while the androgynous guy/gals of Collier Schorr make discipline their vehicle for a profound intimacy.

Thus the uniform becomes the pretext for talking about society, and those who are part of society attempt to organize their weaknesses and doubts through the necessity of dressing, the desire to dress like others out of a fear of remaining alone, a fear of becoming formless. Fashion with its armies, art in flight with its deserters.

HELMUT LANG JEANS
KHAKIS CHINOS DENIMS
WORK WEAR CASUAL WEAR
FUNCTIONALS
PROTECTIVE WEAR

ROBERT, EAGLE SCOUT,
IOWA TROOP, 1996

PHOTOGRAPHED BY
BRUCE WEBER

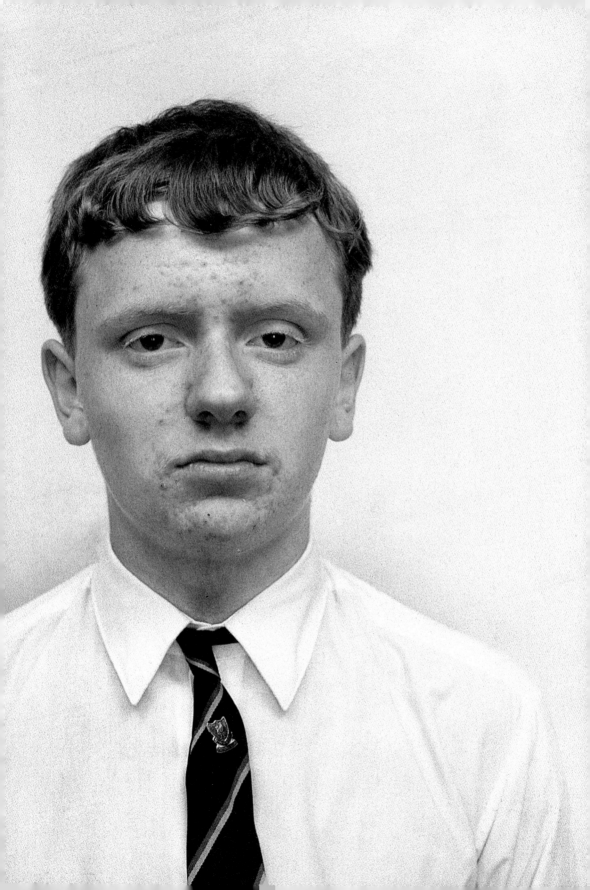

 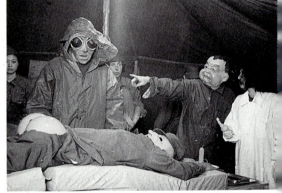

Paul McCarthy, Mike Kelley,
Sod & Sodie Sock, 1998.
Performance at Wiener Secession, 1998.
Courtesy of the artists.

What are we? Humans?
Or animals? Or savages?
What're grown-ups going to think?

William Golding,
Lord of the Flies, 1954

Luther and Johnny Htoo brothers.
© SYGMA/Grazia Neri.

Inez Van Lamsweerde, Vinoodh Matadin,
Gerard Philippe, 2000.
Print on plexiglass, 126 x 161 cm.
Courtesy Matthew Marks Gallery, New York.

Cossack cadets at military school.
© Robert Kowaleski. Agenzia Grazia Neri.

USA, Valley Forge Military Academy, Wayne,
Pennsylvania - Plebes, 1989.
Wirtz Philadelphia Inquirer/Matrix. Agenzia Grazia Neri.

سپاه ما مخصوص به برادران ارتشی

ما نیست ، زن و مرد ما کوچک وبزرگ

ما سپاه اسلام اسد و پاسدار

سلام .

آیت الله طالقانی

Our army does not belon
only to our brothers in th
armed forces. Men and women
young and old in our countr
are the members of Islami
Army, and are guardians o
Islam.

Ayatollah Taleqani

"Our Army Does Not Belong Only To Our Brothers...,"
in Peter Chelkowski, Hamid Dabashi,
Staging a Revolution, The Art of Persuasion in the Islamic Republic of Iran,
London: Booth-Clibborn Editions, 2000, p. 7.

Farewell as the USS Theodore Roosevelt sails from
Norfolk, Virginia for the Persian Gulf, 28 December 1990.
Photo Les Stone.
In *In the Eye of the Desert Storm*,
New York: Harry N. Abrams, Inc., 1991.
Agenzia Grazia Neri.

"Bombshell,"
in *Vogue Italia*,
n. 568, December 1997, p. 250.
Photo Bruce Weber, fashion editor Joe Mckenna.

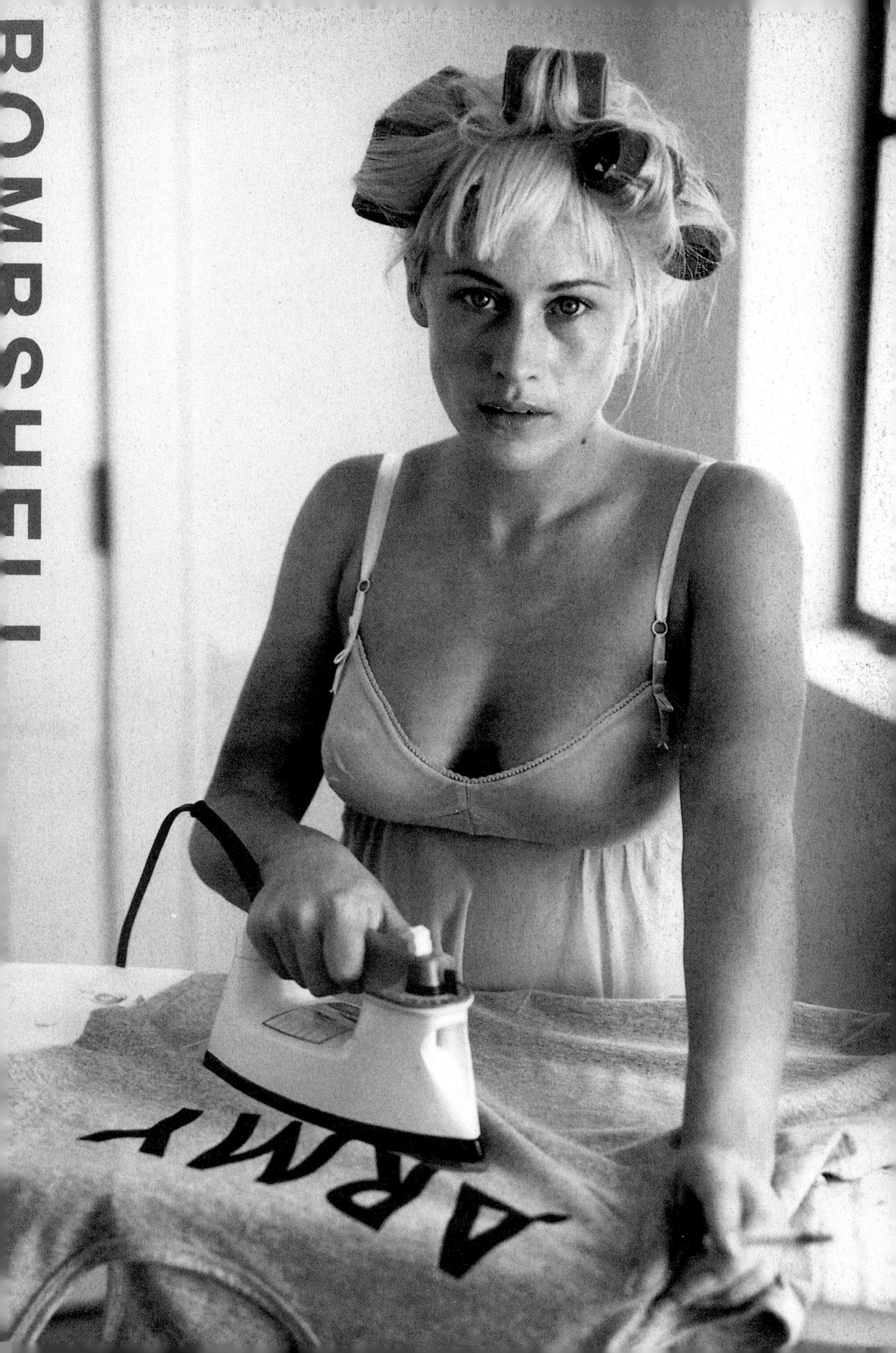
BOMBSHELL
ARMY

Marylin Monroe performs for U.S. troups
in Korea, February 1954.
Snap Photo/JR. Agenzia Grazia Neri.

Apocalypse Now, 1979.
Directed by Francis Ford Coppola.
Photo Chas Gerretsen. Agenzia Grazia Neri.

Goldie Hawn,
in *Private Benjamin*, 1980.
Directed by Howard Zieff.
©Yoram Kahana, USA. Agenzia Grazia Neri.

As a zone of conflict and testing of the relations between the sexes, the military has always been indicative of the changes in progress in civilian society and, specifically, in the process of female emancipation. While the traditional image focused on a woman patiently waiting at home for the return of the warrior, beginning with the Second World War there was an acceleration that led to a reduction of subordination in favor of a gradual equalization in the division of tasks and responsibilities. Obviously this process – which for evident reasons appears to be unstoppable – met and continues to meet with forms of resistance that seem to confirm anthropologist Margaret Mead's observation at the end of the Forties that in many societies the security of the sexual role model of men is connected to the right, or the ability,

to practice certain activities from which women are excluded a priori. Therefore a defensive interpretation can be applied to certain male gazes which, reconfirming the traditional role of the woman, have offered a contribution on this subject. The girl as seen by Bruce Weber (the woman at home, busy helping her warrior mate); the showgirls of *Apocalypse Now* and the country singer Dolly Parton surrounded by adoring soldiers (the woman as an element of escape from the harshness of the front and as an object of desire); *Private Benjamin*, with Goldie Hawn at first as a soldier by mishap, then as the model recruit, an example of courage and dedication to the cause; the goodbye of a Marine on the way to the Gulf War, drying the tears of his woman, emotionally transcending any possible temporal specificity...

If, as we have seen, the military is a territory that plays an important role in the question of relations between the sexes, the ultimate battle, that of interchangeability of roles, is accompanied by the appearance of a new female icon. Simultaneously pin-up, virago and Lolita, this heroine confuses and mixes clichés, playing the role of the intelligent, independent, tough, and even violent but also sensual woman, bordering on the grotesque and the scurrilous. The battle for equality of the sexes is fought by appropriation of male aggressiveness, but also by utilizing the arms of seduction and the strategies of entertainment. The key characters of this revolution are Lara Croft and Tank Girl, neo-feminist models and perfect incarnations of the most sexist fantasies. Straight out of the hyperbolic, synthetic realms of video games and comics, the two wear high-tech clothing or recycle second-hand pieces according to a post-atomic rebel style. These creatures and their clones, which are gradually springing up throughout the universe of merchandising gadgetry, are perhaps distant relatives of

the Guerrilla Girls, who since 1985 have scattered advertising campaigns, print ads and posters designed to dismantle male dominion of the US art scene. But Lara Croft & Co. are fighting a guerrilla war without ideology, stratified, a remix, like many Nineties phenomena. An ideological leftover also in terms of the use of the uniform by the heiress Patricia Hearst, kidnapped by the Symbionese Liberation Army and then convinced to join them, which was above all the expression of a desire for flight from her "family of origin." Of all the real and imaginary heroines, there is little doubt that the most extreme position has been taken by the toymaker Mattel, which in 1989 for the thirtieth anniversary of the Barbie doll, launched a military version complete with uniform and galloons. In the words of one of the company's marketing managers reported in a short piece in the *Chicago Tribune*, it appears that this version was produced "by popular demand" of women in the army, who wanted a doll that would remind their daughters of them. *edc*

A soldier's life In 1970 only 1.4 percent of the US army were women; the current figure stands at 11.8 percent. Barbie's military career began in 1989. She has served as an officer, pilot and Thunderbird squadron leader. Here, she appears as a fully qualified army medic. Her authentic uniform is based on those worn by the 101st Airborne Division during the Gulf War. Barbie is ready for any emergency with two handy medical shoulder bags and a large, white hairbrush.

Vita da soldato Nel 1970, solo l'1% dell'esercito americano era composto di donne: attualmente la percentuale è dell'11,8%. La carriera militare di Barbie è iniziata nel 1989. Barbie ha prestato servizio come ufficiale, pilota e capo di un gruppo di Thunderbirds. Qui ci appare come medico dell'esercito a pieno titolo. La sua uniforme autentica si rifà a quella indossata dalla 101ª Divisione Aviotrasportata durante la Guerra del Golfo. Barbie è pronta per ogni emergenza, equipaggiata con due pratiche borse a tracolla con medicinali e una grande spazzola per capelli bianca.

us$24

COLORS

"Vita da Soldato," in *Colors,*
n. 9 - Shopping, p. 35.

Nova, September 1971.

NOVA

SEPTEMBER 1971

ONE MAN'S MEAT IS
ANOTHER MAN'S
GLUCONO-D-LACTONE
DRESSED TO KILL
PETER WALKER,
CABINET SUPERSTAR
FIND THE
FACE THAT FITS YOU
MISSIONARIES
IN THE MELTING POT

From left, top to bottom
"The All American Hit Parade,"
in *Vogue*, August 1991, pp. 204/211.
Photo Max Vadukul,
fashion editor Elizabeth Saltzman.

Kevin Sussen, "Good Golly, Miss Dolly!"
in *Vanity Fair*, June 1991, pp. 106/111.
Photo Annie Leibovitz,
styled by Marina Schiano.

On the right
Esquire, August, 1965.

Following pages
Speak Out About Violence Against Lesbians!
Party invitation for the Lesbian Avengers,
USA, early 1990's,
in Liz McQuiston, *Suffragettes to She Devils*,
Women's Liberations and Beyond, London.
Phaidon Press, 1997, p. 168.

Cady Noland, *Tania as a Bandit*, 1989.
Serigraph on alluminum, 180 x 120 cm.
Courtesy Galleria Massimo De Carlo, Milano.

AUGUST 1968
PRICE 75¢
GREAT BRITAIN 4/6

Esquire

THE MAGAZINE FOR MEN

Revisit beautiful Bataan, Guadalcanal, Iwo Jima, Corregidor, Okinawa, Guam, Tarawa, and Wake Island. For details, see page 50.

10)NEW YORK, May 20-NOW A SUSPECT-The FBI charged <u>Patricia</u> Hearst with violation of the federal firearms law Sunday in Los Angeles. The charge claims that Miss Hearst sprayed bullets at a sporting goods store in Los Angeles after a clerk attempted to stop William and Emily Harris, suspected Symbionese Liberation Army members, from shoplifting a pair of socks. This photo is a copy of one received in April in San Francisco by radio station KSAN and purports to show Miss Hearst in front of a Symbionese Liberation Army insignia. (AP Wirephoto)(See AP AAA Wire Story) 20115fls)1974

DID SHE RISK HER LIFE FOR GOVERNMENTS THAT ENSLAVE WOMEN?

A PUBLIC SERVICE MESSAGE FROM **GUERRILLA GIRLS** 718 LaGuardia Pl. #237, NY 10012

Guerrilla Girls,
*Did She Risk for Governments
That Enslave Women*?,
1980, poster, in Liz McQuiston,
Graphic Agitation, London: Phaidon Press,
1993, p. 168.

Demi Moore,
in *G.I. Jane*, 1997.
Directed by Ridley Scott.
Agenzia Grazia Neri.

"The Bit Girl," in *The Face*,
n. 5, June 1997, pp. 62/69.

"New Boots and Panzers. Tank Girl is Finally
Hitting the Big Screen (…)," in *The Face*, n. 74,
November 1994, pp. 54/59.

"Vita Moderna? Vita da Tute,"
in *L'Uomo Vogue,*
n. 45, March 1976, pp. 193/194.
Photo Oliviero Toscani.

Moschino advertising,
in *Vogue Italia,*
n. 564, August 1997, p. 17.

Cheap and Chic by MOSCHINO

**One of the hardest parts of being a military woman
is just the constant scrutiny ad criticism.
Act too masculine and you're accused of being a dyke;
act too feminine and you're either accused
of sleeping around, or you're not serious;
you're just there to get a man.**

**Lieutenant, US Navy,
in *Camouflage Isn't Only for Combat*, 1998**

Navy male and female basic training, 1992.
© Eli Red/Magnum Photos, New York.
Agenzia Contrasto.

Catherine Opie, *Renee*, 1994.
C-Print, 155 x 78 cm.
Courtesy the Photographers Gallery, London.

From top to bottom
Richard Gere and Debra Winger,
in *An Officer and a Gentleman*, 1981.
Directed by Taylor Hackford.
Agenzia Grazia Neri.

Jennifer Jones and Rock Hudson,
in *Farewell to Arms*, 1957.
Directed by Charles Vidor.
S.S. Archives Shooting Star.
Agenzia Grazia Neri.

Robert De Niro and Meryl Streep,
in *The Deer Hunter*, 1978.
Directed by Michael Cimino.
Snap Photo/JR. Agenzia Grazia Neri.

David LaChapelle,
V-J Day, 1994.

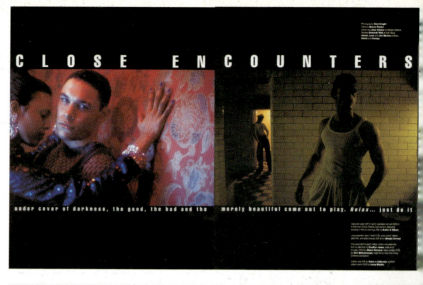

CLOSE ENCOUNTERS

under cover of darkness, the good, the bad and the   merely beautiful come out to play. *Relax... just do it*

"Close Encounters,"
in *Arena Hommes Plus*,
spring/summer 1995, pp. 72/79.
Photo Nick Knight,
fashion editor Simon Foxton.
Esquire, October 1951, p. 66.

Robert Mapplethorpe,
Brian Ridley and Lyle Heeter, 1979.
C-Print, 51 x 41 cm.
Courtesy Studio Guenzani, Milano.
©The Estate of Robert Mapplethorpe,
New York.

Jean-Claude Van Damme,
in *Street Fighter*, 1994.
Directed by Steven E. De Souza.
© Jim Townley/SYGMA. Agenzia Grazia Neri.

Steven Zeeland,
Military Trade,
New York: The Haworth Press, 1999.

MILITARY TRADE

Steven Zeeland

In *Yanks* Richard Gere plays the role of a young soldier who, having reached Lancashire with the American troops shortly before D-Day, falls in requited love with an English girl, and comes to terms with a series of prejudices about his country. The comparison between Americans and English is the red thread that runs through the narrative, and the love story unwinds around language and attitude differences that, for the girl, are an element of attraction, but for her family represent a cause for distrust. In this film as in *An Officer and a Gentleman*, Richard Gere perfectly embodies two aspects that are inseparably connected in the collective imagination: the uniform as an evocation of patriotism and respect for the rules, and the transgressive and therefore irresistible charm that approaching this garment implies. As the script would have it, there is always a girl, hopefully of working class origin, who gets trapped by this charm and overcomes the reluctance of the military man after having gotten past the initial rigidity of the game of roles. In the case of Frankie Goes to Hollywood, the military uniform takes on a different connotation, where the erotic element and the explicitly homosexual perspective combine with an intentional irreverence regarding the macho rhetoric implicit in the traditional idea of the military and the codes that regulate military behavior. It is no coincidence that the pose of the members of the group is reminiscent of sculptural groupings commonly used for war memorial monuments. *edc*

Richard Gere,
in *Yanks*, 1979.
Directed by John Schlesinger.

Frankie Goes to Hollywood.
© Retna. Agenzia Grazia Neri.

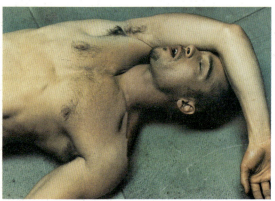

"Brad Pitt Unleashed,"
in *W*, July 1999. Photo Steven Klein.

"A Close Look at the Handcrafted
Prototype GI Joe Figure,"
in John Michlig, *GI Joe. The Complete Story
of America's Favorite Man of Action*,
San Francisco: Chronicle Books, 1998.

INFORMATION
    A closer look at the hand-crafted
    prototype GI Joe figure.

PHOTO TITLE:

PAGE /49

LOG NO. a9E

POSITION:
this page

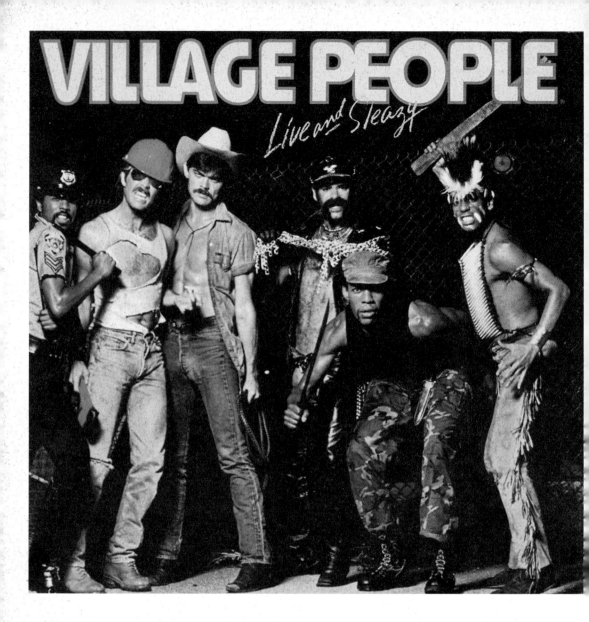

Village People, *Live and Sleazy*, 1979.
Mercury Records, a Polygram Company.

Sylvester Stallone, in *First Blood*, 1982.
Directed by Ted Kotcheff.
© Action Presse, Hamburg.
Agenzia Grazia Neri.

Apocalypse Now, 1979.
Directed by Francis Ford Coppola.
© Shooting Star, Agenzia Grazia Neri.

The Green Berets, 1968.
Directed by John Wayne.
SYGMA. Agenzia Grazia Neri.

A. Schwarzenegger, in *Red Heat*, 1988.
Directed by Walter Hill.
Snap photo/JR. Agenzia Grazia Neri.

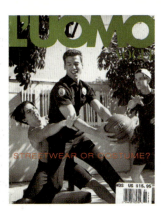

"Cops,"
in *L'Uomo Vogue*,
n. 281, May/June 1997.
Photo Bruce Weber,
fashion editor Joe McKenna.

COPS

or

WAKE UP
AND SMELL THE
FLOWERS

BY BRUCE WEBER

rom day one

wanted to be a cop..."

Lieutenant Jason Shaw

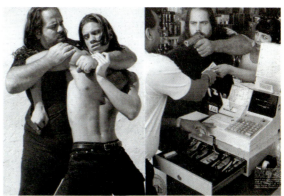

The uniform and the army are frightening: behind the insignia and the medals, the ribbons and the stripes, there is always a sense of discipline that involves a relationship with death. This is the secret of the terrifying charm of the uniform, but it can also lead to a carnival-like, ridiculous side of appearances: to exorcise the looming figure of death, in fact, the popular imagination creates an antidote, coming to terms with the phantom of war by using the weapons of humor. Thus in stories and jokes, in movies and artworks, the military world is often associated with base, vulgar impulses, mixed with four-letter words and off-color comments, or is parodied as the ultimate stronghold of stupidity, a space where the rules serve only to conceal the empty futility of actions. In the hope of never having to serve in the armed forces, the civilian world makes fun of the hierarchies of the army and the police, attempting to corrode their order and reveal their absurdities: soldiers are thus transformed into grotesque caricatures, plastic puppets with broken strings and vacant gazes, mutely pleading for help.
mg

Gillian Wearing,
*Signs That Say What You Want to Say
and Not Signs That Say What Someone Else
Wants You to Say*, 1992/1993.
C-Print, 40.5 x 30.5 cm each, about 600 photos.
Courtesy Maureen Pauley, London.

Daniel Oates, *Cops*, 1993.
Plaster, hair, neoprene, polystyrene, acrylic.
Thin cop (116.8 x 40.6 x 45.7 cm);
Fat cop (99 x 55.8 x 60.9 cm).
Courtesy 303 Gallery, New York.

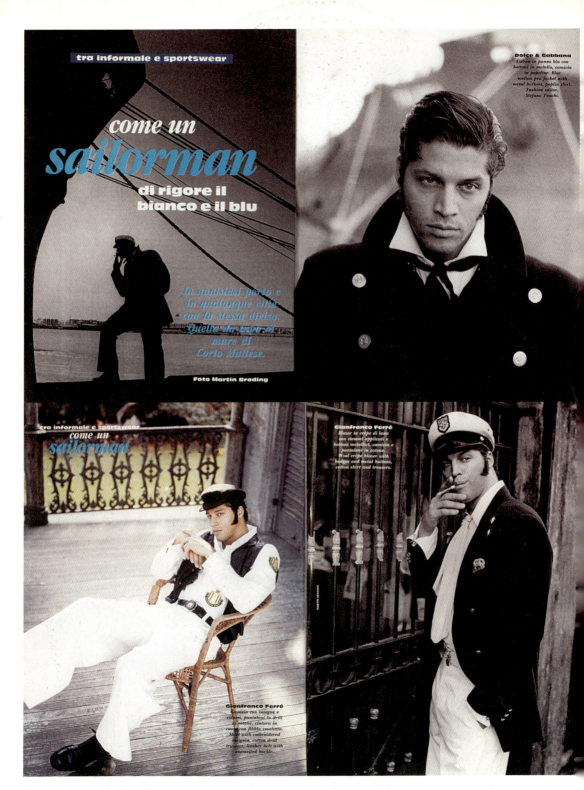

tra informale e sportswear

come un
sailorman
di rigore il
bianco e il blu

*In qualsiasi porto e
in qualunque città
con la stessa divisa.
Quella dei lupi di
mare di
Corto Maltese.*

Foto Martin Brading

Dolce & Gabbana
*Caban in panno blu con
bottoni in metallo, camicia
in popeline. Blue
melton pea jacket with
metal buttons, poplin shirt.
Fashion editor,
Stefano Tonchi.*

tra informale e sportswear
*come un
sailorman*

Gianfranco Ferré
*Camicia con insegne e
ricami, pantaloni in drill
di cotone, cintura in
cuoio con fibbia smaltata.
Shirt with embroidered
insignia, cotton drill
trousers, leather belt with
enamelled buckle.*

Gianfranco Ferré
*Blazer in crepe di lana
con stemmi applicati e
bottoni metallici, camicia e
pantaloni in cotone.
Wool crepe blazer with
badges and metal buttons,
cotton shirt and trousers.*

"Come un sailorman," in *L'Uomo Vogue*,
n. 240, May 1993, p. 68.
Photo Martin Brading,
fashion editor Stefano Tonchi.

Hugo Pratt, "Royal Marines," in *Corto Maltese*,
n. 11, November 1990, p. 4.

GREAT BUYS:
BREAKING RAN

Designers award menswear-inspired uniforms priority status for fall, marching everything from military styles to English dandy looks down the runways. The order of the day: distinctive mixes that throw masculine basics some decidedly feminine curves— and prices that make the grade

272

"Breaking Rank,"
in *Vogue*, August 1992, pp. 272/279.
Photo Dewey Nicks, fashion editor Elizabeth Saltzman.

Jack Pierson, video-still from *Celestial Child*, 1995.
Courtesy of the artist.

One of the few opera triumphs of the recording century. They were giving an example around the world that guys can be friends. They have conveyed the realisation that the world and human consciousness had to change. After the apocalypse of Hitler and the apocalypse of the Bomb, there was an exclamation of joy, a rediscovery of joy and what it is to be alive... They showed an awareness that we make up our own fate, and they have decided to make a cheerful one. They have decided to be generous to Lovely Rita, or be generous to Sgt Pepper himself, turn him from an authority figure to a figure of comic humour, a vaudeville turn.

Remember, this was in the midst of the Sixties; it was 1967 when some of the wilder and crazier radicals were saying "Kill the pigs." They were saying the opposite about old Sgt Pepper. In fact the Beatles themselves were dressing up in uniforms, but associating themselves with good old-time vaudeville authority rather than sneaky CIA, KGB, MI5 or whatever. It was actually a cheerful look round the world... for the first time, I would say, on a mass scale.

Allen Ginsberg, *The Lost Beatles Interviews,* **1995**

Beatles, *Sgt. Pepper's* sleeve, 1967.
© London Features International.
Agenzia Grazia Neri.

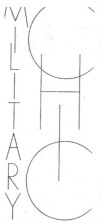

Avanzano a passo di marcia, impettiti e disciplinati, generali di corpo d'armata e samurai, ufficiali e granatieri, capitani d'alto bordo e tenenti di cavalleria, ussari e avieri, cosacchi e soldati semplici: fervono i preparativi, si studiano strategie, si mettono a punto le grandi manovre, eppure il bollettino - o sarebbe meglio chiamarlo comunicato? - non annuncia venti di guerra. Perché se è vero che l'esercito sta invadendo le sale del Costume Institute del Metropolitan Museum di New York, è altrettanto certo che si tratta di una conquista assolutamente pacifica, con un approccio puramente estetico. In pratica, stiamo assistendo agli ultimi ritocchi della mostra «Swords into Ploughshares: Military Dresses from Civilian Wardrobe», che dal 7 settembre fino al 26 novembre metterà in luce la profonda e radicata influenza dell'abbigliamento militare nella moda contemporanea sia maschile che femminile. «Sono influenze fondamentali e spesso dimenticate», afferma Richard Martin, curator del Costume Institute. «Per esempio, quando oggi indossiamo una sahariana o un pantalone kaki non è automatico pensare alle loro origini. Sono capi che hanno letteralmente conquistato il quotidiano e, di conseguenza, la memoria collettiva si è per così dire atrofizzata. Comunque, i reclutamenti stilistici sono stati a tal punto numerosi che è difficile immaginare il guardaroba del Ventesimo secolo senza la storia americana.

Disegni di Ruben Toledo

MARINES STORY

STORIA DI UN'ARMA E DELLA SUA DIVISA

«Dovere, onore, patria». Come abbiamo detto, il corpo dei marines è forse il più famoso tra quelli che compongono l'esercito americano, con la fanteria l'aviazione e la marina. E il corpo addestrato per le missioni più difficili, per le operazioni tattiche particolari, come truppe d'assalto o sabotatori. La loro storia inizia parallelamente alla storia americana.

Nascono nel 1775, durante la Revolutionary War, e la loro prima divisa era costituita da una giacca a code verde con la pettorina bianca per gli ufficiali e rossa per la truppa. La seconda data importante fu la guerra anglo-americana (1812-1815); la divisa subisce alcuni cambiamenti, più che altro decorativi come il cappello piumato e le decorazioni in broccato sul davanti della corta giacca. Nella guerra civile (1861-1865) la giacca si allunga fino a diventare un tre quarti, stretta in vita da una fascia di colore rosso con paramani blu; il cappello diventa il famoso berretto con frontino.

Il 1898 è la guerra ispano-americana. La giacca si accorcia, diventando simile alle camicie cinesi per i fregi che ne ornano il davanti. Durante la prima guerra mondiale (1917-1918) per la prima volta la divisa assume quell'aspetto, sia per il colore grigio-verde sia per i particolari tecnici, tasche ganci ecc., che conserva tutt'oggi. In questo periodo la divisa si diversifica a seconda dell'uso (l'ultima foto della pagina accanto rappresenta la fanteria, la prima della pagina seguente l'aviazione, sempre dei marinai).

Nella seconda guerra mondiale (1941-1945) la specificazione tecnica della divisa si affina e per la prima volta compaiono i famosi colori mimetici. Altra data importante è quella della guerra di Corea (1950-1953) e infine quella che per i marines è probabilmente più tristemente legata a loro, la guerra nel Vietnam (1961-1973).

GUERRA D'INDIPENDENZA	GUERRA ANGLO-AMERICANA	GUERRA CIVILE	GUERRA ISPANO-AMERICANA	1a GUERRA MONDIALE
1775/83	**1812/15**	**1861/65**	**1898**	**1917/1**

"Military Chic," in *L'Uomo Vogue*, n. 263, September 1995, pp. 416/417. Drawings by Ruben Toledo.

"Marines Story," in *L'Uomo Vogue*, n. 60/61, 1977, pp. 96/99. Photo Oliviero Toscani.

tesimo secolo privo di una matrice militare». L'allestimento metterà in evidenza come determinate forme e dettagli siano stati importanti e spesso inospettabili fonti di ispirazione per moltissimi fashion designer. «Abbiamo lavorato al progetto circa sei, sette mesi. Un'esperienza entusiasmante anche se abbastanza complessa proprio per la ricchezza di implicazioni, espropriazioni, riadattamenti», racconta Martin. «L'idea, invece, l'avevo in mente da molto tempo, per me è sempre stata un chiodo fisso, una magnifica ossessione: già cinque anni fa, quando stavo ancora al Fashion Institute of Technology, mi ero buttato a capofitto sull'argomento per scrivere un articolo, uno dei pochi dedicati a questo tema». Ma eccoci al punto: se è vero che gli abiti molto spesso sono la proiezione dei nostri sogni e delle nostre aspirazioni, come mai la divisa ha esercitato un'attrazione così forte e tangibile? «Perché il suo fascino è duplice», spiega Martin. «Da una parte identifica l'eroe - e penso ai cappotti Napoleonici, alle Eisenhower Jackets - dall'altra, proprio perché studiata per il combattimento, esalta i criteri di praticità. È, insomma, una emblematica fusione dei valori epici e comfort, echi di gloria e funzionalità». Non a caso Diana Vreeland, amante delle definizioni perentorie tanto quanto della moda, era solita dire che «le uniformi sono lo sportswear del Diciannovesimo secolo». Ed ecco in parola pea jacket e bomber, tute mimetiche e trench-coat, austeri doppiopetto color oliva e completi coloniali: più di cento divise provenienti da tutto il mondo e catalogate per temi, dalla marina all'aviazione all'esercito. Mixate a queste, le creazioni più significative degli stilisti, da Armani - e basterà citare la sua sfilata Giappone dei primi anni ottanta e le infinite varianti della giacca da aviatore - a Yves Saint Laurent, che «include sempre una pea jacket in ogni sua collezione», dice Martin. «C'è poi il caso di Jean Paul Gaultier», continua, «che ha nei confronti del militare un interesse particolarmente complesso. Prendiamo il suo tipico completo da marinaio - maglietta bianca e blu, pantaloni a vita bassa, giacca da lupo di mare. È evidente un'idea di comodità, ma nello stesso tempo anche una suggestione erotica; il suo "sailor" è in bilico tra l'iconografia ironica e scanzonata di un Popeye e certe reminiscenze intriganti e hot alla Jean Cocteau». L'elenco potrebbe continuare con Issey Miyake e le sue incredibili armature plastificate, Ralph Lauren e le rivisitazioni degli outfit della prima Guerra Mondiale, fino all'uso della divisa per una professione anti-establishment - chi non ricorda, durante gli anni sessanta, il boom degli army & navy surplus e gli abiti da battaglia indossati in maniera provocatoria dai movimenti pacifisti? La mostra mette anche in evidenza in che modo il guardaroba contemporaneo abbia liberamente «saccheggiato» alcuni tipi di tessuto: il nylon impermeabile dei paracadute (un home su tutti Prada) e il camouflage. «Particolarmente interessante», puntualizza ancora Martin, «è un completo di Stephen Sprouse - giacca e pantaloni, cartia - dove l'originaria ispirazione è mediata da precisi riferimenti pop. Il risultato è un mix tra il tipico pattern mimetico da Desert Storm e quello rielaborato nei quadri di Andy Warhol». Altri «slittamenti stilistici» sono evidenti nel riutilizzo di particolari dettagli ▶ S10

S
W
I
S
H

A
R
M
Y

UERRA MONDIALE
1917

2a GUERRA MONDIALE
1941/45

2a GUERRA MONDIALE
1941/45

COREA
1950/53

COREA
1950/53

VIETNAM
1961/63

Following pages
Do-ho Suh, *High School Uniform*, 1997.
Fabric, plastic, stainless, casters,
701 x 551 x 137 cm.
Courtesy Lehmann-Maupin Gallery, New York.

CHANEL

Preceding pages
Chanel advertising,
in *Vogue Italia*, n. 554, October 1996.

Dolce & Gabbana advertising,
in *Esquire*, October 1993, p. 142.

Sean Connery,
in *The Hunt for Red October*, 1990.
Directed by John McTiernan.
SNAP Photo JR/Agenzia Grazia Neri.

Ralph Lauren advertising,
in *Vogue Italia*, n. 478, April 1990.

"Great Coats,"
in *Vogue*, August 1992, pp. 194/202.
Photo Hans Feurer,
fashion editor Jenny Capitain.

It's official: falling in line with skirt lengths, coats drop right down to the ankles without surrendering shape on top. Teamed with high-climbing boots, officers' caps, and decorative badges, these romantic swashbucklers assume military airs

great coats

monete e medaglie

Stampate su seta o applicate su giacche e pantaloni. Ma anche come insoliti gioielli.

CAMICIA, GONNA E SCARPE DI SETA, STAMPATA: TUTTO GIANNI VERSACE, COLLANT PIERRE MANTOUX. NELLA PAGINA ACCANTO BORSETTA DI CAMOSCIO DECORATA, FENDI, BIJOUX E MONETE, MONNAIE DE PARIS. FASHION EDITOR MANUELA PAVESI.

BLAZER E PANTALONI CON DECORAZIONI, ICEBERG. COLLANE BARBOZA, CROCE DI STRASS, YVES SAINT LAURENT. SCARPE BLUMARINE. NELLA PAGINA ACCANTO BLOUSON, JEANS, CINTURA E BRACCIALI: TUTTO CHANEL. COLLANE, MONETE E MEDAGLIE, MONNAIE DE PARIS.

"Monete e medaglie,"
in *Vogue Italia*, n. 491, July 1991, p. 174.
Photo Walter Chin, fashion editor Manuela Pavesi.

The Face, n. 55, November 1984.

THE fACE

BOLD

NEW!

TRENDSPOTTER'S
GUIDE:

MENSWEAR AT T
OUTER LIMITS

THE ENGLISH PU
DEATH BY DISCO

WHO ARE
THE M·U·D·S·?

nes Brown
le Council
n DMC
aragua: The Revolution of Youth
am Ant
ida
der Still!

Photo **Jamie M**

Roxanne Lowitt
Uniforms:
as a part of society
as a part of fashion
as a part of life.
Uniforms unite people. They create order in our society.
There is a uniform for practically everything and everyone,
and today's fashion has helped to make it even more so.
Uniforms also make it quite easy to be stylish.
Traveling the world and working day and night,
a uniform makes it all so effortless.
My basic uniform is black: it matches everything
and I can go from day wear to evening wear.
The crucial parts of my uniform are my sunglasses,
which have several purposes, my Chinese jacket –
with big pockets to hold lots of film, and of course
a camera or two!

Chantal Thomas, Jean Paul Gaultier.
John Galliano for Dior Couture, July 2000.
Wigstock, New York, September 1997.

From left to right
March, 1998;
Bridget Hall, Louis Vuitton, Paris, March 1998;
May, Miu Miu, Milan, October 1998;
Tina and Michel Chow, December 1984;
Claude Saba at Naomi Campbell's party, New York 2000.

From left to right
Stella Tenant, VH1 Fashion Awards, October 1996;
Guinevere, Balmain, Paris, July 1996;
Navia, Karl Lagerfeld, Paris, May 1996;
Scott Barrie;
Walter Van Berindonk, Paris, October 1998.

From left to right
Shalom Harlow at Valentino, Paris, July 1998;
Ewa, Fendi, Milan, March 1998;
Thierry Mugler, Paris, January 1998;
John Galliano, Paris, March 1997;
Madonna, Apla, Jean Paul Gaultier Show, Los Angeles, 1992.

From left to right
Kate Moss at Versace, Paris, January 1993;
Istante, March 1996;
Naomi at Ralph Lauren, New York, November 1991;
Jean Paul Gaultier, Paris, October 1997;
Christy Turlington, Ralph Lauren, New York, November 1991.

The Brigade of Guards.
Photo Patrick Lichfield.
Camera Press, London. Agenzia Grazia Neri.

Annual reunion of the Household Cavalry, Hyde Park, London, 1994.
© Neil Libbert/Network. Agenzia Grazia Neri.

Thatcherian Great Britain.
© R. Hutchings/Network. Agenzia Grazia Neri.

While in the Club Monaco campaign the uniform worn by the smiling models is a bit military, a bit boy scout, evoking a Fifties atmosphere, superimposing the need to convey a style and a product on the future-confident gazes of the young people, the efficacy of the Benetton advertising is based on an opposite procedure: the models, in fact, are replaced by "normal" people, most of whom were found in the street. This image is part of a series of 56 photographs of men and women, old and young people, taken by Oliviero Toscani for the Benetton advertising campaign for 1995/96 in Beijing and Manchuria. Thanks to the absence of redundant elements, the soldier evokes the memory of the People's Republic of China, intertwining it with recent history, the fall of Communism, the introduction of fashion and personalization of dress in a country that lived in uniforms during the Mao years. The image takes a neutral, documentary stance, but at the same time its impact is based on ambiguity, with equal doses of the charm of the uniform, the elegance and discipline it suggests, attention to ethnic differences and an idea of their possible coexistence under the same trademark. *edc*

Club Monaco advertising,
in *L'Uomo Vogue*, n. 283, September 1997.

Wu Wen Quing (sailor),
United Colors of Benetton in China,
autumn/winter 1995/1996, in *The Face*, n. 85,
October 1995, p. 25.

ITED COLORS OF BENETTON IN CHINA
L-WINTER 95/96

UNITED COLOR
OF BENETTON.

Emporio Armani billboard,
autumn/winter 1985/1986.

Following pages
Clegg & Guttman, *The Financiers*, 1986.
Cibachrome, 191 x 270 cm.
Courtesy Lia Rumma, Napoli. Private Collection.

The army celebrates the continuous trespass of the Self into the Other: the steps of marching, the color of the uniform, the ritual of the salute impose the rhythms of the group on the individual. But when artists look at the world of the army, their attention often lingers over the small fractures that interrupt uniformity: the uniform thus becomes the special territory for a clash of gazes. In her performance in 1998, Paola Pivi packed one hundred Chinese people into a room, obliging them to all wear the same gray jersey and to line up in ranks, composing a new version of the famous army of terracotta. But the involuntary actors in this happening seem to react with intolerance: their faces betray an unexpected hardness, scornful, proud. The differences immediately spring to the fore, the little imperfections that shatter the homogeneity of the image. The gaze is even more severe: pointed directly at the audience, it seems to respond with decision to the voyeurism implicit in this operation, laying claim to the independence of an individual point of view. Alighiero Boetti's is another reversed gaze, but in an opposite sense, though still wavering between exoticism and stereotype. The image, shot by an anonymous photographer during a trip to Japan in 1985, catches the artist as he mingles with a group of students in uniform: Boetti's face peeks out from the crowd, and we can almost glimpse a mocking smile, which also seems to have been communicated to the students. An accidental image, little more than a snapshot, yet it almost emblematically conveys the sense of Boetti's career, his passage from persona to persona, his cheerful schizophrenia of alter egos and working companions. The group and the uniform become reassuring company, an escape route from the boredom of consistency, from the weight of the Self.
mg

Preceding pages
Do-Ho Suh, *Who Am We I?*, 1996.
Wallpaper, variable dimensions.
Courtesy Lehmann-Maupin Gallery, New York.

Paola Pivi, *100 Cinesi*, 1998.
Courtesy Galleria Massimo De Carlo, Milano.
Photo Attilio Maranzano.

Alighiero Boetti in Japan, 1985.
Courtesy Archivio Boetti, Roma.

Wang Du, *Sketch for Red Army*, 2000.
Courtesy Jeffrey Deitch, New York.

The Chinese Army; how many for Mao?
© Camera Press, London.
Agenzia Grazia Neri.

Giorgia Fiorio, *897/7; 13e D.B.L.E., C.M.E., "F1,"*
Platoon Cadet Corporal, Myriam, Dijibouti,
October 1995, in Giorgia Fiorio,
Legio Patria Nostra,
Paris: Marval, 1996, p. 82.
Agenzia Grazia Neri.

Giorgia Fiorio, *891/4; 13e D.B.L.E., C.M.E., "F1,"*
Platoon cadet corporal, Myriam, Dijibouti,
October 1995, in Giorgia Fiorio,
Legio Patria Nostra,
Paris: Marval, 1996. p. 82.
Agenzia Grazia Neri.

1. Legionnaire: you are a volunteer serving France faithfully and with honor.
2. Every Legionnaire is your brother-at-arms, irrespective of his nationality, race or creed. You will demonstrate this by an unwavering and straightforward solidarity which must always bind together members of the same family.
3. Respectful of the Legion's traditions, honoring your superiors, discipline and comradeship are your strengths, courage and loyalty your virtues.
4. Proud of your status as a Legionnaire, you will display this pride, by your turnout, always impeccable, your behavior, ever worthy though modest, your living-quarters, always tidy.
5. An elite soldier: you will train vigorously, you will maintain your weapon as if it were your most precious possession, you will keep your body in the peak of condition, always fit.
6. A mission once given to you becomes sacred to you, you will accomplish it to the end and at all costs.
7. In combat: you will act without relish of your tasks, or hatred; you will respect the vanquished enemy and will never abandon neither your wounded nor your dead, nor will you under any circumstances surrender your arms.

Code of Honor of the Foreign Legion

With an unprecedented capacity for penetration, the Vietnam War produced a short-circuit between the news and its reworking in industrial culture that took the form of rock music, cinema, fashion, and communication. This event played a fundamental role in the changing awareness of the counterculture years. Many voices were raised against the war on the front of popular music: the *Feel Like I'm Fixin' to Die Rag* (1967) by Country Joe and the Fish, in which the narrative voice identifies with a drafted soldier forced to die far from home, followed by a range of different references. *Izabella* by Jimi Hendrix, *Four Dead* by Crosby Stills and Nash, *Lucky Man* by Emerson Lake and Palmer, *Running Gun Blues* by David Bowie represent a true soundtrack for a generation. But the greatest visibility was for *Give Peace a Chance* by John Lennon who, with Yoko Ono, had attracted attention with their *Bed-Ins for Peace*. Rock played a central role with respect to the invasion of Vietnam,

although in a tortuous path that often reveals the contradictions between pacifist desires and the interests of the entertainment industry. The circle closes with the identification of Bruce Springsteen with the figure of the veteran-hero in *Born in the USA*: not by chance, this song unintentionally became a sort of hymn for Reagan's presidential campaign in '84. On the other side of the fence, the entertainment industry cooked up propaganda like the nationalistic *Green Berets* (John Wayne, 1968), a film greeted with protest demonstrations all over Europe. The two ways later met in a gradual process of critical reinterpretation of the war that was to become a genre and a proving ground for leading Hollywood directors. The show must go on, even in the wake of an unprecedented event: the United States had never before found itself so full of doubts and questions, mortified by the outcome of a clash with an enemy that was supposed to be much weaker, at least on paper... *edc*

H. Hoarn, "Strive to Train Soldiers
to Be in a Position to Defend the Nation," 1971,
in *Decade of Protest*,
Santa Monica:
Smart Art Press, 1996, p. 61.

In Country, 1989. Directed by di Norman Jewison.
Photo Compix/Agenzia Grazia Neri.

Tom Berenger, in *Platoon*, 1986.
Directed by Oliver Stone.
Copyright Photofest/Retna Pictures/Agenzia Grazia Neri.

"Vietnam by Bruce Weber,"
supplement of *L'Uomo Vogue*,
n. 272, July/August 1996, p. 37.

Saturated colors, backdrops of red marble as in some secret corner of the Taj Mahal, and khaki uniforms reinvented by Hugo Boss, Prada, Cerruti... When the colonies have all but disappeared and terms like "diaspora," "orientalism," and "exile" become the key words of the new criticism, the winds of globalization begin to blow in the fashion world as well. Naturally the accent falls on the eccentric details, the exotic atmospheres, sashes, scarves, striped shirts, humid, monsoon hues, and the somewhat decadent freedom of military men stationed in Madras. The code of the uniform is compromised, leaving room for the affectations of these dandies abandoned in the holdings at the far reaches of the empire. And then the olive skin, obtained with sunlamps, a few scars, the glassy, sensual gaze worthy of the lover of Marguerite Duras. As if this wasn't enough, in the tropical heat of this imaginary India it is always best to wear a winter overcoat.

This is the dream of an East seen through the backward spyglass of the West: projection of our desire for escape, like a watercolor by Delacroix or an adventure tale by Emilio Salgari. *mg*

"Omar God! Campaign Shots from the Modern Militia," in *Arena Hommes Plus*, n. 6, autumn/winter 1996/1997. Photo Jean Baptiste Mondino, fashion editor Karl Templer.

page: khaki double-breasted raincoat £1,400 by Giorgio Armani; stone cotton shirt £105 by Prada; silk club tie £45 by Hugo by Hugo Boss; military brooch to hire from Angels & Bermans *Opposite:* double-breasted stone raincoat approximately £800 by Dolce & Gabbana; stone cotton shirt £75 by DKNY; silk club tie £75 by Hugo by Hugo Boss; military brooch to hire from Angels & Bermans

Free time is a recent invention, which appeared straddling the Fifties and Sixties, when newsstands began to offer installments of guides for hobbyists and do-it-yourselfers, voyages became organized tours and highway rest stops sprouted cloned cafeterias and service stations. In a mechanism of compensation, the appearance of leisure time coincided with the birth of new structures and organizations designed to give an order and a style to new freedoms.

Starting in the Eighties free time began a dialogue with what should have been its number one enemy, military organization: aided and abetted by an American cowboy president and a film industry busy celebrating heroes like Rambo and gentlemen officers like Richard Gere, shop windows began to offer accessories and garments borrowed from the locker of some unknown soldier. Leather jackets, khaki trousers, thick and durable, even wrinkle-free, Zippo lighters and RayBan sunglasses: all objects with a rugged charm, to be treated with the disregard typical of "real men."

At first glance these seem like garments and accessories selected for their practicality, but the implications are much more complex: the print campaigns, slogans and advertisements all dipped into the stores of memory, using faded photos of grandpa the pilot mixed with second-hand recollections gathered from cinema. The images all have a retro atmosphere, as if after having achieved a state of order free time felt obliged to invent itself a glorious past. In this way every time we take a walk in the country, with our leather jacket and sunglasses, we can feel that we deserve this rest, the rest of the warrior after the battle. And our hours of leave from the gray walls of the office have the pungent aftertaste of adventure: without getting our hands dirty, we are all heroes of a past that never existed, lost in the great American dream, in a present masquerading as nostalgia. *mg*

Avirex advertising,
in *Per Lui*, n. 29,
July/August 1985.

Japico advertising,
in *L'Uomo Vogue*,
n. 35, April/May 1975.

★ MILITAR ★

★ JAPICO ★
diffusione

Una proposta *japico* per l'estate 1975

U.S. AIR FORCE

LA DIVISA MILITARE: DESIGN E TECNOLOGIA DELLA CONFEZIONE

U.S. NAVY

U.S. ARMY

"U.S. Army, U.S. Navy, U.S. Air Force,"
in *L'Uomo Vogue,*
n. 60/61, 1977, pp. 82/94.
Photo Oliviero Toscani.

U.S. AIR FORCE

Nella esta grande e piccina: uno a giubbotto da volo caratteristico della maintenza inglia e pre-inis inizial, anche la sottozizzina è dato marcio, capo tedesta da volo i vende americano. Particolari: il cappello e particolare. L'aeroponente del pilota, su cui si rilleva i gambi di pelle il giubbotto è molto americano, caratteristica dell'Aviazione americana: nelle sopraminatilizza aicorreo, sotto grigio, indossato e luggione al interno.

Nelle foto in alto, sull'ordine da sinistra: l'impermeabile di volare, il cappotto di pano, il capte Maestro d'ordinanza di classe, e le foto sotto, la giacca d'ordinanza. L'arrivi da aiammaminatizza, la quadian active a l'orderata con nastrici bianchetti. Nelle foto grande a destra: la testa da volo in aiu, il portano bianco, grigi e particolari inisio; le particolati uniche militari in ditaoniato e le periodo anche color di uscine nelle servizie.

U.S. NAVY

Nella foto grande, la turbina giacca da lavoro P.E.A., usata in Marina; tutte il più bottoni tra i capo bianchi nelle vesi esele dagli stessi soldati: già esono in questa almeno divisa della marina, da quelle da lavoro a quelle di riutizziaa.

U.S. ARMY

LA DIVISA: COSA NE PENSA IL SOLDATO

Lo detoriano il vestiario è profondamente in attesa per tutte le farce, siamo incontro di oggi, e le idee, i modelli, nasciono nei vari laboratori e vengono poi controllati dell'esercito.

Noi reciproco vestiti esempio: Il vestiario dei cari fabbricati e la distribuzione dei estulli che vurreno all'altra aria dei che vedo loro anche in tutero. Questi più ranci anche a giurdia dei fornetti i more armati la parti di tentare avvicitazione, hai più a resinala avvicitazione aicenalmente al tegelabbre loro con i individuli di restare i attivitute, fatto il morbicha aperta, inviato inini antagoni ai riparano, ed uno che presi rifugione. I tardini in quanti substanzia soldatici i respiaginti delle loro delema, ma aloro anche il nessun ni effetti della vario sani, che vitere peno guadita determinata.

Induccono el questi abiti nella vita civile?

La ascese «No! Pecce a questi testamini ve ne ad assilottato; I vi detuno personal; ma spazi al lavoro».

Un tervitore «Si, d'aran cui il indumenti ancillissi, trasa i cui distanza». Ma con l'outoli persona lo diveo nelle sue implamento «Una palanca dell'oscibi «Indovimo la divisa in festa per fa i altri sportti».

Un recinto «Sono guerriero che capi sono le piazze di viti e i pantaloni, postati sorvere per la vita di certi ! giorni».

Come considera il tuo vestiario?

Un avante «Indabilazano, bene la tua ani bisogno, di cambiarsaris».

Un mecanico «A ditorio pei ti gettarsa a più uvazi, pei sia il mano decspinata».

Un soldato dell'avanno «I vitesti, una giudigioli, fesse casubbico; la aglie delle attive, si trespi i fivassi».

Un morrino «Fino recibici; già che si subire il vande di aizascazione, specifimente le riuzzata a s' licenzia».

Sarebbi sostituzzma diemsabre tri giovani?

Un mecanic «Ai me pense che senza riuda aprezzi a scampavirsi da quando ! fosto a guerra nei Viet Nam?».

Un magiore «Si, ho arro al mantiene bre? ». Un motevie «Si, qui in Italia la gente reclita in verda, oltre da avri. La giacca Pea italia Marina è stata in avinnio spagini». Un soldato dell'escelte «Per ll'effido-meliero che guadano abiti verdi di aizasere una divisa».

Tutte dve foto grandi, almeno particolari delle divise da contabilizzato; gli stivaletti neri e le povertia patro-altre. Elementi caratterizzati del divisa minuto dell'endente militare. Nelle tue piccole di centro: le alto il contabrio (l'uso militari a sinistra la Beina ad divisa; pene motti quella da contabilizzato; sotto a distitta la divisa cosi e perigri, assatta l'alta origine degli officieri.

Gianfranco Ferré Man advertising,
autumn/winter 1987/1988.
Photo Herb Ritts.

Lina Bertucci,
Accademia di guerra, 1998.
C-Print, 100 x 75 cm.
Courtesy of the artist.

Jacket, Flying, Type,
A-2

東部イタリア地方のシルク・スクリーン技法で美しくプリントされたパッチを全身にまとったA-2。第2次大戦当時、米陸軍フライトジャケットに残されたウォーアートは、戦場の将兵の創意によって芽吹いた。そのもうひとつの魅力は、それぞれの部隊が展開していた戦域現地に存在した技術と、将兵の創意の融合にあった。なかでも、CB戦線のレザー・ハンドクラフト、イタリア戦線のシルク・プリントは代表的なものである。

歌の題名から取ったのか、"Me My Gal"とペイントされたA-2フライトジャケット。B-17フライング・フォートレス爆撃機と、第8空軍をあらわす数字、それとウイングをモチーフに、出撃回数をあらわす爆弾のシルエットを美しく配置したウォーアートの秀作である。前面には、"トミー"、それにガールフレンドまたは夫人だろうか、"ベティ"のニックネームが描かれている。青年飛行士の甘い思い出が伝わる1着である。

⑳220

㉑221

Jacket, Flying, Intermediate, Type,
MA-1 (RIVERSIBLE MODEL)

インディアン・オレンジのライニングもこのMA-1着をモデル、スペックMIL-J-8279D、1950年代におけるジェット戦時救難部隊の遭出に求められなかったが、それにだけ機能を発揮した。米出版物の一40により、事務物の放出は容易になったため、問題はその後の発行がの現在と登出けっにこれられても登場にてもよるし、同時にMA-1アレ、2着といったフライトジャケットも派生のオレンジ面カラのリバーシブル仕様に変更された

成立までのステッチなどに特徴をもつMA-1着をモデル。スペックMIL-J-8279D、その後は1952年2月に締む付な締は約でられた。"DSA (80"で終るようなコード・ナンバーからわかるように、写真の着をモデルは、スポーツマスターズ社がDSA (国防経理会社) から引起を受けた1949年ものである。多くの場合、支給品の新入地を予示している。は、契約以上の社在者を出量とはには同一きるものとも、半値開水ないの前品着、合理者ともにけを着出に内側によって、再色を停止することがある

㉒312

Jacket, Flying, Intermediate, Type,
MA-1 (THE LAST FLIGHT STATUS MODEL)

このMA-1は、米空軍試部(SP)部の短行士が装備にしたシリーズ最もモデム(スペックMIL-J-8279D)、1971年の社事新契約ら、アルフ・インチェットリーズを記念である。同社は、MA-1(米国部の-65をはじめ、その装備や出ット生産してきたメーカーで、その内容を生かした電動装がンの機場所で全生をリン料然的に行なってきた

MA-1着をモデルは、シリーズ最後の短行仕様として、CWU-45/P の空軍を1970年代の終ま出で産された。写真は、海軍の短速性陸部ガ装置である、ヘリコプター、SH-20Tと官場地具が装備したものである

㉓313

"Suit Up! The Flight Jacket," in *World Mok*, n. 1,
fashion editor Kesaharu Imai, pp. 310/313.

丹念に刺しゅうされたロックミシン使用の手製パッチを左胸に、美しいペイントを背中にのせた第2次大戦中の南西太平洋戦域、第5空軍、第90爆撃航空群・第320爆撃飛行隊〝ジョリー・ロジャース〟のA-2フライトジャケット。オーストラリアを拠点に対日反攻作戦を開始した第5空軍の重爆撃機部隊、B-24を使用する第320飛行隊は、1942年から43年にかけて、精鋭日本海軍航空隊の零戦が待ち受けるパプア・ニューギニアやソロモン、

ガダルカナルなどの激戦地を転戦した。この戦域の戦いは、日本軍の快調な進撃が終わりを告げ、連合軍が前進を開始する転機となったが、損失も大きかった。同飛行隊のB-24の1機は、撃墜されたときのままの姿で、いまだにニューギニアのジャングルに放置されている。またその後、同飛行隊は、フィリピン戦線に転戦し、ミンドロ島およびルソン島に展開、日本軍の拠点に対する集中爆撃と対艦艇攻撃を行った。

BY SAINT LAURENT

DESIGN
APPLI-
CATO
ALL'ABITO

Y.S.L.- LA SAHARIANA: UN CLASSICO

YVES

"By Saint-Laurent,"
in *L'Uomo Vogue*,
n.18, July 1972, p. 93.
Photo Oliviero Toscani.

"Design applicato all'abito,"
in *L'Uomo Vogue*,
n. 23, May 1973, p. 195.
Photo Alex Chatelain.

"YSL – La Sahariana: un classico,"
in *L'Uomo Vogue*,
n. 29, April 1974, p. 197.
Photo Richard Imrie.

War photographers
Robert Capa and George Rodger,
Naples, 1943.
Magnum/Agenzia Contrasto.

Wherein one well-dressed bwana shows off—thanks to a little photographic magic—a multiplicity of looks that are perfect for weekends in the urban jungle

City Safari

The fitted khaki jacket, a garment that's something of a cross between sport coat and overshirt. It looks best worn with more of the same khaki and olive-drab-type stuff. *Opposite page, left:* Four-button single-breasted silk-and-linen jacket by Wilke-Rodrigues, $185. *Right:* Four-button cotton-and-polyester jacket with peaked lapels by Dolce & Gabbana, $610.... The short trench. Think of it not as an officer's but as a gentleman's raincoat, with a chic civilian length that makes for easy in-and-out of the car. *This page, from left:* Six-button double-breasted cotton-and-polyester trench by Dolce & Gabbana, $980. Six-button double-breasted cotton-and-rayon trench. Nautica by David Chu, $225. Six-button double-breasted nylon trench by D Squared, $850.

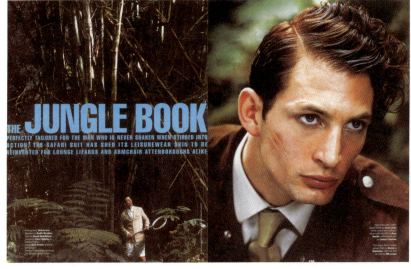

THE JUNGLE BOOK

PERFECTLY TAILORED FOR THE MAN WHO IS NEVER SHAKEN WHEN STIRRED INTO ACTION: THE SAFARI SUIT HAS SHED ITS LEISUREWEAR SKIN TO BE REINVENTED FOR LOUNGE LIZARDS AND ARMCHAIR ATTENBOROUGHS ALIKE

From top to bottom, left to right
"City Safari," in *GQ,* January 1997, pp. 134/135. Photo Peggy Sirota.

"Jungle Book,"
in *Arena Hommes Plus,* spring/summer 1995, pp. 138/139. Photo Schoerner, fashion editor David Bradshaw.

"Summer Safari/ Military Green," in *Esquire,* March 1975, pp. 123,125. Photo Oliviero Toscani.

"Commando Performance," in *Esquire,* February 1976, pp. 126/127. Photo Ladner/Blake.

"Tenute da safari per le escursioni all'interno," in *L'Uomo Vogue,* n. 18, July 1972, p. 82. Photo Oliviero Toscani.

SUMMER SAFARI

MILITARY GREEN

COMMANDO PERFORMANCE

The men's fashion industry calls this the Survival Look and bets you'll be wearing a lot of it this winter on your vacation in the sun and during off-hours next spring and summer. It's rugged sportswear made from natural fabrics and influenced by the cut of Army clothes or the outfits worn by hunters, auto racers, mountain climbers and paratroopers. Wear it for action and comfort; pair it with boots and heavy socks.

Shorts are cut fuller this year and come in any length you can think of. One man opposite, shown in the cane fields of the Dominican Republic, roughs it in pleated khaki shorts ($25) and a short-sleeve battle jacket ($89), both by Scotts Grey Ltd. Under the jacket he sports a long-sleeve crew-neck T-shirt ($14) by Al B. Arden. Workman's boots ($40) from Sears, Roebuck. His leader's shirt and shorts are by De Noyer. As you are here, denim has made the transition from work clothes to high fashion to sportswear. For making his way through the sugarcane, our hero smartly wears an indigo denim fly-front jumpsuit ($50) by Landlubber; over a cotton-gauze shirt ($16) by Scotts Grey Ltd. The companion he carries wears drawstring pants and top by De Noyer.

Out of the cane and into battle, or battle dress at least, with a little help from the army of the Dominican Republic. Our soldiers of fortune are turned out for weekend adventure in their military best. At far left, he wears Nik Nik's quilted-poplin jacket ($100), cotton pants ($49) and overshirt ($33). As ease for the summer, our middle man looks ready for anything in Bert Pulitzer's water-repellent cotton-poplin jacket ($240) and cotton cargo pants ($165) that unzip above the knee to make shorts. The suede bullet vest ($75) is from Hunting World. His pal at right favors a cotton survival jacket ($89) and matching pants ($25), both by Male, and Creighton's khaki shirt ($39). For added protection, he wears boots ($40) by Kaufmann Footwear and sunglasses from Ultimate Spectacle. Pith helmets by Tex Tan. She wears a De Noyer safari suit, Olof of Sweden boots, and a Hunting World hat.

ESQUIRE: FEBRUARY 157

UNA VACANZA ALLA HEMINGWAY

Tenuta da safari per le escursioni all'interno. Il raggruppamento, sullo piro ghe decorate, laguna uniseriae, villaggi primitivi colori, dal verde, al va a cascia di coccodrilli, è più semplicemente di immagini e sensazioni forti e economiste. Sul piano, sui terminali, trasmitti a naturisme tipo militare, in colore mimetico. 1. Da cintura corsé ampia: Max, il biondo, dietro, impeccabilmente imbattuto del Mr. con Caroline Jim: tute a completi di cotone cachi militare, a contene a sottolineatura sport di Monnalisa: Organizza i tessuti a 2. vi ripresa il perché, con short militari sentori e Rhythm rupe stalli, City (milanci), la shellatura a diretti di Monnalisa. Per Patrick, cottonira-seturi la divena leggero di Fonica, pantalone misumisi, attuali tutti di Fonotel. Per Gérard Guenani, a capello corte e a del Club, il cameo delle pinghe, tatto un posta di cottone Levi's da Bramati. Randolph (nelleta) Su bilioletto-top e pantaloni di Monnalisa, stretti di tela a deste dopo il cotone Levi's Jeans City legitatti, con amici su Museum tipo militari di Monnalisa e pantalone minutare. 3. Leggera cantuta in cotone con nuschio, di Max: O'Polo da Browto's e, dietro, cintata in seta grassa di Cassuè. 4. Poli intra ampia a maniche corte, in seta di De King, a stato una cannica-tuta di Browto's. 6. Cintini naturale lente con la tris coperchi, per la maglia di De King. Il palo la sua verde militare di 7. 6. Dua belliissimi tessuti naturali: interno potione dei fili di magistra spaccio per la prima cannica, di Browto's, tela grezza diseguali e riglia appresentava l'altro di Cassuè. 7. Si mimetizza tra la palma la voglietta di cinque tinti a melone con colori vegetali, in vendita alla boutique del Club. Orologi di Longines.

design e tecnologia d'avanguardia

DI GIORGIO ARMANI NUOVE DIVISE PER UN ESERCITO NUOVO

Giorgio Armani, su invito dell'«Uomo Vogue», ha studiato e realizzato delle ipotetiche uniformi che potrebbero essere quelle adottate dalle Forze Armate di domani, qualora il servizio militare venisse considerato, da parte delle autorità e dei giovani, in modo democratico e aderente ai tempi. E cioè un anno formativo d'addestramento, di studio, di sport, un periodo utile, e non più mal sopportato, di preparazione alla vita. Ringraziamo lo Stato Maggiore dell'esercito italiano che ha collaborato con noi e ci ha permesso di realizzare il servizio in una caserma milanese.

Negli ultimi anni, nell'esercito, molte cose stanno cambiando e altre stanno cambiando, sotto la spinta di una parte delle forze politiche e sociali. Abbiamo pensato a un ipotetico esercito di domani (un domani forse non così lontano), in cui i giovani, superata la convinzione di battersi in un anno di vita fra chepì e cuori assenti, troveranno invece la possibilità di vivere un periodo della loro vita costruttivo e comunitario, un anno di preparazione fisica e sociale, di riflessione e maturazione utile prima di intraprendere scelte definitive. Un anno cioè di attività più realistico, dove accanto alla conoscenza di armi e metodi bellici, abbiamo la possibilità di apprendere tecnologie utilizzabili nella vita civile, di sviluppare il fisico con sport che oniti non avrebbero probabilmente mai il tempo e il modo di fare.

Partendo da questo presupposto, siamo arrivati al nostro servizio. Utilizzando esperienze e ricerche delle industrie e sportswear più avanzate e considerando le necessità della vita militare e ancora tenendo presente l'indissolubile fascino che certe divise — le più funzionali, vedi l'esercito americano — hanno sui giovani, anche al di fuori del loro contesto, Giorgio Armani ha realizzato una dotazione-tipo che dovrebbe coprire ogni esigenza del soldato. Sono rinnovamenti che corrispondono a una effettiva esigenza: da settembre, ad esempio, nelle Forze Armate italiane verrà abolito il rigido capotto tradizionale (che nessun soldato più indossava) e sostituito con un più pratico impermeabile doppiopetto foderato di pelo, che ha molti punti in comune con quelli proposti da Armani. In Francia, recentemente, tutti designers di moda sono stati invitati a concorrere per disegnare le uniformi di servizio dell'esercito per usi di città: il progetto prescelto è firmato da Ted Lapidus, seguito da quelli di Cardin, Courrèges, e da altri che...

Lo studio di queste divise di Armani ha seguito criteri tecnico-estetici, adottando in maniera più esasperata negli accorgimenti e quei materiali che l'industria del casual e già utilizza. Ma non vuol essere un vero progetto per rinnovare la immagine dell'esercito italiano. Si tratta semplicemente di una proposta, dell'indicazione di una via da seguire, di un contributo agli argomenti e quei materiali che si già in atto. Se sia valido è permesso di oggi, alle uniformi dell'esercito di domani queste potrebbero dare molti spunti, in tutti i settori.

Uniformi da lavoro: nel disegnare le mute Armani ha tenuto presenti le tenute da officina, con relativa esigenza: che forniscano la maggior libertà di movimenti, che in funzione dell'uso militare. Ne è uscita più di una soluzione, e tutte bellissime e al alto grado di praticità.

Per il combattimento: divise «totali» che non temono i cambiamenti meteorologici. Con fodera termiche, che tengono fresco al caldo e caldo al freddo. Con imbottiture di pulfisco sintetiche: funzionali, di poco conto, nessuna usura, e esteticamente valide. Con materiali leggeri, piacevoli, tiepidi.

Tenute sportive. Armani ha dato loro molta importanza, in quanto sottolineano quanto sia utile e necessaria questa pratica nell'educazione e nella formazione dei giovani, per valorizzare la componente sportiva come base fondamentale della vita comunitaria.

L'uniforme ordinaria, quella della libera uscita è stata risolta in modo polemico. In contrasto con la divisa attuale, secondo cui si riveste il soldato con giacca quattro bottoni, pantaloni regolabili, alla zip che nasconde un collo dilatabile per una maggiore aerazione, all'uso del doppio tessuto, impermeabile fuori, caldo dentro.

segue a pag. 171

Nella foto: tuta da lavoro kaki piena di accorgimenti speciali: delle molte tasche a soffietto regolabili, alla zip che nasconde un collo dilatabile per una maggiore aerazione, all'uso del doppio tessuto, impermeabile fuori, caldo dentro.

Giselia Bottoli

SPECIALE MILITARE

NUOVE DIVISE

NUOVE DIVISE

NUOVE DIVISE

NUOVE DIVISE

"Speciale militare: di Giorgio Armani
nuove divise per un esercito nuovo,"
in *L'Uomo Vogue*, n. 60/61, 1977, pp. 100/112.
Photo Aldo Fallai.

NUOVE DIVISE

soluzioni pratiche per sport impegnativi. In queste pagine (ma adatte anche ad altre pratiche sportive) le casacche di tela, differenziate seconda le diverse qualità, da portarsi sulle T-shirt di fila che assorbiranno il sudore. Pantaloni da cavallo tradizionali, ancora i migliori.

NUOVE DIVISE

per lo sport e il tempo libero nella nuova stagione: elle e selvaggi territori, matic e non. I comfort multitasche, il design comico degustatistica attenuto coordinando diverse toni di kaki. Sotto a sinistra e a destra: per il trapeza libero blusotti che indica casualmente, alle pantaloni larghi scelti pratici; manovre funzionare utilizzabili anche fuori dalla mischia. In questa pagina per le divise anche nelle camicie e pantaloni d'ordinanza pronti nuovi tessuti. Tutti colori d'ordinanza rustici, anticipando interni di confortevole e leggero poliestere sintetico.

Be prepared!
When military equipment becomes a style for confronting the metropolis.
The spread of items from the military wardrobe among persons of different ages, social backgrounds and ethnic groups, as seen in these images gathered in one randomly selected ordinary day in the center of Milan, would seem to indicate that a significant style has taken hold among ordinary people, which has nothing to do with questions exclusively linked to fashion.
To be precise, the evidently out-of-context use of camouflage pants, backpacks and jackets, combat vests, army boots, is associated with the idea each of us has regarding moving about in urban space today. Someone who leaves his apartment dressed as if he were on his way to the jungle approaches his day, or a simple stroll in town, in a state of mind that could be compared to that of a soldier at the front. The difference between this individual and the true soldier, but also between him and the counter-cultural attitude of those who, in past decades, declared war on the system and on the conformity of dress codes of the middle classes, is that in both cases the enemy still had a face. Today, the danger is diffused, and the enemy has disappeared, and therefore could be anywhere. There are no more heroes, no more medals for valor or bravery, no more welcome-home ceremonies for the veterans.
The small/large enemies to engage are all the difficulties associated with everyday life. The dream of widespread affluence promoted by the modern era has been replaced by a decidedly normal struggle for survival, and it is always better to be prepared, to expect the unexpected. *edc*

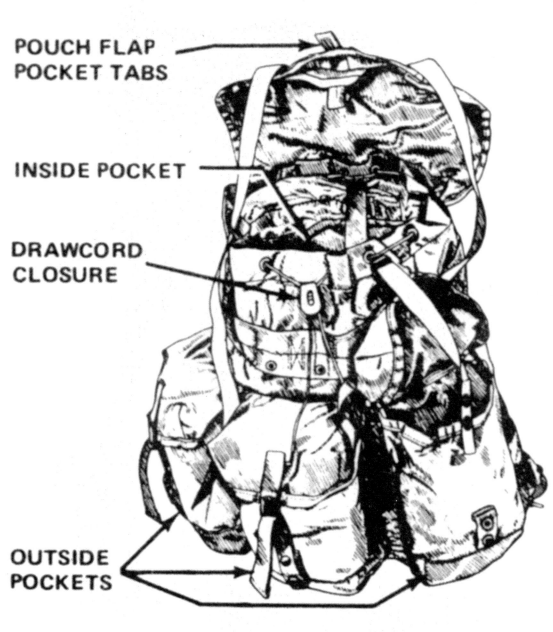

POUCH FLAP POCKET TABS

INSIDE POCKET

DRAWCORD CLOSURE

OUTSIDE POCKETS

"Medium Combat Field Pack,"
in *Care and Use of Individual Clothing
and Equipment, Field Manual n. 21/15*,
Headquarters Department of the Army,
Washington, D.C., 22 February 1985.

Prada advertising,
in *L'Uomo Vogue*, n. 288,
February 1998, p. 75.

Argun, Chechen. Russian soldiers
of the Tula Air Division,
5 km from Argun.
© Luc Delahaye/Magnum.
Agenzia Contrasto.

"Les gilets d'interventions et d'Assauts,"
in *Doursoux. Aviation, Armée, Securité, Expedition,
Equipment Civils et Militaires, cat. 9,*
Paris, 1993/1994, pp. 33/34.

The Face,
n. 81, January 1987, p. 68.
Photo Marc Lebon.

Following pages
CP Company/ Urban Protection advertising,
autumn/winter 2000/2001.

Stone Island advertising,
autumn/winter 2000/2001.

Maharishi advertising,
technical fibers,
autumn/winter 1999/2000.

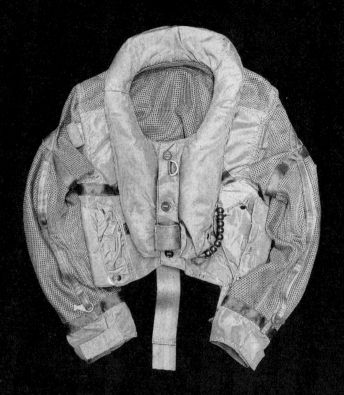

The best clothing design moulds pure functic
theatre into the same form, into a
This is what fashion takes from utility, v
fashion

uniforn

"Uniform = Utility,"
in *Arena Hommes Plus*, n. 6,
autumn/winter 1996/1997, pp. 94/97.
Photo Toby Mac Farlan Pond.

hole.

...

n =utility

Following pages
Lucy Orta, *032. Mobile Cocoon - Polar Fleece.*
Microfiber,1996.

CP Company advertising,
Urban Camouflage, autumn/winter 2000/2001.

CP Company advertising,
Transformable, spring/summer 2000.

32187208
Lunga mantella arancione con cappuccio in "CRISTAL WIND",
leggera rete di nylon indemagliabile gommato antivento e
antipioggia. Dalla mantella tramite giochi di velcri e zip si estrapola
un aquilone (profili in carbonio forniti) logo 000 C.P.riflettente
stampato a caldo.

Orange long hooded cloak in "CRISTAL WIND", windproof and
rainproof light rubberised runproof nylon mesh. A system of velcro
and zips is used to turn the cloak into a kite (carbon frame
supplied) bearing a hot-pressed reflecting 000 C.P.logo

C.P.
COMPANY
autumn _ winter '000 _'001

Andrea Zittel, *A-Z Seasonal Uniforms*, 1991/1994.
Fabric, leather suspenders, variable dimensions.
Installation view. Deichtorhallen, Hamburg, 1999.
Courtesy Andrea Rosen Gallery, New York.

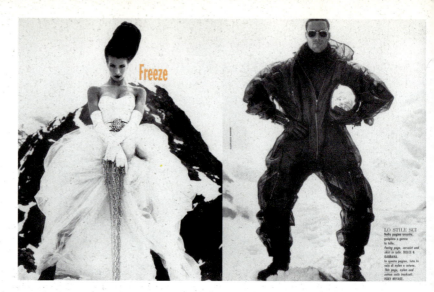

Freeze

Freeze

Freeze

"Freeze," in *L'Uomo Vogue,*
n. 232, September 1992, p. 168.
Photo G. Barbieri,
fashion editor Marco Reati.

Elite Teams, U.S. Navy Seals,
California, 1996.
© Louis Psihoyos, Matrix.
Agenzia Grazia Neri.

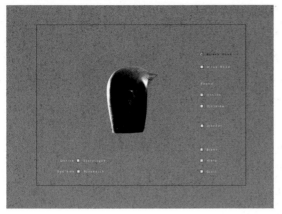
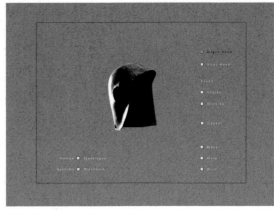
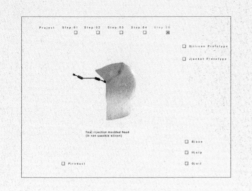
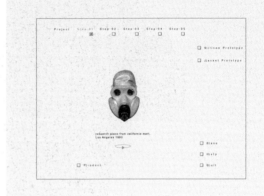
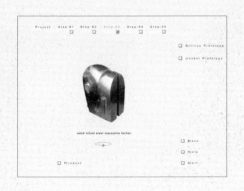
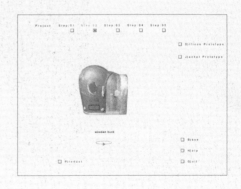

Stone Island advertising,
autumn/winter 1999/2000.

Casper Van Dien, in *Starship Troopers*, 1997.
Directed by Paul Verhoeven.
Courtesy Douglas Kirkland.
Agenzia Grazia Neri.

The Japanese designer Kosuke Tsumura makes creations for his Final Home line of garment-equipment for the urban jungle and all its possible associated risks. All the garments are easy to wear, and come with a tag on which the wearer can write name and blood group, fundamental information for identification in the extreme case of the discovery of a dead body. The Final Home garments, with their functional efficiency underlined, for example, by the presence of up to 44 pockets, express a response to an environment in which survival seems to be constantly threatened. The disturbing part is that this clothing is conceived for everyday life in cities, imagined as the most hostile possible environment, and not for exotic trips to the equatorial jungles. It is no coincidence that the images in the information brochures for the 2000 collection are pictures of endless urban peripheries, seen from above.

The techno-design of this Japanese stylist, just the tip of the iceberg of a rapidly growing style at the turn of the millennium, makes a true mission out of research on waterproof, thermal, ultralight materials and functional quality. Just another confirmation of the fact that today the territory most densely filled with dangers for man is the landscape he himself has constructed. There is an evident affinity with the special uniforms of the activists of Greenpeace and, more in general, with the uniforms of the special corps trained to combat and prevent environmental disasters, to defuse bacteriological bombs, all invisible enemies and therefore even more dangerous. Friend and foe, technological research permits the construction of devastating immaterial weapons, against which we can defend ourselves only with equally sophisticated technological tools. *edc*

Final Home/Kosuke Tsumura advertising,
spring/summer 2000.
Photo Takashi Homma.

Final Home, *Mother*, drawings, 2000.

Following pages
U2-Greenpeace demo.
© Adrian Boot. Retna Pictures.

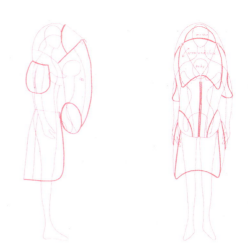

LIVE SURVIVE PROTECT

In the Fifties and Sixties the turbine of capitalistic growth and the spread of industrially produced goods induced new needs and produced the framework for contemporary mass society. The American model spread and promised the realization of a dream of widespread well-being. These were the years of the space race culminating in the moon landing, the years in which behavioral phenomena previously reserved for an elite become accessible to all (air travel, for example). This was the context for the birth of the *Star Trek* saga, where everything happens in uniform, inside a spaceship-world. At the same time, Braniff International Airlines was transformed into a space-age icon. Thanks to an intelligent marketing operation involving the artist Alexander Calder and the Italian fashion stylist Emilio Pucci, the campaign *The End of the Plain Plane* "launched" in 1965 transformed the flying experience into style. Calder designed a DC8, transforming it into airborne artwork, while Pucci created uniforms for the stewardesses, introducing bright colors and creating an image that all the other airlines rushed to imitate: the Braniff stewardesses looked like female astronauts on their way to the moon. Pucci invented a special garment, the "air-strip," which permitted variation of the combination of elements in keeping with the moment and the temperature. "We love our new uniform," a Braniff employee declared for *Life* magazine, "because it makes you feel like a real woman." In 1971 a fan of Pucci's work, the astronaut Colonel David Scott, contacted the designer and asked him to design the official emblem for the coming Apollo 15 mission. Pucci, who during the war had been a pilot, created a design based on the forms of the three spaceships, and the design was approved by NASA. Thirty years later, the American artist Matthew Barney shot the main part of his film *Cremaster 1* inside a space capsule, but the vision is not the same: faith in progress and unlimited development has given way to nostalgia for a dream that reality has frustrated, perhaps forever. *edc*

Astronauts. Katz Pictures.
© Steve Pyke, 1998.
Detail from the Outpost Bar
used by the Astronauts since the 1960's.
Houston, July 1998.

Astronauts. Katz Pictures.
© Steve Pyke, 1998.
Cape Canaveral, October 1998.
A photo with John Glenn next to the old
Mercury suit worn by Gus Grissom.

Corpo Nove advertising, 2000/2001.

Following pages
Yinka Shonibare, *Cloud 9*, 1999/2000.
Dutch wax printed cotton textile,
fiberglass figure, flagpole and flag.
Astronaut: 212 x 63 x 56 cm. Flag: 183 cm.
Courtesy Stephen Friedman Gallery, London;
Neuberger Berman Collection, New York.
Photo Andy Keate.

Bibliography

Acker, J.
"Hierarchies, Jobs, Bodies:
A Theory of Gendered Organizations."
Gender & Society 4 (1990): 139/158.

Acker, J.
"Gendered Institutions."
Contemporary Sociology 21 (1992):
565/569.

Adair, G.
Hollywood's Vietnam:
From the Green Berets
to Apocalypse Now.
London: Proteus, 1981.

Alberoni, F.
"Pubblico&Privato." Corriere della
Sera (Milan), 3 July 2000.

Alleau, R.
La science des symboles. Paris: 1976.

Ammendola, T.
Missione in Bosnia. Le caratteristiche
sociologiche dei militari italiani. Milan:
Angeli, 1999.

Ash, J. and E. Wilson.
Chic Thrills: A Fashion Reader.
Berkeley: University of California
Press, 1992.

Aspesi, N.
"Miles gloriosus." Edited by G. Malossi.
Uomo oggetto. Milan: Bolis, 1999.

Auster, A. and O. Leonard.
How the War Was Remembered:
Hollywood & Vietnam. New York:
Praeger, 1988.

Avanti, 9 March 1953.

"Barbies Salute Military Mothers."
Chicago Tribune, 12 November 1989.

Barhaim, G.
"Action and Heroes: The Meaning
of Western Pop Information
for Eastern European Youth."
The British Journal of Sociology 40
(March 1989): 22/45.

Barnes, R. and J.B. Eicher.
Dress and Gender:
Making and Meaning in Cultural
Contexts (Cross Cultural
Perspective on Women). Oxford: Berg,
1992.

Barthes, R.

Mythologies. Paris: Seuil, 1957.

Barthes, R.
Système de la mode. Paris: Seuil, 1967.

Barthes, R.
Le bruissement de la langue.
Essais critique IV. Paris: Seuil, 1984.

Barthes, R.
Œuvres complètes. Edited by Eric Marty.
Paris: Seuil, 1993, 1994, 1995.

Basinger, J.
The World War II Combat Film: Anatomy
of a Genre. New York: Columbia
University Press, 1986.

Batterberry, A.R. and M. Batterberry.
Fashion, The Mirror of History.
New York: Greenwich House,
distr. by Crown Publishers, 1982.
1st edition, Mirror, Mirror.
New York: Holt, Rinehart and Winston,
1977.

Battistelli, F.
Soldati. Sociologia dei militari italiani
nell'era del peace-keeping.
Milan: Angeli, 1990.

Battistelli, F.
"Ufficiale o gentiluomo? Il militare
come sopravvivenza della società
pre-moderna." Giano 5 (1990).

Battistelli, F., ed.
Donne e forze armate. Milan: Angeli,
1997.

Baudrillard, J.
Les stratégies fatales. Paris:
Grasset, 1983.

Baudrillard, J.
La guerre du Golf n'a pas eu lieu.
Paris: Mayenne, Galilée, 1991.

Baudrillard, J.
Simulacres et Simulation.
Paris: Galilée, 1991.

Baudrillard, J.
"Design et Dasein." Agalma 1 (2000).

Baumann, Z.
"The Making and Unmaking of
Strangers." Postmodernity and
Its Discontents. Oxford: Blackwell,
1997, 17-34.

Belsito, P. and B. Davis.
Hardcore California: A History of Punk
and New Wave. San Francisco:

Last Gasp, 1983.

Berg, R.
"Losing Vietnam: Covering the War
in an Age of Technology."
Cultural Critique 3, 92/125.

Berger, J.
Ways of Seeing. London:
The BBC and Penguins Books, 1972.

Bird Francke, L.
Ground Zero: The Gender Wars
in the Military. New York:
Simon & Schuster, 1997.

Bonnell, V.E.
Iconography of Power. Soviet Political
Posters Under Lenin and Stalin.
Berkeley: University of California
Press, 1997.

Boose, L.
"Techno-Muscularity and the Boy
Eternal: From the Quagmire to the Gulf."
Edited by M. Cooke and A. Woollacott.
Gendering War Talk. Princeton: Princeton
University Press, 1993, 78.

Boynton, A.L.
Religion, Dress and the Body.
Oxford: Berg, 1999.

Breward, C.
The Culture of Fashion. Manchester:
Manchester University Press, 1995.

Bruzzi, S.
Undressing Cinema: Clothing and
Identity in the Movies. New York:
Routledge, 1997.

Burk, J., ed.
La guerra e il militare nel nuovo
sistema internazionale. Milan: Franco
Angeli, 1998.

Buxbaum, G.
Icons of Fashion. Munich,
London, New York: Prestel, 1999.

Calefato, P.
Mass moda. Genoa: Costa & Nolan, 1996.

Calefato, P.
Moda, corpo, mito.
Rome: Castelvecchi, 1999.

Catapano, A.
Fort Apache. Etnografia
di un'amministrazione pubblica.
Milan: Angeli, 2000.

Cardini, F.

Quell'antica festa crudele.
Milan: Mondadori, 1995.

Carman, W.Y.
A Dictionary of Military Uniform.
New York: Scribner, 1977.

Cavallaro, D. and A. Warwick.
"Fashioning the Frame. Boundaries,
Dress and Body." Eicher J.B. Dress, Body
Culture. Oxford, New York: Berg, 1995.

Céline, L.F.
Casse-Pipe. Paris: Gallimard, 1975.

Codeluppi, V.
Sociologia della moda.
Milan: IULM, 1996.

Cooper, W.
Hair. London: Aldus Book, 1991.

Cordwell, J., ed.
The Fabrics of Culture.
The Anthropology of Clothing
and Adornment. The Hague,
Paris, New York: Mouton
Publishers, 1979.

Craik J.
The Face of Fashion: Cultural
Studies in Fashion. London,
New York: Routledge, 1994.

Cucciari, S.
"The Origins of Gender Hierarchy."
S.B. Ortner and G. Whitehead. Sexual
Meanings: The Cultural Construction of
Gender and Sexuality. Cambridge:
Cambridge University Press, 1991.

Curcio, A.M.
La moda: identità negata.
Milan: Angeli, 1994.

D'Amico, F. and L. Weinstein.
Gender Camouflage: Women in the
US Military. New York:
New York University Press, 1999.

Davis, F.
Fashion, Culture, and Identity.
Chicago: University of Chicago
Press, 1992.

Debord, G.
La societé du spectacle.
Paris: Gallimard, 1967.

De Lauretis, T.
Technologies of Gender:
Essays on Theory, Film and Fiction.
Bloomington: Indiana University
Press, 1987.

De Lauretis, T.
Sui generis: scritti di teoria femminista.
Milan: Feltrinelli, 1996.

De Pauw, L.G.
"Gender as Stigma: Probing Some
Sensitive Issues." Minerva:
Quarterly Report on Women
and the Military VI, n. 1 (1988):
29/43.

De Sassure, F.
Cours de linguistique générale.
Paris: 1922.

Dittmar, L. and G. Michaud.
From Hanoi to Hollywood:
The Vietnam War in American Film.
New Brunswick: Rutgers University
Press, 1990.

Dixon Wheeeler, W.
Disaster and Memory: Celebrity
Culture and the Crisis of Hollywood
Cinema. New York: Columbia University
Press, 1999.

Dunivin, K.
"There's Men, There's Women,
and There's Me: The Role
and the Status of Military Women."
Minerva: Quarterly Report on Women
and the Military VI, n. 2 (1988): 43/68.

Dyer, K.
Gays in Uniform: The Pentagon's Secret
Report. Boston: Alyson, 1990.

Eco, U.
La struttura assente.
Milan: Bompiani, 1968.

Eco, U.
Segni, pesci e bottoni. Appunti
su semiotica, filosofia e scienze umane.
In Sugli specchi e altri saggi. Milan:
Bompiani, 1968.

Eco, U.
Stelle e stellette.
Genoa: Il Melangolo, 1968.

Edwards, P.N.
"The Army and the Microworld:
Computer and the Politics of Gender
Identity." Signs: Journal of Women in
Culture and Society 16 (1990): 102/127.

Edwards, T.
Men in the Mirror: Men's Fashion,
Masculinity and Consumer Society.
London: Cassell, 1997.

Eibl-Eibesfeldt, I.
Etologia della guerra. Ital. trans. Turin:
Bollati Boringhieri, 1979.

Enloe, C.
Does Khaki Become You?
The Militarization of Women's Lives.
Boston: South End Press, 1983.

Enloe, C.
"The Politics of Constructing the
American Woman Soldier." Edited by E.
Addis, V. Russo, L. Sebesta. Women
Soldiers: Images and Realities. New
York: St. Martin Press, 1994, 81-109.

Evans, C.
"Dreams That Only Money Can Buy…Or
The Shy Tribe in Flight from Discourse."
Fashion Theory 1, n. 2 (1997).

Ewen, Stuart.
All Consuming Images: The Politics of
Style in Contemporary Culture.
New York: Basic Books, 1988.

Faursch, D., P. Singfey, E. Khoury,
et al., ed.
Architecture: In Fashion. New York:
Princeton Architectural Press, 1994.

Fenner, L.
"Either You Need These Women
or You Do Not: Informing the Debate on
Military Service and Citizenship." Gender
Issues 16, n. 3 (summer 1998):
5-32.

Finkelstein, J.
The Fashioned Self.
Cambridge: Polity Press, 1991.

Finkelstein, J.

After a Fashion. Interpretations.
Carlton South, Vict., Australia:
Melbourne University Press, 1996.

Finkelstein, J.
Fashion: An Introduction. New York:
New York University Press, 1998.

Foucault, M.
Surveiller et punir. Naissance de la
prison. Paris: Gallimard, 1975.

Fox, K.
"Real Punk and Pretenders: The Social
Organization of a Counterculture."
Journal of Contemporary Ethnography
16 (October 1987): 344/370.

Fraboni, M.
"Punks." AA.VV. Bande, un modo di dire.
Rockabillies, Mods, Punks. Milan:
Unicopli, 1986.

Francis, M. and M. King, ed.
The Warhol Look. Glamour, Style,
Fashion. Ex. cat., The Andy Warhol
Museum, Pittsburgh. Boston, New York:
A Bulfinch Press Book, 1997.

Frazer, J.G.
The Golden Bough: A Study
in Magic and Religion.
London: MacMillan, 1911.

Frisch, M.
Libretto di servizio.
Turin: Einaudi, 1977.

Frith, S. et al., ed.
Sounds and Visions:
The Music Video Readers.
New York: Routledge, 1993.

Gaines, J. and C. Herzog C., ed.
Fabrications: Costume and
the Female Body. New York:
Routledge, 1990.

Garber, M.
Vested Interests: Cross-Dressings
and Cultural Anxiety. New York:
Routledge, 1992.

Geertz, C.
The Interpretation of Cultures.
New York: Basic Books, 1973.

Giancola, A.
La moda nel consumo giovanile.
Milan: Angeli, 1999.

Gilas, M.
Se la memoria non mi inganna.
Bologna, Il Mulino, 1987.

Girard, R.
La violence et le sacré. Paris:
B. Grasset, 1972.

Gobbicchi, A., ed.
La professione militare oggi.
Caratteristiche sociali e nuovo
contesto. Milan: Angeli, 1995.

Goffman, E.
The Presentation of Self in
Everyday Life. Garden City,
N.Y.: Doubleday, 1959.

Goffman, E.
Asylums. Chicago: Aldine, 1961.

Goffman, E.
"The Arrangement Between the
Sexes." Theory and Society 4

(1977): 301-331.

Gooding-Williams, R.
*Reading Rodney King,
Reading Urban Uprising.*
New York: Routledge, 1993.

Greco, L.
"Praticabilità di uno studio
semiologico/antropologico
della cultura militare."
Il Ponte 6 (1994):102.

Greco, L.
"Gesti della vita militare e codici letterari."
Il Ponte 12 (1995): 115.

Greco, L.
La cultura militare. Segni, codici, valori.
Leghorn: Accademia Navale, 1998.

Greco, L.
*Homo militaris. Antropologia
e letteratura della vita militare.*
Milan: Angeli, 1999.

Hall, M.
"The Lesbian Corporate Experience."
Journal of Homosexuality 12 (1986): 59-75.

Harvey, David.
*The Condition of Postmodernity:
An Enquiry into the Origins of Cultural
Change.* Oxford: Blackwell, 1989.

Hebdige, D.
Subculture: The Meaning of Style.
London: Methuen, 1979.

Hendrickson, H., ed.
*Clothing and Difference. Embodied
Identities in Colonial and
Post-Colonial Africa.* Durham:
Duke University Press, 1996.

Herr, Cheryl.
"Terrorist Chic: Style and Domination
in Contemporary Ireland." Edited by S.
Benstock and S. Ferriss. *On Fashion.*
New Brunswick: Rutgers University
Press, 1994.

Hewitt, A.
*Fascist Modernism: Aesthetics, Politics
and the Avantgarde.* Stanford: Stanford
University Press, 1993.

Hicks, S. J., ed.
*It's Our Military too! Women
and the U.S. Military.* Philadelphia:
Temple University Press, 1996.

Hobsbawn, E. and T. Ranger.
The Invention of Tradition. Cambridge:
Cambridge University Press, 1983.

Hollander, A.
Seeing Through Clothes. Berkeley:
University of California Press, 1975.

Hollert, T.
"Material World: Tom Holert Tells
a Tale of Textile Wars." *Frieze* 53
(June, July, August 2000).

Holm, J.
*Women in the Military:
An Unfinished Revolution.*
Novato: Presidio Press, 1982.

Holmberg, C.B.
Sexuality and Popular Culture.
Thousand Oaks: Sage Publications, 1998.

Humphrey, M.A.

My Country, My Right to Serve. New
York: Harper Collins, 1990.

"Invisible Soldiers. Military Technology."
The Economist (4 June 1994): 87.

Isernia, P.
*Dove gli angeli non mettono piede.
Opinione pubblica e politiche
di sicurezza in Italia.*
Milan: Angeli, 1996.

Jakobson, R.
Essais de linguistique générale.
Paris: Minuit, 1963.

James, D.
*Power Misses. Essays Across
(Un)Popular Culture.*
London, New York: Verso, 1996.

Jameson, F.
*Postmodernism, or the Cultural Logic of
Late Capitalism.* Durham, N.C.: Duke
University Press, 1991.

Jeffords, S.
*The Remasculinization of America:
Gender and the Vietnam War.*
Bloomington: Indiana University Press, 1989.

Jeffords, S. and L. Rabinovitz.
*Seeing Through the Media: The Persian
Gulf War.* New Bruswick: Rutgers
University Press, 1994.

Jobling, P.
*Fashion Spreads: Word and Image in
Fashion Photography Since 1980.*
Oxford, New York: Berg, 1999.

Kaiser, S.
*The Social Psychology of Clothing:
Symbolic Appearances in Context.*
New York: Macmillan, 1990.

Kopytoff, I.
"The Cultural Biography of Things:
Commoditization as Process."
Edited by A. Appadurai. *The Social Life
of Things: Commodities in Cultural
Perspective.* New York: Cambridge
University Press, n.d.: 64/91.

Kroker, A., M.Kroker, and D.Cook.
*Panic Encyclopedia: The Definitive Guide
to the Postmodern Scene.* New York: St.
Martin Press, 1989.

Kuhn, A.
*The Power of Image: Essays
on Representation and Sexuality.*
London, New York: Routledge, 1985.

Lakoff, R.
Language and a Woman's Place. New
York: Harper Colophon Books, 1975.

Lanternar, L.
Festa, carisma, apocalisse.
Palermo: Sellerio, 1983.

Leach, N.
"The Architect as Fascist."
The Anaesthetics of Architecture.
Cambridge, Mass.:
MIT Press, 1999,17-32.

Ledda, G.
Padre padrone.
Milan: Feltrinelli, 1975.

Lévi-Strauss, C.
Les structures élémentaires de la parenté.
Paris: Presses Universitaires, 1949.

Lodato, S.
*Vademecum per l'aspirante
detenuto.* Milan: Garzanti, 1993.

Long Bonita, C.
"Sex-Role Orientation, Coping
Strategies and Self Efficacy of
Women in Traditional and Non-
Traditional Occupations."
*Psychology of Women
Quarterly* 13 (1989): 307/324.

Lotman Jurij, M.
"O semiosfere." *Trudy Poznakovym
Sistemam* 17. Tartu: 1984.

Lurie, A.
The Language of Clothes.
New York: Random House, 1981.

Mablen, J.
*Getting Iron: The Clothing of
Rock'n Roll.* New York:
Abbeville Press, 1987.

Mac Donald, S.
"Drawing the Lines - Gender,
Peace and War: An Introduction."
Edited by S. MacDonald, P. Holden,
S. Ardener. *Images of Women in
War and Peace: Cross-Cultural and
Historical Perspectives.* Madison:
University of Wisconsin Press, 1987, 1/26.

Magherini, G.
"Codice della donna e codice
militare: un punto di vista
psicoanalitico."
Edited by F.B. Battistelli. *Donne e forze
armate.* Milan: Angeli,1997.

Maguire, J.A.
*Art of the Flight Jacket: Classic Leather
Jacket of Second World War.* Atgen:
Schiffer Publications, 1985.

Marcou, L.
Staline, Vie privée. Paris: Calmann-Levy,
1996.

Marcus, G.
*Mystery Train: Images of America
in Rock'n Roll Music.*
London: Omnibus Press, 1977.

Marcus, G.
*In the Fascist Bathroom: Writings
on Punk 1977/1992.* London:
Viking Penguin, 1993.

Marchi, V.
Nazi-Rock. Pop music e Destra radicale.
Rome: Castelvecchi, 1997.

Mari, M.
Filologia dell'anfibio. Diario militare.
Milan: Bompiani, 1995.

Marsh, P., et al.
The Rules of Disorder.
London: Routledge, 1978.

Marshall, K.
*In the Combat Zone: An Oral History of
American Women in Vietnam 1966/1975.*
Boston: Little Brown, 1987.

Martinez, T.
"Popular Culture as Oppositional
Culture: Rap as Resistence." *Sociological
Perspective* 40, n. 2 (1997): 265/286.

May, D.
"Women Police: The Early Years."
Police Review (9 March 1979): 358/365.

Mc Robbie, A., ed.
Zoot Suits and Second-Hand Dresses: An Anthology of Fashion and Music.
Boston: Unwin Hyman, 1989.

McVeigh, B.
"Wearing Ideology: How Uniforms Discipline Minds and Bodies in Japan."
Fashion Theory 1, n. 2 (1997).

Mereghetti, P.
Il Mereghetti. Dizionario dei film 2000.
Milan: Baldini & Castoldi, 2000.

Mitchell, B.
Weak Link: The Feminization of the American Military. Washington, D.C.: Regnery Gateway, 1989.

Morace, F.
Fashion Subway: il destino dei percorsi incrociati nel paesaggio della moda avanzata.
Milan: EM, 1998.

Morris, D.
L'uomo e i suoi gesti, la comunicazione non verbale nella specie umana. Ital. trans., Milan: Mondadori, 1978.

Moskos, Ch. C.
Sociologia e soldati.
Ital. trans., Milan: Angeli, 1994.

Mulvey, L.
Visual and Other Pleasures.
Bloomington: Indiana University Press, 1989.

Nathan, J.
Uniforms and Non-Uniforms: Communication Through Clothing.
New York: Greenwood Press, 1986.

Nathan, J. and A. Nicholas.
"The Uniform, A Sociological Perspective." *American Journal of Sociology* 77 (1972): 719/730.

Niessen S. and A. Brydon.
Consuming Fashion: Adorning the Transnational Body, Dress, Body, Culture. Oxford, New York: Berg, 1998.

Oliver A.M. and P. Steinberg.
"A Geography of Revolt."
Public Culture 3, n. 1 (fall1990): 139/143.

Omodeo, A.
Momenti della vita di guerra.
Turin: Einaudi, 1968.

O'Neill, W.
"Sex Scandals in the Gender Integrated Military." *Gender Issues* 16, nos.1/2 (winter/spring1998): 64/85.

Palazzeschi, A.
Vita Militare. Padua: Rebellato, 1959.

Paris Match, 21 March 1953.

Pesch, M. and M. Weisbeck.
Techno Style: Musik, Grafik, Mode und Partkultur der Techno-Bewegung.
Zürich: Olms, 1996.

Peterson, D.
"Waffen-SS Camouflage Uniforms and Post-War Derivatives."
Europa-militaria 18. London: Windrow & Greene, 1995.

Philbin, M.
Give Peace a Chance: Music and Struggle for Peace. Chicago: Chicago Review Press, 1983.

Polhemus, T.
The Body Reader: Social Aspects of the Human Body.
Harmondsworth: Penguin, 1978.

Polhemus, T. and L. Procter.
Fashion & Anti-Fashion: Anthropology of Clothing and Adornment.
London: Thames & Hudson, 1978.

Polhemus, T.
Streetstyle: From Sidewalk to Catwalk. Ex. cat., Victoria and Albert Museum, London. New York: Thames & Hudson, 1994.

Pozzi, E.
"La caserma come istituzione sociale manipolante." *La critica sociologica* 19 (1971).

Preto, P.
I servizi segreti di Venezia.
Milan: Il Saggiatore, 1994.

Quick Collins, W., et al.
More Than a Uniform: A Navy Woman in a Navy Man's World, 1997.

Ragone, G., ed.
Sociologia dei fenomeni di moda.
Milan: Angeli, 1992.

Reed, J.
"Annie Gets Her Gun."
Vogue, July 1997, 42.

Reynolds, S. and J. Press.
The Sex Revolts. Gender, Rebellion and Rock'n Roll. London, New York: Serpent's Tail, 1995.

Reynolds, S.
Energy Flash.
London: MacMillan, 1998.

Roach, M.E.
Eicher Bubolz J., New York.
London: John Wiley & Son, 1995.

Rosenwasser, S.M. and N. Dean.
"Gender Role and Political Office: Effects of Perceived Masculinity/Feminity of Candidate and Political Office."
Psycology of Women Quarterly 13 (1989): 77/85.

Ruddick, S.
"Pacifying the Forces: Drafting Women in the Interests of Peace."
Signs: Journal of Women and Culture in Society 8 (spring 1983): 471/489.

Rugoff, R.
"Arrested Artifacts: The LA County Sheriff's Museum." *Circus Americanus.*
London, New York: Verso, 1995, 109/113.

Saba, U.
Antologia del canzoniere.
Turin: Einaudi, 1963.

Sabin, R., ed.
Punk Rock: So What?
New York: Routledge, 1999.

Sanga, G.
"Gerghi." Edited by A. M. Sobrero.
Introduzione all'italiano contemporaneo. La variazione e gli usi.

Rome-Bari: Laterza, 1993.

Schneider, D. and C. Schneider.
Sound Off: American Military Women Speak Out.
New York: Dutton, 1988.

Schur, E.
Labeling Women Deviant: Gender, Stigma and Social Control. Philadelphia: Temple University Press, 1984.

Segal, D., M. Segal, J. Bachman, P. Freedman-Doan, P. O'Malley.
"Gender and the Propensity to Enlist in the U.S. Military." *Gender Issues* 16, n. 3: 65/87.

Segal, D.R. and W.M.Segal.
I soldati di pace e le loro famiglie.
La partecipazione americana alle Forze multinazionali: aspetti sociologici.
Milan: Angeli, 1995.

Segre, S.
Mode in Italy: una lettura antropologica.
Milan: Guerini Scientifica, 1999.

Selzer, M.
Terrorist Chic: An Exploration of Violence in the Seventies. New York: Hawthorn Books, 1979.

Shilts, R.
Conduct Unbecoming: Gays and Lesbians in the U.S. Military. New York: St. Martin, 1993.

Simmel, G.
"Die Mode." *Philosophische Kultur* (1911).

Souvarine, B.
Staline. Aperçu historique du Bolchévisme. Paris: Champ Libre, 1997.

Stam, R.
"Mobilizing Fictions: The Gulf War, the Media, and the Recruitment of the Spectator." *Public Culture* 4, n. 2 (spring 1992): 101/126.

Strizenova, T.
Moda e rivoluzione.
Milan: Electa, 1979.

Taormino, T.
"Dress Blues, Disciplines and Demerits, New York." *The Village Voice*, 11 January 2000.

Tasker, Y.
Working Girls: Gender and Sexuality in Popular Cinema. New York: Routledge, 1998.

Thorne, T.
Fads, Fashions & Cults: From Acid House to Zoot Suit - Via Existentialism and Political Correctness - The Definitive Guide to (Post) Modern Culture.
London: Bloomsbury, 1993.

Tondelli, P.V.
Pao Pao. Milan: Feltrinelli, 1982.

Trompf, G.W., ed.
Cargo Cults and Millenarian Movements: Transoceanic Comparisons or New Religious Movements. Berlin, New York: Mouton de Gruyter, 1990.

Turner, V.
The Ritual Process. Structure and Antistructure. Chicago: Aldine, 1969.

Vazzoler, E.
La maschera del boia.
Genoa: Herodote, 1982.

Vignola, G.
I riti di iniziazione.
Milan: De Vecchi, 1972.

Virilio, P.
Esthétique de la disparition.
Paris: Galilée, 1989.

Virilio, P.
*Guerra e Cinema. Logistica della
percezione.* Ital. trans., Turin: Lindau,
1996.

Volkov, S.
San Pietroburgo. Ital. trans., Milan:
Mondadori, 1998.

Yarmolinsky, A.
The Military Establishment.
New York: Harper & Row, 1971.

Yoder J. and J. Adams.
"Women Entering Non-Traditional Roles:
When Works Demands and Sex-Roles
Conflict: The Case of West Point."
*International Journal of Women's
Studies* 7 (1984): 260/272.

Warwick A. and D. Cavallaro.
*Fashioning the Frame: Boundaries,
Dress and the Body.*
Oxford, New York: Berg, 1998.

Weiner, W.
Cloth and Human Experience.
Washington, D.C.: Smithsonian
Institution Press, 1989.

Wheelwright, J.
*Amazons and Military Maids: Women
Who Dressed as Men in Pursuit of Life,
Liberty and Happiness.*
London: Pandora, 1989.

Williams, C.
*Gender Differences at Work: Women and
Men in Non-Traditional Occupations.*
Berkeley: University of California Press,
1989.

Williams, V.
*Warworks. Women, Photography and
the Iconography of War.* Ex. cat.,
Rotterdam, Nederlands Photo Institut,
London, Victoria & Albert Museum.
London: Virago Press, 1994.

Wilson, E.
*Adorned in Dreams: Fashion and
Modernity.* London: Virago, 1985.

Wilson, E.
"Bohemian Dress and the Heroism of
Everyday Life." *Fashion Theory* 2, n. 3
(1998).

Wolinski, N.
"Art et camouflage: les grandes
manoeuvres." *Beaux Arts* 169 (June
1998): 58/63.

Woods, J.
*The Corporate Closet: The Professional
Lives of Gay Men in America.*
New York: Free Press, 1993.

Woolf, V.
Three Guineas.
Richmond: Hogarth Press, 1938.

Zavlasky, V.
Il dottor Petrov parapsicologo.
Palermo: Sellerio, 1984.

Zeeland, S.
*Barrack Buddies and Soldier Lovers:
Dialogues With Gay Young Men in the
U.S. Military.* London, New York:
The Haworth Press, 1993.

Zeeland, S.
*Masculine Marine: Homoeroticism in the
U.S. Marine Corps.* London, New York:
The Haworth Press, 1996.

Zizek, S.
"Slavoj Zizek, Modernism and Stalinist
Sublime." *Parkett* 58 (2000): 6/10.

Printed in Italy by Tipografia Rumor Spa, Vicenza
December 2000 for Edizioni Charta